Finding Fox Creek

An Oregon Pilgrimage

by

William Nichols

@@@

Pagescape Press

2015

To Nathan, Ana, Toby, and Jack

And grandchildren everywhere

Finding Fox Creek: An Oregon Pilgrimage

Contents

Prologue

Born in San Francisco, I soon moved with my parents to Portland, Oregon, where I had the advantage of listening to my grandfather's stories about hunting deer as a youth in western Montana. If storytelling began around campfires among hunting and gathering tribal groups, my grandfather's spellbinding accounts of tracking deer through deep snow as a boy probably shaped me in ancient ways although I've never hunted deer. But among other things, mine is a story of white male privilege

Like most stories in this 21st Century, this is partly a tale of technology too. The western men in my family have been drawn to modern technology. My grandfather left his family's Montana ranch early in the twentieth century to drive trolley cars through the streets of Missoula, moved to a railroad job in Seattle, and settled down as a city bus driver in the streets of Portland. My father spent most of World War II in Portland's shipyards, moved after the war to a job on the Hanford Nuclear Reservation, and worked finally for Stubbs Electric, a wholesale electrical appliance distributor in Portland. My brother David owned a small wholesale lighting fixture store in Portland for several years and then took work as a computer technician. My brother John sold hydraulic equipment to operators of lumber mills and fishing boats on the west coast.

I became an academic. Some academics, mainly scientists, are comfortable with machines, but many of us are not at ease with the devices humans have created for imposing our will on the physical world. We are as likely to be attracted to well-designed machines as anyone, but when they begin to skip, cough, leak, or shake, we're like someone with severe abdominal pain who heads for the nearest emergency room. There are, of course, historians, philosophers, and literary scholars who will tear into a troublesome fuel injection system with relish. But I am not one of them.

More than thirty years ago the contrast between those at ease with machines and those who, like me, approach them with great ambivalence came home to me. My brother John's Volkswagen bus broke down when he was visiting our family on the Oregon coast, and he asked me to drive him into Portland to buy a book about fixing Volkswagens. By the time we returned to the silent engine in the rear of my brother's bus, he had concluded the problem was electrical. It took little more than a day of chasing down parts and replacing wires before he got the bus moving, and what impressed me more than his success was his patience and calm during a time of trial and error. I think I know certitude when I see it, and my brother was sure he could get the job done.

There are similar stories about Dave, who lifts the hood on most machines and looks inside with an air of confidence. Part of this gift probably has to do with his assurance that he can find his way through unfamiliar territory. A few years before John worked his magic on the bus at the beach, Dave led Marine reconnaissance missions in Vietnam, and he had long been skilled at finding his way with a map or using a set of directions. He once stopped by our Oregon cabin to help me install a woodstove. It needed a brick wall behind it, I told him, and I had never laid a brick. He hadn't either, but he was sure we could figure out how to do the job. It took us longer than he expected, nearly all night, but to my eye the brickwork looked almost professional.

My skepticism and humility in the face of most technologies might have something to do with the Bomb.

As the oldest brother by several years, I'm the one who remembers two nuclear explosions in Japan that punctuated the horror of World War II. Later, in 1947, I took a train from Portland to visit our father, who moved after the war from a shipyard to the Hanford Nuclear Reservation. A fourth grader, I felt something ominous in the tall wire fences, the many security guards, and the sense of secrecy. A few months later, Dad resigned and came home, troubled not so much by the fact that Hanford was the source of plutonium for the atomic bomb we dropped on Nagasaki but by the wastefulness and sloppy workmanship he found there. Until he died in 1986, he told stories of engineers who criticized designs or materials and were promptly fired or transferred. Those stories help to explain my skepticism when it comes to nuclear technology and why one of my earliest publications, "Skeptics and Believers: The Science-Humanities Debate" (1976) takes the side of humanist-skeptics despite my continuing admiration for engineers.

Along with the influence of technology on our lives, this is partly a story of places where our family has lived. It is haunted by the powerful tension in American culture between our love of technology and our deep regard for pastoral places and wilderness like the Fox Creek forest, which figures importantly here. It's a story that grows in part from our country's good fortune: our ancestors came to this beautiful land convinced they were bringing civilization to a wilderness. Part of the deep shock so many of us felt on September 11, 2001, came from living in a land that has been almost unscathed since 1865 and the end of the Civil War by many wars fought elsewhere.

My attempt to understand our family's relationship with places has been influenced by Kentucky farmer and writer Wendell Berry, who adopted terms used by his Stanford teacher, Wallace Stegner: *boomers* and *stickers*. Boomers, according to Berry and Stegner, have provided the major theme in American history with their restless mobility and their greed. In his 2012 Jefferson Lecture at the Kennedy Center for the Performing Arts, titled "It All Turns on Affection," Berry says: "Stickers . . . are motivated by affection, by such love for a place and its life that they want to preserve it and remain in it." But our family, like many in our country, has moved around a lot. I've lived for extended periods in California, Oregon, Missouri, Maryland, Ohio, Illinois, Connecticut, New York, Massachusetts, and New Hampshire, where I live now. I want to believe we've been more *seekers* than *boomers*, hoping to connect with the many places where we lived in ways consistent with something else Berry said in his Jefferson Lecture: "To have a place, to live and belong in a place, to live from a place without destroying it, we must imagine it. By imagination we see it illuminated by its own unique character and by our love for it." At our best, we've tried to imagine fully the places where we've lived. This is partly a story of the imagination, where I've always been rooted in Oregon.

In our family only my brother Dave, who commanded the reconnaissance patrols in Vietnam in 1969, has actually lived in a place torn apart by war. With that important exception, it's hard to imagine how we could have been more fully protected from violence and the wars fought in our lifetimes. Neither of my grandfathers nor my father fought in a war. We told stories in Oregon during World War II of people killed by explosives carried by balloons released from Japanese submarines, but no one in our family knew anyone who encountered one of them. No one from my family was sent to the wars in Iraq and Afghanistan.

There was a painful debate within our family about the Vietnam War although we would probably have disagreed more fiercely if Dave had not been living in the midst of it. Dave told stories for a few days after his return from Vietnam in 1969, while he stayed with my wife and daughters and me in Ohio. In these pages I offer

4

my view of that war's effects on Dave and the rest of our family although he doesn't agree with me. I believe the war in Vietnam affected him profoundly, and one important piece of evidence for me is this: Dave was probably drawn to dangerous Marine reconnaissance partly as a chance to use his impressive skills in woodcraft. He seemed most himself as a youth when he was backpacking or climbing mountains in the Pacific Northwest, but after he came back to Oregon from Vietnam he didn't return to the woods for twenty years. Well before I knew of Oregon's old growth Fox Creek forest and hoped Dave would lead me there, I'd begun to wonder if my brother's healing after the war might require him to find his way once again into wild nature.

Considering the influence of war in our family, I recall a statement by the unnamed "whiskey priest" in Graham Greene's novel *The Power and the Glory*: "Hate was just a failure of imagination." And I think of *collateral damage,* a phrase meant to bypass the imagination, which can "get mired/ in scum and ashes,/ sofa springs,/ splintered glass,/ and bloody rags," as Polish poet and 1996 Nobel laureate Wislawa Szymborska says in "The End and the Beginning." Bombs, bullets, and drone-fired rockets kill and wound far more noncombatants than soldiers in warfare as we know it, and it is difficult to push on with war-making if your mind is weighed down by such unintended consequences. In 2006, when our military killed notorious terrorist Abu Musab al-Zarqawi in Iraq with two 500-pound bombs, we also killed his five companions, including a mother and child. To fix one's mind and heart on a dead child is to question war itself so we distance ourselves with language like *collateral damage.* Our increasing use of drones for "targeted assassinations," is partly an attempt to limit the troubling constraints of imagination on making war. Osama bin Laden grew too large in our imaginations to be "droned."

We needed DNA evidence and post-mortem photographs to convince ourselves he was dead.

In his novel *Hannah Coulter* (2004) Wendell Berry considers the connection between war and imagination. Hannah, the narrator, says: "Want of imagination makes things unreal enough to be destroyed." Recently widowed, she is explaining why she has devoted her old age to studying the World War II battles on Okinawa, where her husband, Nathan, fought. Nathan returned safely to their farm in Kentucky, and she's trying to understand what lay beneath his lifelong silence about the war. "By imagination I mean knowledge and love," Hannah adds. "I mean compassion. People of power kill children, send the young to die, because they have no imagination." Maybe when we're uprooted and displaced, imagination fails us because it's grounded in actual places.

Finding Fox Creek focuses on our family and the places where we've lived more than on the "people of power" who make wars. I write during our nation's partly metaphorical "war on terror," which led us into actual wars in Iraq and Afghanistan and might yet justify other wars. Considering Iraq and Afghanistan and the war in Vietnam has brought to mind all the other wars, literal and metaphorical, that have shaped our lives within my memory. They include World War II, the Korean War, the Cold War, our "low intensity" war in Nicaragua, the "war on poverty" (for which there seems to have been an unannounced armistice), the "war on drugs," the Persian Gulf War, the "war on terror," and even Oregon's "Trojan War," a battle over commercial nuclear power in which I unintentionally became a participant. *War* has provided a powerful metaphor for tackling difficult problems and describing important conflicts. But we've learned from the "war on terror," as we should have learned from the "war on drugs," that such a powerful metaphor has a way of shading into literal reality. As a result, our privileged middle class family in this very protected country has lived in our imaginations on the edge of war zones as long as I can remember.

By *imagination* I mean a way of knowing grounded in complex knowledge, powerful feelings, and direct experience that differs as much from free-floating fantasy as from narrowly specialized thinking. Imagining at its best is an act that thrives on balancing solitude and participation in actual communities embodied in geographical places, not just metaphorical versions of community like those found online. Acts of imagination produce results as down-to-earth as changing one's mind, understanding another's perspective, finding the limits of one's knowledge, or recognizing the need to seek help in understanding something difficult. Sometimes imagination provides glimpses of the wholeness of creation and insight into the injustices that betray wholeness. Imagination offers glimpses of the importance of communities that include whole ecosystems. Because acts of imagination are human acts, they are bound to be flawed, insufficient, imperfect, but humility is built into acts of imagination, a natural consequence of recognizing our human dependence on much in creation over which we have no control.

Finding Fox Creek is partly the story of how our family has imagined the world we live in. The ranch in western Montana where my grandfather, William Martin Watson, grew up must not have been prosperous because his father sometimes worked as a teamster, driving horse-drawn wagons through the mountains into Idaho and back. But the ranch and the land around it were a rich repository of my grandfather's stories about deer, coyotes, wolves, and rattlesnakes. After my grandfather married my grandmother, Louise Brown Watson, who was briefly a teacher after she completed the eighth grade, they had my mother, who was delivered by a Native American midwife we remember as Mrs.

Tinklepaw. Their family moved from western Montana to Seattle, and then settled in Portland, Oregon.

As a bus driver, my grandfather was a heroic figure in my childhood. In a framed photograph on my desk he wears the uniform of the Portland Traction Company, a light gray dress shirt and dark tie with black twill trousers. His sleeves are rolled up almost to the elbow, and his right fist rests on his hip. He stands on a curb and leans slightly into the open door of the bus, his left hand probably resting on the handle passengers might use to pull themselves up onto the first step. His heavy driver's hat is pushed back on his head at a mildly rakish angle, and he looks ahead, not into the camera, as though he is considering roads yet to be traveled.

My grandfather was a garrulous, energetically sociable man. He believed there were people who rode the buses with the purpose of reporting drivers who talked too much with their passengers, but he also believed he could recognize these "stool pigeons," and he seldom stopped telling stories. One of his favorites in the years I knew him was an account of being robbed at the end of the line by a young man with a pistol. The part of the story my grandfather seemed to relish in the telling was about the official hearing, where someone from the Portland Traction Company asked him why he didn't grab the kid's gun. My grandfather's youth as his family's hunter, when venison got them through the winter, led him to have great respect for guns. The question, he thought, didn't warrant much of an answer, and when the company forced him to repay the stolen eighty dollars, he chalked their decision up to foolishness rather than corporate greed.

He was a mildly flamboyant, athletic man who, as he neared retirement, used to bet younger drivers a dollar he could stand in the aisle of a bus and kick the ceiling. He seemed unworried, even a little fearless, and only his stomach ulcers and then his sudden death from a heart attack revealed, not long after he retired, that he felt the pressures of bus schedules and traffic jams.

He can't have been an easy father-in-law for a man who was shy and quiet, a Republican who never lost his suspicion of Franklin Roosevelt and labor unions. My father, Alfred Ishmael Nichols, came to Oregon during the Great Depression. He was a bookish man from rural Pennsylvania, and he took a degree in journalism from the University of Colorado because he was seeking a cure in the mountain air for tuberculosis, which had recently killed his mother. He later traveled the Pacific Northwest as a bill collector and, improbably, a repo man for the Grolier Society. He met the woman who would be my mother, Grace Watson, in a doctor's office in Portland, where she was a receptionist. He deliberately left his hat in the office, the story goes, and returned at closing time to ask her out to dinner. She accepted, and soon they were married and on their way to San Francisco, where he continued to work for the Grolier Society, and my mother worked with the Campfire Girls until my father became ill from what may have been an undiagnosed infection left over from his tuberculosis. They returned to Portland with me, their infant son. We lived for about a year in a tent under an oak tree on land where my grandfather had built a house at the southeast edge of Portland.

Photographs of my mother as a young woman suggest sadness, a beautiful, dark sadness. The first thing I remember learning about her youth was that just after she graduated from Portland's Franklin High School, which would be my high school too, she went swimming in the Sandy River with two Baptist friends, and one of them, Dolores, drowned. My mother feared deceptive holes and currents in rivers for the rest of her life, and we generally stayed away from the Sandy River. But once, when I was eight, we stopped on our way back to Portland from a picnic on Larch Mountain, and my father and a friend from the shipyard where Dad worked took me down to the bank of the Sandy to cut a willow branch for making a whistle. When we returned to our 1931 Graham car, where my mother had stayed with my little brother, she didn't see me with the men and assumed at once I had drowned. It was as though she had a sudden, hysterical flashback, and it took a while to convince her I'd survived. The drowning that haunted my mother linked her powerfully to the Baptist faith of her childhood and youth.

My mother's fundamentalist Baptist vision, which she seemed to embrace even after she joined a more liberal church, was probably as influential in our family's political imagination as my father's suspicion of government and unions. When they decided to leave Lents Baptist Church, where my mother had grown up, my parents chose Mount Tabor Presbyterian Church, a large, rather affluent congregation some two miles from our neighborhood. Their preference probably had something to do with a longing for middle class respectability, as did their decision to move to the suburbs when I was a senior in high school. At Mt. Tabor Presbyterian Church my father became a ruling elder, my mother a Sunday school teacher, but she was not satisfied with the curriculum, which seemed to her insufficiently Bible-centered. When they moved to the suburbs in 1955, my father once again became an elder, in the Milwaukie Presbyterian Church. My mother no longer taught Sunday school. About this time I think she began to struggle with a depression that was not diagnosed until the last months of her life, after she had suffered a stroke that took away most of her language.

Six years after my birth in 1938, Dave was born, and eight years after that came John. Because I left Oregon for college in 1956 and returned for only brief stays, I didn't know them well as they grew into adulthood.

Chapter One

Saddle Mountain

Shortly after the New Year in 1959, on a train bound to Kansas City from Oregon, I talked with a Marine who wore his uniform with style. He was a handsome young man, full of himself, and I found his self-confidence deeply appealing. I was in the middle of my junior year at Park College, a tiny Presbyterian college in Missouri. (Now called "Park University," it is no longer Presbyterian and has campuses and programs in nineteen states, many on Air Force bases.) Returning from a Christmas vacation in Portland, I was confused about what I wanted to do with my life. I envied the Marine's self-assurance, and he made the Marine Corps sound more interesting than college. Later, he left for the club car, and as we pulled into Kansas City, he returned to introduce an attractive young woman who had agreed to spend the night with him in the city.

I began to wonder how I'd look in uniform. It was a possibility consistent with our family's conservative Republicanism, and my mother had often said a few years of military life might teach me to make my bed properly. The idea seemed risk-free in 1959, when our country wasn't at war, but my parents thought it made no sense, given the fact that I was doing well enough in college to be able to think about medical school. I finished college, married Nancy Shea from Massachusetts, and instead of going to medical school, went to graduate school in English at Johns Hopkins University.

Almost eight years later, in the fall of 1967, my brother Dave graduated from St. Olaf College and joined the Marines without consulting anyone in the family. After finishing officer's training, he wore dress whites at his wedding in Hibbing, Minnesota, hometown of Bob Dylan,

11

and I was his best man. Within weeks, Dave flew off to fight in Vietnam. By then, my own view of military life had changed. Along with millions of others, I'd begun to question the wisdom of this particular war, and I'd begun to argue with my parents about it. But once Dave was leading reconnaissance missions north of Phu Bai, our family stopped arguing about the war in Vietnam. When he returned from combat in 1969 and joined his wife to stay at our house for a few days in Granville, Ohio, where I was teaching at Denison University, it seemed the wrong time to resume our debate. Dave had survived deadly encounters, and his wife, Karen, had been working as a psychiatric nurse with veterans. We listened to Dave's stories and jokes about crawling through rainforests at night, setting Claymore mines, and calling in air strikes, and it felt as though his experience in Vietnam and Karen's encounters with war's aftermath in the hospital trumped our growing objections to the war. If I had imagined that for years afterward Dave, who seldom talked about anything that worried or frightened him when he was a kid, would be silent about his Vietnam experience, I might have asked more questions.

Dave's letters from Vietnam were so infrequent that Karen sometimes contacted the Red Cross to be sure he was still alive, but when he wrote, he acknowledged the war's horror. He told of losing a young rifleman, drowned on a training mission just after they arrived in the country, and he mentioned his revulsion at seeing "crispy critters" after calling in a napalm air strike close to his own position.

In our Ohio living room, however, just out of combat, he gave us a version of war lite. One of his stories about a reconnaissance mission suggests his narrative strategy. Two helicopters put Dave and his men into a clearing somewhere in a mountainous region in late afternoon. Shortly after the choppers lift off, they radio back that Dave's patrol has been spotted, and soon the Marines can tell someone is following them. They set up an ambush, but the people tracking them are too skillful to walk into it. So Dave and his men move slowly down into a valley and dig in as though they plan to spend the night by a stream. When darkness settles in, they begin to crawl silently beside the stream that runs through the valley. They crawl for hours, listening for clicks and whispers, and then suddenly they hear automatic weapons firing and grenades exploding back where they pretended to bivouac. There is the sound of so much firepower they figure the people who followed them waited for reinforcements.

Dave and his men continue crawling, and pretty soon they can tell the enemy has guessed what they are doing because they hear people moving above them on the ridges, and occasionally a grenade comes down into the valley. No one is hit, and they continue moving for the rest of the night, not standing up to walk until it is almost dawn. At full light, they set up a perimeter and stop to rest. But after they settle down, they hear noises, as though someone is moving carelessly in their direction. Dave has put two of the newest members of his squad, Owen and Adams, at their rear in the direction of the sounds, so he crawls back to join them. As he is crawling, he realizes the noise is coming from up in the trees. It's a troop of monkeys. Although Owen and Adams are tired and frightened, they hold their fire. Dave ends the story by saying if he ever hunted elk, he'd be pleased to hunt with Owen and Adams. He never hunted, and after he returned from Vietnam, he favored the idea of a police force that doesn't carry guns.

Although Dave tried to put something like the monkeys in all his stories, most of his comic twists didn't work for me. He told of setting a Claymore mine that killed two young girls traveling with a group of Viet Cong and added that his men claimed they'd have to watch out for horny VC for a while. And he told of capturing an old

13

man on a trail used by the VC and bringing him in for questioning. The translator told him the old man expected them to kill him, and when they let him go, he kept whirling around like a dancer to face them as he walked away.

But Dave seemed more confident during their visit to Ohio than he ever seemed as a student. He knew he was good at the dangerous art of reconnaissance. After the young Marine drowned on the training mission, Dave lost no more men even though the patrols he commanded drew fire so often other officers gave him the nickname "Magnet." He tried unsuccessfully to extend his stay in Vietnam. For two years afterwards, while he and his wife were stationed in Hawaii with the Marine Corps, he sounded content.

When Dave returned to Portland, where we both grew up, he had difficulty finding jobs that played to the strengths he'd found in combat. He tried banking and then selling insurance before he bought a small wholesale company, Fox Lamp and Fixture. It seemed wonderful and strange to me that the most rebellious of my parents' three sons would come home and follow the lead of our father, who had taken a position in Portland with Stubbs Electric in the late 1940's after he left his job on the Hanford Nuclear Reservation.

Even though Dave had used the woodcraft he loved in the Marine Corps, he seemed unwilling to go back into the forest after his return. He coached his two children's baseball, softball, and soccer teams, and when I watched Dave with a tee ball team early in his years of coaching, I was reminded of what a gentle, thoughtful little brother he'd been when I wasn't teasing him. A tiny shortstop panicked at the plate and flailed away briefly without hitting even the tee, and I saw evidence that Dave had schooled his team to deal gently with each other's errors. While his players yelled encouragement, Dave walked out to say something quietly to the boy and give him a hug. The little shortstop flied out respectably to second base. Dave's approach, which he explained to me exhaustively over dinner afterwards, was to work hard on the fundamentals in practice and focus on achievements in games. No need, he said, to point out mistakes. His teams played with great abandon. When they made mistakes, it was not because their nerves were frazzled.

Dave's nerves *were* frazzled, in my opinion, even though he claimed they were not. He would have laughed at me if I said he suffered from post-traumatic shock syndrome. But he started smoking in Vietnam, and he didn't stop for years after he came home even when he developed severe asthma. When we talked politics, he was uncharacteristically abrupt, impatient, and sarcastic. Our best times together came when he showed me how to build the brick wall or I helped him shingle a roof, and we could focus on the work. He suffered from depression. Years later he would be diagnosed and briefly medicated for attention deficit disorder although he'd done good work as a history major at St. Olaf College in Minnesota. I wondered how anyone pays attention to anything after fighting in a war.

It took years for me to entice Dave to return to the woods after he came back from Vietnam. The place I had in mind, the Fox Creek forest, is a community of ancient Douglas fir, cedar, spruce, and younger hemlock, hidden on the northwest shoulder of Oregon's Saddle Mountain. My first memory of Saddle Mountain, a faint one, goes back to the late spring of 1955. I was sixteen then and behind the wheel of my parents' 1951 Plymouth coupe on Highway 26, heading toward the beach. The Plymouth had slick nylon seat covers and no seat belts so passengers slid sideways when we rounded curves at high speed. Even with both of my hands on the wheel, I could feel my rear end slide toward the girl by the window when the road swung left. We were part of a church group, and later, at the beach, the minister told me he tried to catch us after I passed him, but he gave up when his speedometer went above 80.

We hurtled past Saddle Mountain that day, giving it little more than a glance. On such a clear, sunny morning, Saddle Mountain comes into view on the right side of the highway as you start down the western slope of the Coast Range some fifteen miles from the ocean. The mountain's triple summits, the tallest just 3283 feet, are higher than any of those around it. Saddle Mountain has a large variety of wildflowers, but most of them don't appear until July, and in 1955, even walking on the mountain, I probably wouldn't have noticed if they were blooming.

Years later, the poet Gary Snyder told me he once parked on a Saddle Mountain logging road with a woman friend when they were undergraduates at Reed College in Portland. Snyder's early connection with Saddle Mountain was more interesting than mine, and it reminds me of something he said in *The Practice of the Wild* (1990) about the ecological impoverishment of civilizations in the East and West. By the time of the sixteenth century, he wrote, "The people were rapidly becoming nature-illiterate. . . . The leaders of these civilizations grew up with less and less personal knowledge of animal behavior and were no longer taught the intimate wide-ranging plant knowledge that had once been universal." Hurtling heedlessly past Saddle Mountain in 1955, I was part of a movement already well underway 500 years earlier.

Meriwether Lewis and William Clark resisted that movement on their famous military expedition to the Pacific Northwest. Owing partly to the influence of Thomas Jefferson, who was deeply curious about what they might find along their way, they worked skillfully to know plants and animals and indigenous cultures along the route of their Expedition. But in 1805-06, when the

Corps of Discovery wintered at Fort Clatsop in Saddle Mountain's watershed and their hunters walked the mountain's western slopes, Lewis and Clark learned little about the indigenous people and almost nothing about the mountain. For one thing, they had an extraordinary run of fog and rain during their stay on the coast, and Saddle Mountain was probably not often visible to them, as it was to me on that morning in 1955. For another, the explorers' relations with tribal societies near the mountain were strained. Expecting people like those in the warrior societies of the Great Plains with whom they were more familiar, Lewis and Clark misunderstood the northwestern cultures, and they seem to have been oblivious to indigenous views of the Northwest landscape. If they understood that Saddle Mountain was sacred to the Clatsops and Chinooks, they said nothing of it in their journals.

The first white person to write about indigenous views of Saddle Mountain may have been a Methodist missionary, Gustavus Hines, who arrived in the region some thirty-five years after Lewis and Clark. Hines was so repelled by these tribal societies that within days of traveling thousands of miles to save their souls, he believed nothing could protect them from the darkest of destinies. "Under the impression that the doom of extinction is suspended over [t]his race," he wrote in *Life on the Plains of the Pacific* (1852), "and that the hand of Providence is removing them to give place to a people more worthy of this beautiful and fertile company, we arrived at our place of encampment. . . ." Some years later, in *Oregon and Its Institutions* (1868), Hines commented on the local tribes' conception of Saddle Mountain:

> The most remarkable [mountain] in the vicinity of the Columbia River is one named "Swallalahoost," concerning which they have a singular tradition. One of their

great and mighty chiefs a long time ago, according to the tradition, after having accomplished the most wonderful exploits in behalf of his people, was finally killed by his enemies; but after death he assumed the form of a monstrous eagle; and, taking wing, flew to the top of his mountain, and there became the creator of the lightning and the thunder at the top of this peak. From this tradition, as well as from the appearance of the mountain, it is supposed by some that it might probably have once been an active volcano. Commodore Wilkes, on his exploring visit in the country in 1842, gave it the name of "Saddle Mountain" from the resemblance of its top to the shape of a saddle.

To say I was ignorant of the mountain's history as we swept by it in 1955 is an understatement. Even in 1973, when our family began visiting Saddle Mountain, our walking and talking in that place seemed just one of many gestures we made as we tried to learn about the land and heal the wounds from our family's disagreements about the Vietnam War. But in the years that followed, my wife, our daughters, and I returned so often to Saddle Mountain from our home in Ohio that our journeys had the character of pilgrimages. By 2010 I would publish *Fleeing Ohio*, a prison novel that revolves around Saddle Mountain.

It took me several years to begin to understand why Dave never joined us on the mountain. It would be almost twenty years before we knew about the Fox Creek forest, and by the time we learned of that beautiful ancient forest on the mountain's northwest shoulder it was under attack.

Chapter Two

The Kaiser Aluminum Skirmish

In late 1967, before Dave went to Vietnam, I wrote to Mr. T.J. Ready, then president of Kaiser Aluminum & Chemical Corporation, about an apparent injustice. Two years out of graduate school, settling in at Ohio's Denison University as an assistant professor in English, I'd just gotten to know an engineer at the nearby Kaiser plant when he was fired. The engineer, I told Mr. Ready in my letter, had resisted pressure within Kaiser to buy U.S. Savings Bonds, explaining to his superiors that his opposition to our government's policy in Vietnam made the required purchase of the bonds "an assault on his conscience." However, I told Mr. Ready, the engineer agreed to buy a few bonds when he was told continued resistance would cost him his job. Shortly after he yielded on the savings bonds, he grew a beard. "It is a rather handsome, red beard," I wrote, "but my understanding is that he was told by the management of the Newark plant to remove it. He did not yield, and he was dismissed."

What gave my letter to Kaiser's president impressive authority, as I saw it, was my claim that Mr. L had been promoted the week before he was fired, and Kaiser's Division Industrial Relations Manager, Mr. J.O. Presley, addressed that point on behalf of President Ready in his surprisingly prompt reply on December 29, 1967. After commending me on the sincerity of my concern and acknowledging that it was "somewhat justified," given what I had been told by the engineer, Mr. Presley wrote:

> I would, however, like to point out that you have heard only one side of the story—a rather incomplete and inaccurate one at that. As an example, Mr. [L] was not

promoted just prior to his departure, as he apparently contends. In fact, he has not been promoted since joining our company in 1964.

It was true: I had misunderstood L's account of an offered promotion, but this mistake gave me an opportunity to make a point that, at the time, seemed to me decisive:

A question remains in my mind: you pointed out—quite accurately, I have discovered—that Mr. [L] has not been promoted since he joined your company in 1964. However, he was indeed offered a promotion to Senior Engineer just prior to his dismissal; and the offer was contingent on his shaving off his beard. If you did not know this when you answered my letter, is it possible that there are other factors in his dismissal that have not come to your attention?

I asked Mr. Presley next why Mr. L would have been offered a position at IBM with more responsibility if his work were unsatisfactory at Kaiser. Kaiser headquarters is in Oakland, and I concluded this power-packed letter by wishing the Oakland Raiders well in Super Bowl II, which they were destined to lose rather decisively to the Green Bay Packers.

Before I go further with this correspondence between Kaiser management and my assistant professor self, I should say something about my defense of Mr. L's beard. If there is a photograph on this book jacket, it might lead a reader to think I was defending my own personal appearance, but it would be several years before I grew a beard. I had tried to grow one in college without success; in fact, a young woman I hardly knew volunteered one day in the dining hall to give me some eye shadow to make it more visible. So I was clean-shaven at the time I corresponded with Mr. Presley, and I would not have entered a classroom without first girding myself in shirt, tie, jacket and well pressed pants. Indeed, this is the explanation, the *only* explanation I can offer, for how I became Assistant Dean of the College when I was barely out of graduate school. While some of my colleagues were drawn to denim work shirts and jeans or tie-died shirts and brightly colored bell-bottoms, I dressed with the austere dignity of a politician or a perhaps Kaiser executive.

My second letter to Kaiser seemed to stir up dust. Mr. Presley came close to offering a concession:

> You state in your letter Mr. [L] was offered a promotion if he would shave off his beard. My information is that this is not the case. This does not mean that the subjects of his promotability and his beard were not discussed with him, the distinction being the context in which they and other aspects of his total performance were discussed.

Following that delicate distinction, Mr. Presley announced he had set up a meeting for me with the Industrial Relations Superintendent at Kaiser's plant in Newark, Ohio, where Mr. L was once employed.

When I arrived at the Kaiser parking lot for the meeting, a security guard greeted me by name, and I soon found I was actually meeting with two men. The superintendent, a short bulldog of a man, sat behind his desk, and the other man, seated just to my right, was very large. I was dressed as if I were about to teach a class, which in a sense I was hoping to do. The two Kaiser men wore ties but no jackets, and their shirtsleeves were rolled up, a fact that seemed increasingly significant as our meeting progressed.

That one-hour meeting was as close as I've come to being mugged. The superintendent led off by saying they had been in touch with A. Blair Knapp, president of Denison University, where I'd begun teaching. I let that go at first because I hadn't identified myself as a Denison employee in my letters, and I was surprised. Then the superintendent and his associate set out to convince me that Mr. L was an incompetent engineer and his firing was a result of that fact alone. Had they been willing to share information with me to make their case, I probably wouldn't have understood it anyway because I wasn't a good judge of engineering skills, but they relied instead on repetition and rising volume as though they were American tourists ordering food in a restaurant where the waiter doesn't understand English.

When I realized they had pretty well exhausted their arguments with their first sentence or two, I asked why they had contacted my employer since I had written to Kaiser as a private citizen. With that, the bulldog offered the most memorable line in our long conversation: "So you want to get down in the dirt." It was a statement, but I treated it as a question and said I really *didn't* want to get down in the dirt. But the truth was, he continued, that he and his big buddy thought I should not have contacted *their* employer. When I explained that Mr. L believed he'd pretty well exhausted his appeals there in Newark, and I'd decided to take the case to Kaiser's supreme court in Oakland, they were not persuaded. Our meeting ended unpleasantly.

Although I knew our meeting was supposed to be the end of the line, I wrote a letter to the superintendent with a copy to Mr. Presley in Oakland, registering my dissatisfaction:

> You probably guessed that I was not entirely reassured by meeting with you.

That is, I received the impression from your remarks that Mr. [L] was dismissed for reasons that were not at all clearly matters of professional competence.

I undertook my correspondence with Kaiser Corporation as a private citizen, and I want to say again that your decision to contact my employer, Dr. A. Blair Knapp of Denison University, constitutes the sort of confusion between public and private, corporate and individual, that was probably responsible for Mr. [L's] dismissal.

In general, my experience with you has helped me to understand why bright young people are becoming less and less interested in pursuing careers with large corporations.

That last paragraph turned out to be less than prophetic: soon some of my best students were happily taking jobs with large corporations, and there was a period not long after the 1960's when students greeted a job with the Leo Burnett ad agency in Chicago as though they had won a Rhodes Scholarship. Had I guessed when I wrote my letter, which proved to be the last in our exchange, that Kaiser would file for bankruptcy protection under Chapter 11 in February of 2002, I might have claimed their cultural insensitivity was likely to have long-term financial implications, but that possibility didn't even occur to me.

There were two additional matters I didn't mention: (1) I understood their concern about the symbolic power of beards better than I let on in my meeting with the managers. Three years earlier my father had told me he was worried about my oldest friend, Terry, because he had grown a beard. Facial hair was generally a sign, Dad said, that someone had gone off the deep end politically. Terry and I had been close friends since the first grade, and after his family moved away from Portland, he often came to stay with us. I spent much of a summer living on the farm run by Terry's parents and grandparents. That my father would apply his beard theory to my friend, knowing as he did that Terry had worked his way through the University of Oregon as a math major by giving music lessons, taught me something about the emblematic power of beards. It was probably one reason why I longed to grow one myself. (2) My hunch, and Mr. L's as well, was that the real cause of his firing was not the beard but a Black Power button he wore to work. It was just four months before the assassination of Martin Luther King, and the Civil Rights Movement had been torn by disagreements about strategy. Black Power was very controversial. Many people identified it with a call to answer violence with violence. The button may well have been the straw that broke the back of Mr. L's career at Kaiser, but I was so concerned about the fear induced by Mr. L's association with Black Power even though he was white that I was silent about it, and no one from Kaiser brought it up.

There was something both troubling and encouraging about the rise of Black Power in the 1960's and its academic rendering in Black Studies. I'd just devoted several years to studying the fabric of American culture while ignoring African American culture, one of its most important threads. Just a few decades earlier biology and anthropology had been used to justify segregation, but now colleges were beginning to offer courses that explored African American culture. Martin Luther King had begun to call attention to a connection between the war and the civil rights movement he had been leading. On April 4, 1967, in a speech to Clergy and Laymen Concerned About Vietnam, King spoke of his growing awareness of the link and its irony. "We were taking the black young men who had been crippled by our society," he said, "and sending them eight thousand miles away to guarantee liberties in Southeast Asia which they had not found in southwest Georgia and East Harlem." Spotting such connections involves a painful act of imagination, and our family struggled to understand.

26

Chapter Three

God and Mom at Yale

In 1969-70, while Dave and his wife lived in Hawaii with the Marine Corps after the end of his tour in Vietnam, we moved from Granville, Ohio, to New Haven, Connecticut. It was an exciting time for us. Nancy tutored adults and audited a course at Yale. Daughter Judy started the second grade, and her sister, Annie, not yet in school, made friends with Maryknoll priests who lived on our street. I was a post-doctoral fellow in Afro-American Studies at Yale because I had suddenly become the campus "expert" at Denison University in this rapidly developing field.

My new expertise began to blossom in the fall of 1967, when a student asked to write her senior essay on the Ralph Ellison novel *Invisible Man*. Although I'd been a graduate student in American literature and American intellectual history, I hadn't read a single slave narrative, and my knowledge of modern African American writers was superficial. But I admired Ellison's essays in *Shadow and Act* and was glad to have an excuse to study *Invisible Man*. By the time the Danforth Foundation decided to help people like me understand what we were teaching, I'd written a scholarly article, "Ralph Ellison's Black American Scholar," which explored the influence of Ralph Waldo Emerson on Ralph Waldo Ellison, and I was coordinating the college's first Black Studies course, an interdisciplinary class that enrolled every African American student at Denison in 1968, along with some 60 white students, bringing the total enrollment to about 75. The course generated much controversy, punctuated by a student boycott near the end, when the African American students objected to having their understanding of their own culture graded by white faculty. With the help of a senior, Charles P. Henry, who would go on to a distinguished career in African American Studies at the University of California at Berkeley while working with Amnesty International and the National Endowment for the Humanities, we managed to find a compromise, but no one claimed the class was a success. The college's serious but flawed effort to offer its first course in Black Studies probably increased the Danforth Foundation's eagerness to send me to Yale in Afro-American Studies.

We lived that exciting year in a drafty summer cottage on Long Island Sound, and my mother flew out from Oregon to visit us. She showed Judy and Annie, who were eight and four, the magic of the place, sleeping in a room with them that looked east over the water, and as they watched the sun rise out of Long Island Sound, she told them she had lived all her life in the West without ever seeing the sun come out of the ocean. She walked with them by the water and showed them shells and rocks that couldn't be found on the Oregon coast. Watching her with Judy and Annie, I recognized for the first time what she must have missed by having three sons who came home from church and read the Sunday paper while she made dinner. She worried aloud about fire danger in our cottage, but perhaps because Dave was safely out of Vietnam, she seemed filled with hope.

In the spring of 1970, when Mom arrived in New Haven, the town was swept by much political and intellectual excitement. The local Black Panther organization was preparing for a murder trial that included Bobby Seale, one of their national leaders. There were large demonstrations against the Vietnam War on the New Haven green. Nancy and I attended a lecture course, "Revolutions and Revolutionary Thought," taught by Isaac Kramnick, and one day he shared the platform with uninvited members of the Black Panther Party, who were there to let the class know revolution would soon be coming to New Haven. On the day of a student strike Kramnick came to a depopulated class and expressed his disappointment that even so few were there. When a student asked why he was disappointed, he said both bodies and language were being assaulted in America. He didn't have to mention the recent killings of students at Kent State and Jackson State because they were on everyone's minds. Another student asked why Professor Kramnick was going on with business as usual by meeting our class, and he said he supported the student strike, but he was unwilling to make moral choices for his students. Five or six students walked out after that, but about one-fifth of the usual class population remained to hear Kramnick talk half-heartedly but thoughtfully about revolutionary thought.

As Mom struggled to make sense of the political and cultural controversies swirling about us that year, she turned to a new book by Francis A. Schaeffer, *The Church at the End of the Twentieth Century* (1970). Schaeffer, a Presbyterian who claimed to fear the growing power of a "left-wing elite," shared my mother's sense that many Christians had turned their backs on "the historic, Bible-believing minority." The assertion at the heart of Schaeffer's book was this: the Bible is "objective, absolute truth." Mom urged me to read Schaeffer, and I did. But I was troubled by the cultural criticism he built on his fundamentalist premise. Almost thirty-five years later, Thomas Frank described something similar in explaining the backlash against the "liberal establishment" in *What's the Matter with Kansas?* (2004). "In this tragic land," Frank says, "unassuageable cultural grievances are elevated inexplicably over solid material ones, and basic economic self-interest is eclipsed by juicy myths of national authenticity and righteousness wronged." Schaeffer's social commentary was steeped in righteous indignation. Commenting on campus disruptions in the 1960's, for example, he said liberal faculty members teach "man is a machine" and treat students themselves like machines, providing no ground for values. "Liberalism has committed suicide," he insisted, "because it has cut away its foundation. So the faculty screamed with glee when students stormed the administrative offices, but squealed once they turned against the faculty."

The professors whose courses I attended that year at Yale didn't say anything about people as machines, and I didn't hear them screaming with glee about the disruptions. Like me, they seemed to be struggling to make sense of rhetoric and activism that confronted neglected problems in our society but also seemed in danger of spinning out of control. Even C. Vann Woodward, the genteel, highly respected historian of the American South, seemed to be thrown off his stride in a graduate seminar that focused on slavery when members of the class made connections between the history of American slavery and issues being raised outside the windows of our classroom. Arna Bontemps, a writer in the Harlem Renaissance, was teaching at Yale, and he spoke of his puzzlement on reading Norman Mailer, who mixed autobiography and fiction in *The Armies of the Night,* which condemned the war then haunting our country. "It would be a pity," Bontemps said of an important African American autobiography, "if Richard Wright had decided to fictionalize *Black Boy.*"

Bontemps was in his late sixties, and he quietly resisted some of the rhetoric used by young black intellectuals at Yale. When William Styron came to Yale to talk about his novel *The Confessions of Nat Turner* (1967), and his critics said a white writer had no business trying to imagine his way into the life of a revolutionary black slave, an assertion that worried me years later, when I set out to write *York's Journal,* a novel about the only slave to accompany the Lewis and Clark Expedition, Bontemps spoke up to defend the power of imagination.

Austin Clarke, a black writer from Barbados who was more than thirty years younger than Bontemps, interrupted, shouting, "That's irrelevant!" Later, Bontemps stumbled over the phrase *cultural nationalism*, and there was laughter and whispering among students and young faculty.

Even the articulate Isaac Kramnick, a young political scientist who might have been expected to fit Francis Schaeffer's stereotype of a liberal faculty firebrand, struggled to find language. One day he ran into trouble, for example, talking about the changing meaning of "race riot" in the United States. Before the 1960's, he said, race riots were really communal lynchings: whites would go into a black neighborhood, burn houses, and shoot black people who fled their houses. When he started to describe race riots of the 1960's, Kramnick seemed momentarily tongue-tied. He struggled to find words for the violence, and students, recognizing the cause of his difficulty, began to laugh. What he probably meant to say was that "race riot" in the 1960's meant destructive and unpredictable force initiated by black people within their own communities. But he was understandably concerned about offending black students, and he also must have wanted to acknowledge that the race riots in Watts (1965) and Detroit (1967) were touched off by less visible forms of violence directed against black people. What he said, finally, was something like this: "They engaged in rioting within their own black ghettoes." Perhaps because it seemed euphemistic, several students hissed.

In an undergraduate course that focused partly on slavery, historian Stanley Elkins came to visit one day. The students were familiar with his controversial and influential book *Slavery: A Problem in American Institutional and Intellectual Life* (1959). A student asked him if his background, his cultural "whiteness," had prepared him adequately to understand slave psychology, a crucial theme in his book. It was a skeptical question that troubled the eight white Danforth Fellows every day, and it sometimes made us angry. I imagine Elkins felt something close to what Henry Kissinger might have felt several years later on a visit to a Johns Hopkins seminar, when a student asked if he considered himself a war criminal, and Kissinger walked out, saying he had come expecting an "academic exercise." Elkins didn't walk out. He led a discussion, often heated, of problems encountered in the study of slavery. One part of the discussion remains fresh in my mind. A student asked why Elkins made little use of slave narratives in writing his book, and Elkins' answer seemed to rely more on traditions of historical research than on the trustworthiness of the narratives. After that discussion, several members of the class, including me, began reading and discussing slave narratives. I wrote an essay for C. Vann Woodward, later published as "Slave Narratives: Dismissed Evidence in the Writing of Southern History."

I was fascinated by the conflicts both inside and outside the classroom that year, and I was humbled by the experience. Near the end of the year the Danforth Foundation organized a conference for the nine Yale Fellows in Afro-American Studies, a chance to meet with several senior scholars and educators. Some forty-five people attended, almost evenly divided between black and white, and we sat around a large banquet table at the Showboat Inn in Greenwich, Connecticut. I read a statement on behalf of the eight white participants in our program, an attempt to summarize our humbling, sometimes traumatic, experience. It was not meant to be a keynote address, but our scheduled speaker arrived late so I kicked things off. "We have come to recognize," I said, "that the Black Studies movement, as it is understood by many black students and professors, is a radical challenge to our traditional views of higher

32

education and to our legitimacy as teachers." I pointed out that black students at Yale had questioned our motives for being in the program, and I concluded with a gloomy prediction: "In fact, some of us will probably approach the teaching of individual courses in Black Studies with a renewed humility bordering on paralysis. I would not be surprised to hear in a year or so that members of our group have no direct contact with Black Studies programs at their colleges." I said very little about what an extraordinary privilege it had been to spend a year at Yale studying material that should have been part of our earlier educations.

Seated on my left was Herman Branson, an African American who was just moving from the presidency of Central State University in Ohio to Lincoln University in Pennsylvania, both black universities. Branson's response to my opening remarks was impatience with my pessimism about the roles we could play in Black Studies. There were a few Yale undergraduates present for the discussion, including the late Armstead Robinson, who was influential in the development of Yale's Afro-American Studies program and who went on to an influential career as an historian at the University of Virginia. (He was instrumental too in nurturing my humility.) The presence of undergraduates may have led to some posturing by young faculty members who seemed eager to display their radical credentials, and Branson was as impatient with their bluster as he had been with my pessimism. He spoke with a firm, evenhanded caution, and each time he began, he turned on a small tape recorder. This struck me as vain, and once, when he dismissed something said as romanticism, I longed to lean over and whisper *bullshit* in his recorder.

Fortunately, I was silent. A few weeks later *The New York Times* reported that Branson had joined a group of fifteen Black college presidents who met with

President Nixon, and it was Branson who read an angry statement criticizing several of the administration's policies. The quick revision of my perspective on Herman Branson was a sign of things to come, for within a few months I realized the year at Yale had given me new confidence, as well as humility, and some of my most interesting work over the next twenty-five years would grow out of my work in Black Studies.

But I still had no clarity to set against Francis Schaeffer's certitude or my mother's. If I had come away from that wonderful, perplexing year with revolutionary fervor, I might have decided our family's conflict was insignificant in the larger scheme of things, or I might have had the evangelical zeal required to bring family members along. But the year at Yale seemed to complicate my own thinking and to deepen our family divide. It was difficult to imagine a way to bridge it. Our disagreement about racial conflict and injustice at home seemed inseparable from our disagreement about the war in Vietnam.

Chapter Four

Finding Our Way Home

In late August of 1973, sleeping in a motel in Alexandria, Minnesota, I had a dream that gave me a strange sense of hope: I was on President Richard Nixon's staff, kneeling on the floor with several other workers, trying to remove watermarks from a carpet in the Oval Office. In my waking life I had begun to wish the President would be impeached as a result of the Watergate scandal, which was gaining momentum. But Nancy, Judy, Annie, and I were on our way from Ohio to Oregon, planning to spend a year living near my family, and my dream suggested that at some deep level of my being I held onto Republican loyalties from my childhood. Maybe if I could tap into the remnants of those old allegiances when our family gathered, we could talk.

Within a week of my dream we were talking with my parents about the Watergate hearings, in which White House staff members testified and senators tried to expose the cover-up. We were driving along the Columbia River Highway with my parents, and I asked what they thought about the many hours of televised hearings with the Senate Select Committee on Presidential Campaign Activities. Dad, recently retired, said Senator Sam Ervin, who chaired the hearings, was an "old self-seeking charlatan." Sam Dash, Ervin's appointee as chief counsel to the committee, did not appear to be very bright, Dad insisted. But his main complaint was that the committee's hearings endangered the defendants' rights to a jury trial. My memory of this conversation has me in the role of respectful, curious son, but my journal includes a note that Nancy later told me our daughter Annie, almost eight years old, quietly asked if we were fighting.

A few days later, on Labor Day weekend, the six of us drove up to Tilly Jane Forest Camp, near the timberline on the northeast side of Mount Hood. (I hadn't yet begun to wonder why Dave, now living in Portland, excused himself from such outings.) It was chilly, rainy weather, and my parents, skilled campers, would normally have relied on their tent to keep them warm and dry. Some of my most pleasant memories of childhood are of holing up with them in their old tent in heavy Oregon rainstorms. Once on a beach when I was very young, Dad improvised a surprisingly effective shelter out of driftwood when we were caught in a sudden rainstorm. On Mount Hood Mom and Dad were probably concerned about our ability to keep their granddaughters dry in the rain, and we stayed in a big log shelter, where we met two young, longhaired men from Denver. They were traveling through the West, they told us, working when they needed money. They had been picking apples near Hood River, and they planned to spend the winter near New Orleans, hiring out to local farmers. When we joined them, they were cooking over an open fire in the fireplace and one of them said they'd be glad to move if we wanted to put our sleeping bags down by the fire. The other asked if we'd like to share their dinner. Dad said thanks, but we'd sleep up in the loft and we had stuff to cook on our camping stove.

The next morning we walked up to the timberline, crossing a bridge over a powerful stream that came boiling out of a glacier. Although the rain had stopped, it was cold for early September, but the girls found the stark mountain landscape very exciting. Judy, almost twelve, wanted to talk about the young men back at the shelter. She was impressed with their generosity and their apparent ease with the world. While we had settled down for the night, one of them sat by the fire, staring out into the darkness and playing a wooden flute. Judy, who had recently decided she wanted to play both flute and guitar, thought the music was beautiful. Mom told Judy the lifestyle those young men had chosen was selfish. They weren't doing a thing to help anyone or make the world a better place. As I remember, she didn't use the word *hippie*, but she seemed to have in mind the counterculture that worried so many people in the 1960's. (When I was born in 1938, my parents lived at 816 Ashbury Street in the Haight-Ashbury neighborhood of San Francisco, and it may have been particularly troubling to them that the place where they began their lives together in the 1930's had become a hippie Mecca in the 1960's.) Judy would grow up to be a poet, a political activist, and a lesbian, and she seemed troubled by her grandmother's take on the generous young men. She didn't have an answer, and I was silent.

Our encounter with hippies was portentous because we intended to live for the year like Henry Thoreau at Walden Pond. We rented a cabin near Cannon Beach, Oregon, where some of our neighbors seemed to be "rich hippies," as our daughters came to call them, people who claimed to have stepped outside the rat race. They didn't seem to pay much attention to the rigors of earning a living. We planned to live on a half-salary for the year, which came to about $5,000, and although that was a lot compared with Thoreau's meager income during his two years at Walden, it made us a little nervous when the installation of our telephone cost $30.

Within a few days, my brother Dave and his wife Karen came to visit, bringing fruit and vegetables from an old friend's farm, a beautifully sharpened ax, a bucksaw, and a chainsaw. They helped us gather wood for the fireplace and woodstove, and it seemed clear Dave and Karen approved of our plans to live simply. We didn't talk about Watergate or war, but Dave reminded me, surprisingly gently, of how little I knew about war and the business world where he was trying to start a career.

Two days after their visit, we learned the Chilean military, backed by our CIA, had attacked the presidential palace, and Salvador Allende, Chile's democratically elected president was dead. The violent overthrow of Allende came to haunt our family's conversations in Oregon almost as much as the rising tide of Watergate because Judy, in the sixth grade at Cannon Beach School, made Allende the subject of her first term paper.

But in spite of the grim political realities that filled the newspapers, we had good talks with my parents. In late September we visited them in Portland, where they had moved into a mobile home. They were canning peaches and berries they'd picked on local farms. In the past, Dad had helped with the picking and Mom did the canning. He was struggling now to fill his leisure time, and he helped with the canning too. Mom told me Dad had broken down a few days earlier, saying he wasn't worth anything to anyone. But both of them seemed relaxed and happy to have us there, and they could surely tell how much we admired their skills and their resourcefulness, given our experiment in simplicity.

I had begun an essay I called "The New Individualists" about my students, who seemed to be turning away from the activism and the idealism of their predecessors in the 1960's. I told Mom and Dad about the essay and made the mistake of mentioning religion. Those young 1960's rebels were moved by moral ambition, I said, and I added that much of what the rebels said and did could be considered profoundly moral by Biblical standards. Mom responded as she had to the hippies on Mount Hood: young people who opposed war and segregation were concerned about their own skins, she insisted; otherwise they would have done something about child abuse and the highway death toll. This was not the first time Mom had stopped me short with that kind of rhetorical move. A few years earlier, when I was plugging the achievements of Martin Luther King, she asked me what he had done lately about drunk drivers. I was never able to frame a response that took child abuse or traffic deaths as seriously as they deserved to be taken, preserved civility, and insisted on the crucial importance of peace and racial justice.

Still, it was clear Mom and Dad were glad to have us nearby. In mid-October we drove south along the coast to meet them near the beach town of Florence, and they took us rock collecting by Winchester Bay. They encouraged Judy and Annie to run and jump and dance on sand dunes until they were exhausted, and I told them of the time my mother's father had taken me deep sea fishing out of Winchester Bay in a boat that looked as though it hadn't been painted since the Civil War. When we were beyond the sight of land, the captain turned the wheel over to the first mate and climbed up on the cabin to sleep. The sea got rougher and rougher while we fished and the captain slept. He rolled from side to side as the boat leaned with the waves, and I was pretty sure he was about to fall overboard. Instead, he sat up, looked around, and noticed that all the other boats had headed for the harbor. He pointed this out to the first mate, told us all to pull in our lines, and turned the boat back toward Winchester Bay. The swells were huge, but they were dwarfed by the waves on the bar we had to cross, waves that looked to me like impassable, moving mountains. By this time people had gathered on the jetty to watch the returning boats ride the leaping water, and because we were the last boat in, we had their undivided attention. Unfortunately, I told Judy and Annie, I was a kid who preferred not to ride roller coasters so the interminable, lurching journey over the bar was not a great thrill, and I didn't wave to the onlookers.

We camped with my parents that night at Carl Washburn State Park and went the next morning to the Sea Lion Caves. It was a sunny fall morning with light breezes off the water, and after we came out of the caves we stood together at an observation point high above the ocean and talked. I can't remember what we said that morning, but I know we talked for a long time, and it felt to me as though our conflicts were drifting away with the wind. Mom had come to Oregon from western Montana as a little girl, Dad from central Pennsylvania and Colorado after he graduated from college, and they never stopped seeing the coast as magical. Even rambunctious Annie seemed to feel the new family tranquility that morning as she gazed down into the Pacific and asked occasional questions about the behavior of gulls and cormorants and sea lions. By the time we parted, the six of us standing there bathed in autumn sunlight seemed to have found our way back to each other.

Chapter Five

Rooted in the Land

While we lived on the coast of Oregon in 1973-74, we came to know a man who seemed firmly settled in that place. Leon Settem was in his mid-seventies, and he lived in a well-built farmhouse that stood alone on a parcel of land running down into the Pacific. His grandfather homesteaded this piece of land, he told us proudly. When Settem wasn't walking the beach or stopping to talk with us about his memories, he often sat in his window with large binoculars, spotting orange-billed Oyster Catchers, glass Japanese fishnet floats, California gray whales, and in the summer perhaps an occasional nude sunbather on his secluded beach. In February, after weeks of heavy rain, Leon Settem's land slid toward the sea, and the simple lines of his house went nightmarishly aslant. We watched people from the town help him carry his furniture away in pick-up trucks along the beach because a piece of the highway that led south from Cannon Beach past Settem's house had suddenly dropped twenty-five feet. When Settem and I talked in the following months, I recognized a grief that seemed to grow from a relationship with place more powerful than anything I'd known.

During our year in Oregon we spent much of our spare time walking, as we set out to learn the lay of the land and the rhythms of the sea. At low tide, we often walked south, around Silver Point, past Leon Settem's place and Humbug Point, looking for birds and flotsam. Twice we found sea lions that had been shot, probably by salmon fishermen who resented the competition. One day I met a man from the Highway Department who was looking for one of the sea lion corpses so he could haul it away. I told him where he could find it, and he said the year before he had taken a sea lion corpse that someone had decapitated. My interest in his sea lion story led him to tell me a story from when he worked with a logging outfit in the Oregon Cascades and a logger friend shot a bear. They had another friend who was deathly afraid of bears so they took their dead bear to his little house trailer on a night when he was out drinking, and they placed it in a chair at the table with a whiskey bottle next to its paw. Their friend never told them what happened, and they never saw the dead bear again.

On eroded logging roads we walked up Angora Mountain, south of our cabin, and looked down on stark clear-cuts. Sometimes we climbed another road, Tolovana Mainline, to a dumpsite on a small mountain just behind our cabin. Old refrigerators and discarded insulation were strewn in a setting that would have made a magnificent home site. On clear nights from the dump we could see the Astoria lightship at the mouth of the Columbia River, thirty miles north. We walked on Tillamook Head, a great mass of land that reaches into the ocean between Cannon Beach and Seaside, a foothill over which William Clark led Sacajawea, York, and several others to find a beached whale. I sometimes hiked the several miles between the towns, realizing for the first time that when I'd been walking alone for a few hours in a dark forest, a clear-cut could feel warm and welcoming.

We walked repeatedly on Saddle Mountain, twenty miles northeast of our rented cabin, moving through the campground at the head of the trail toward the summit, past big second-growth hemlock and spruce and huge stumps of Douglas fir left by loggers, up into the open fields above the basalt cliffs. More than 300 species of plants have been found on Saddle Mountain, including nineteen plants classified as rare or endangered, and their diversity attracts a wide variety of birds and other wildlife. Years later, on a single day in late July, walking the heavily used trail to the western summit with a biologist, we identified Oregon Juncos, a Western Flycatcher, Red Crossbills, devil's club, a Townsend chipmunk, hawkweed, stone-crop, purple prunella vulgaris, wild onion, a Swainson's Thrush, St. John's wort, monkey flowers, Indian paintbrush, a Winter Wren, pathfinder, tiger lilies, northern inside-out flowers, colt's foot, dutchman's britches, wild cucumbers, a Pine Siscan, columbine, mustard, Chickadees, delphinium, a Rock Wren, tufted saxifrage, blue bells, yarrow, vine maple, mallow, wild blackberries, rock ferns, Noble fir, a Wilson's Warbler, bleeding heart, two Golden Crowned Kinglets, two Common Ravens, a Violet Green Swallow, lomatium, huckleberries, gooseberries, a black-tailed deer, a Douglas squirrel, cow parsnip, goat's beard, and, near the summit, several Purple Finches and a Rufous Hummingbird. We heard, too, the mysterious, percussive sound of a male Blue Grouse near a switchback where the trail begins to rise above the trees. It took us years to appreciate the diversity of life on the mountain. At first our frequent hikes had a lot to do with the chance of looking east to the Willamette Valley and north past the Columbia River to Mount Rainier and St. Helens in the years before St. Helens' 1980 eruption. Sometimes we walked into cloud cover and rain. But we often glimpsed the Pacific and the darkly named Cape Disappointment on the Washington side of the Columbia, past Astoria. We hadn't yet learned about the beautiful Fox Creek forest on the mountain's northwest flank, but we could see it on a clear day.

Part way up the mountain, the "exposure," as climbers call it, the visual sense of precipitous decline into space, comes more abruptly than one expects on a mountain of such humble proportions so we usually rested in the open, accustoming ourselves to the wide-open view. Near the top, the trail grows steep and difficult, giving you a sense of accomplishment when you reach the summit. It was like an athletic event for us. We weren't rushing past the mountain at 80 miles per hour as I had done almost twenty years earlier, but we knew very little about what we saw. It would be several years before we began to know Saddle Mountain in anything like the way Leon Settem came to know the land his grandfather settled.

Mom, who began in Montana, and Dad, from Pennsylvania, moved around a lot in Portland during my lifetime, and in 1973-74 they were living in that symbol of American restlessness, a mobile home. But like Leon Settem, they seemed connected with their home. One day we went with them up the Clackamas River, which joins the Willamette River south of Portland. We packed our lunch along a one-mile trail to their favorite stretch of the Clackamas, Alder Flats, where the river bends in gentle rapids, and its wide reach at high water leaves acres of rocks from the mountain where the river begins. Nearby was the Big Timber Job Corps Center, and while we ate lunch, four teenage boys from the Center arrived and climbed aboard a long, slender log wedged at one end under a huge rock and resting on a smaller rock so that its free end moved like a giant, slow-motion diving board when the boys began to ride it. The boys laughed and shouted as they rode, and they made me nervous. They were teenagers, two Hispanics, one African American, and one white, all dressed in jeans and heavy khaki jackets. They were looking for a way to pass the time, and we were alone with them at Alder Flats.

After lunch, my parents began to wander among the rocks, searching for fossils, and Judy and Annie asked to ride the log the boys had by then abandoned. Despite my unspoken impulse to pull our wagons into a circle, our party divided. As I stood guard to make sure the girls weren't thrown from the moving log, one of the boys approached my father, and they began to talk. Soon all four boys were standing around Dad in a semi-circle,

44

and I was comforting myself with the fact that he had his rock hammer in his hand. But when he shook hands ceremoniously with each of the boys, I began to feel anti-social, and the rest of our party must have felt the same way because Mom, Nancy, Judy, Annie, and I all converged on the center of sociability at Alder Flats. Dad introduced each of us in turn, and we talked for perhaps an hour about their Job Corps experience, their homes in Oregon and California, and their reactions to winter in the foothills of the Cascade Mountains.

It hadn't occurred to my parents to worry about the Job Corps boys. Had we been talking more abstractly about federal job training programs and the problems facing poor youth in our society, I would have been enthusiastic about centers like the one there on the Clackamas, and Dad might have worried about big government and the drift toward socialism he saw in such programs. But faced with actual Job Corps trainees in a remote location, I was nervously inclined to ignore them, and Dad was eager to get to know them.

I wasn't about to confess my fears as we drove back to my parents' mobile home that day, but if I had, Dad would have seen the irony right away. He might have spoken, as he did occasionally, of the ivory tower foolishness one finds in colleges and universities. And one of my discoveries during that year in Oregon was that my parents and my brothers were, in fact, rooted in Oregon, more attuned to its realities than I had ever been. And not only had Dave been in combat, but he could build a house or fix a car. I could do neither.

My other brother, John, was only four years old when I went away to college so I was getting to know him in 1973-74. Like Dave, he was handy with tools, and a few years later he would startle me when we stood together one day on a bridge over the Willamette River near Eugene. He called down to a large man on the shore who was throwing rocks that flew close by us as they arched over the bridge. He told the man one of his rocks had almost hit us, and the man said he ought to mind his own business. My little brother told him he'd be coming down to see him if he threw one more rock near us. Like me, the man must have been startled because he stopped throwing and turned to walk downstream without a word. That was the day I realized John was a full-grown man, his shoulders considerably broader than mine, but I couldn't imagine taking a chance on a fight unless he were enraged beyond all rationality. He seemed comfortable with the violent possibilities he had set in motion with his ultimatum. I had thought of him as the musically gifted brother, a dreamer who seemed more at ease with the world than I was. He told me recently he was actually very angry that day, and one of his great challenges in those years was controlling his anger.

Along with my family's confidence in the face of things I considered daunting reality, I recognized my mother and father's self-assurance in rural settings. I remembered from my childhood their delight when we visited farms to pick fruit and vegetables for canning and their preference for camping in places where the roads were so rough they took the oil pan off a car unless you were very careful. On farms and in wilderness campgrounds my parents sought the company of strangers as they seldom did in the city, and more than once they came home from a camping trip with friends they continued to see. They never seemed altogether comfortable in the working class neighborhood of southeast Portland where I grew up. Like many families in the 1950's, they fled to the suburbs, but I think they would have preferred a small town.

Near the end of that wonderful year in Oregon we spent an evening with old family friends gathered in the living room of my parents' mobile home. This family had once been members of Lents Baptist Church, where

Mom grew up. Jim, the father, was in his seventies and going blind. His wife, Agnes, was recovering from a stroke that had left her partially paralyzed. Their daughter, Genevieve, in her forties, had been blind since she was twelve. They were visiting Portland from Tacoma, Washington, for the funeral of an aunt, whose eighty-four year old husband was also with us that evening. Judy and Annie, who had spent most of their lives in relatively youthful academic communities, found much to think about in the grief, the blindness, and the infirmities of age. Nancy and I realized Annie was fighting back tears, and we began to look for a graceful way to invite her into another room to talk. But the others noticed her distress too. Before we could say anything, the older people began to talk with both girls. Gently, with much humor, the eighty-four year old widower comforted my daughters, perhaps showing them they could comfort him. It felt to me as though the older people had decided to let the children see how they could accept their mortality with dignity and humor. By the end of the evening, Annie and Judy were laughing and talking excitedly with people whose pain confused and frightened them at first. It felt as though we had found our way back into old-fashioned community.

That evening reminded me of something I shouldn't have forgotten: my parents and grandparents' lives had included the aged and disabled as long as I could remember. My grandfather, the bus driver in Portland, spent some of his spare time doing errands for aged widows in their neighborhood, and Sunday dinner usually included two or three of them. My grandfather, who may never have cooked a meal in his life, washed the Sunday dinner dishes with the flamboyance of a flamenco dancer. The ritual began with the folding of the linen, performed with one or more of the Baptist widows. Chins held high, heels clicking, as I remember it, they shook and waved the tablecloth before they folded it like a treasured flag even if it was going in the laundry that week. Then, working with one of the widows, my grandfather prepared the rinse water with as much care and commentary as though he were about to sterilize instruments for major surgery. He used water so hot the dishes and silverware had to be handled with tongs. When he began actually washing the dishes, he seemed to believe he was making up for years of neglect. Somehow he managed to control the flow of dishes and the conversation at the same time so that dishwashing was, for a few shining moments, the center of our lives.

These were traditions adopted by my parents when my grandparents died. Politically and religiously conservative, my parents seemed more open to people in need than I was with my newfound liberalism. Our Oregon family seemed somehow more firmly rooted in community and in the earth than I had remembered or imagined.

Chapter Six

Imagining Community

During our year in Oregon I began to feel as though we were bridging chasms that had divided our family, and it was more than that, more even than finding I could go home again. I began to have a fuller sense of what it might mean to live in a real *community*.

Nancy's parents died soon after we were married, and that drew us close to her older sister, Sylvia, and her large family in Pittsfield, Massachusetts, a town struggling as General Electric abandoned most of its factories there. Nancy and Sylvia's father, Frank Shea, had spent his last working years at G.E., packing parts from missile guidance systems, and a G.E. Vice President, Robert Gibson, paid Nancy's transportation costs so she could attend Park College and meet a young man from Oregon.

Sylvia flew out to Oregon to see us in that January of 1974. A spirited, irreverent woman who loves to dance, she hit it off with a shy, deeply serious undergraduate from Ethiopia, Alemneh Dejene, who had come from Ohio to stay with us for the month. (Alemneh would go on to earn a doctorate, combining international studies and agriculture, hoping someday to return to Ethiopia, but he worked for several years for the World Bank in Geneva and then moved to the United Nations in Rome.) He often sat contemplatively, with his head in his large hands when we talked about international politics.

When Sylvia was with us, we danced and cooked Ethiopian food, and a family of four from Wisconsin, the Nibbelinks, joined us for a while. Herm Nibbelink had spent two years in Ethiopia with the Peace Corps so he had much to talk about with Alemneh, and the children seemed fascinated by their stories. More than once,

Nancy and I have tried unsuccessfully to remember where all of us slept in our small, rented cabin, but however we accomplished that little miracle, it must have been comfortable enough because a year later we began to correspond with the Nibbelinks and two other families about the possibility of building a communal experiment and a business we proposed at first to call simply the Institute. Our joy in Oregon grew partly from discovering a taste for living with other families.

For me, the wonder of that year had much to do with my daughters. We explored the beaches and hiking trails and began to play music together. One of my writing projects was a children's story that Nancy illustrated, and we consulted the girls as it grew. Inviting Judy and Annie to weigh in on our project reminded me of the days when my grandfather, the bus driver in Portland, let me ride in the seat behind him to see how he worked. One windy night in our beach cabin something frightened Annie, and she called for me instead of Nancy, a call that felt like a coronation.

But my nostalgic view of Oregon as an Eden I'd left when I went off to college was jarred that year too. One evening Alemneh and I drove into Portland to play volleyball with my brother Dave and several young men from the bank where he was then working. All the men were white, and initially they were polite to Alemneh, who was a gifted athlete. But he hadn't played volleyball in a long time, and he tried to spike from difficult positions well back from the net. Once he blasted a spike into one of the men on his own team. After a bit I realized the men had begun to make him the butt of a running joke. They would stop the game to laugh if he made an error, and they began to talk about him as though he weren't there or couldn't speak English. I didn't know the men, and I couldn't think of a way to call attention to what they were doing without risking a difficult scene. Alemneh pretended not to notice, and he continued to play aggressively. I was reminded of something the African American novelist Ernest Gaines said to me in Ohio, when we were talking about a visit he made to Portland. "Oregon," he said, "is the Alabama of the West." I read in the *Oregonian* that two members of the Portland police had left dead raccoons at the entrance to a restaurant owned by African Americans. In Martin Luther King's last years he revealed that anywhere in the U.S. could be like Alabama, where malignant racism was visible in places like Selma, Montgomery, and Birmingham during the Civil Rights Movement. I was ashamed of Oregon the night Alemneh and I played volleyball with the young bankers.

In early May, Dave and I set out to climb Mt. Hood, an ascent he had made several times before he went to Vietnam. It was my first attempt to entice Dave back into the arms of the wilderness, where I thought he might find healing from the war. Both of us worked hard to get in shape, and we practiced roping up. We started at 2:30 a.m. from Timberline Lodge, and the mountain glowed white in the darkness above us, giving me a sense of one kind of pleasure mountain climbers experience. By five o'clock the sky had brightened enough that the mountain looked dark and dull, but earlier, in the moonlight, we could see the white, glowing trail in the snow, where climbers went up toward the summit. When we got to 9000 feet, however, I began to have chest pains and nausea, and we had to come down. Dave couldn't seem to shake his disappointment, and it would be several years before I developed the alternative plan that would lead us into the Fox Creek forest.

Dave and I grew closer that year, and I got to know John, who had dropped out of college and was working in Portland. He was a gifted musician, and we played guitars and sang a lot together. He had fallen in love with the girl he would marry, a feisty, beautiful farm girl from Perrydale, Oregon, and they sometimes came to visit. John considered himself a "born again" Christian,

51

but he lacked the rigid certitude I associated with the Christian right. He wasn't put off by my increasingly liberal politics, and he had doubts about a college-age Bible study group he had joined, a spin-off from the Bible Study Fellowship that was increasingly the center of our mother's life. He told Nancy and me of a meeting where a married couple described a train wreck in which they'd had to sacrifice their own child to save a whole trainload of people. It was a long, moving story, and John found it totally convincing. In the hush that followed their story, the husband said they had made it up to help the students understand the significance of John 3:16: "For God so loved the world, that he gave his only begotten Son, that whosoever believeth in him should not perish, but have everlasting life." My brother acknowledged that he felt manipulated. Still, he tentatively tried to save my soul. And when I suggested that it might not need saving, he allowed I might be right.

The year in Oregon gave me a chance to renew my friendship with my oldest friend, Terry, who had worried my father by growing a beard in the late 1960's. We'd had a yearlong reunion in 1963-64 at the University of Missouri, where we both taught English. During our year in Oregon, Terry, his wife, and two daughters were living in Sacramento, California, but they had recently been living in a rural commune near Oroville, California, leaving when tensions in the group made them feel isolated.

Terry and his family were living in a suburban apartment when I rode a bus south to visit them, and he worked for the Social Security Administration. It seemed to me they had learned a lot about being good neighbors from their year in the commune. Although they shared a pessimistic vision of our society, convictions that led them to try out life in the rural commune, they seemed to have built an open, hope-filled environment for their daughters. Surrounded by broken marriages and troubled children in their apartment complex, they opened their doors to their neighbors in ways not typical of suburban life. During my two days with them, they offered advice, baby-sitting services, and practical assistance to their neighbors. They appeared to have become a source of stability in their neighborhood.

After a Greyhound ride back to Oregon with a storyteller so gifted I've ridden buses occasionally ever since in the hope of finding raconteurs as skillful as Rusty Webb, I had a disappointing brush with show business. Dallas McKinnon, who played Cincinnatus in the "Daniel Boone" television series, lived in Cannon Beach, and he had been writing a pageant he hoped to produce as Oregon's contribution to the nation's Bicentennial in 1976. McKinnon invited me to spend an afternoon taking notes while he talked and sang his way through his draft of the pageant. Then while Nancy packed for our return to Ohio, I sat at a typewriter, writing a proposal for a grant to fund McKinnon's pageant. It was ultimately unsuccessful.

In return for my work on the pageant proposal McKinnon invited Judy to go with him and his family to a rodeo in Sheridan, Oregon, where he was to be the grand marshal in a parade. It was an exciting, wonderful day for Judy, but the McKinnons didn't return until 3 a.m., and Nancy and I were expecting them by midnight. Images of an accident on the twisting roads of the Coast Range made us panic, and my farewell to McKinnon, when they finally brought Judy home, was not warm.

Saying goodbye to my parents was even more difficult. We went out to breakfast at a pancake house, and Mom was pale and haggard, seemingly almost beyond sadness. Dad came as close to crying as I'd ever seen. They seemed almost angry, as though we'd deliberately rebuilt family ties only to tear them apart again by returning to Ohio.

Chapter Seven

Return to Rush Hour

Although my grandfather was a city bus driver for all the years I knew him, he told those stories set in western Montana about deer, elk, coyotes, and rattlesnakes that could hold a grandchild spellbound for hours. I think he never adjusted fully to life in the city, and the stories he told adults about life aboard the buses sometimes focused on rush hour. I listened closely to those stories too, maybe hoping to understand something about the adult world. The grown-up tale I remember best takes place around five o'clock on a hot day during World War II. My grandfather's bus is crowded with people standing in the aisle, and most of those standing are wedged near the front of the bus. Among the passengers standing in front are two young boys, their chests jammed against the metal bar that protects my grandfather. It's difficult for a new passenger to get through the door, and when a man elbows his way onto the bus, my grandfather is barely able to close the door. So he stands, turns around, and shouts, "Move to the back of the bus, please!" When he sits down and begins to drive, one of the boys at my grandfather's elbow asks his friend, "Does he mean us?" "Nope," his friend says, "he's talking to the *people*." My grandfather, accustomed to being ignored when he tells passengers to move to the back of the bus, roars with laughter and tells the boy *nobody* thinks they're the *people*.

Judging from the number of times I heard him tell that story, it was one of his favorites. It was not one of mine, but when we returned to Granville after our year on the Oregon coast, I remembered it. Driving a bus was stressful work for my grandfather, and rush hour was the emblem of that stress. He went to considerable lengths to avoid driving a crowded bus in heavy traffic even though it often meant going to work when most people were getting ready to go to sleep. I thought I was following his lead when we moved to Granville, Ohio, a small town that looks like the transplanted New England village it is. Dogwoods and redbuds bloom in the spring, and autumn is so colorful a United Airlines pilot from Michigan who often approached the Columbus airport on a flight path over Granville was so taken by the town's autumnal beauty he encouraged his daughter to attend Denison. She did, and when she told me how her father found the college, I told the Director of Admissions he should encourage the college to plant bushes that spelled out "Try Denison" to observers from the air.

After we returned from Oregon in 1974, I quickly fell into a hectic routine that seemed almost to be a simulated rush hour on our bucolic campus. In 1983, when I began a term as Dean of the College, my view of the problem had become more melodramatic. I compared the frantic schedules we made for ourselves to sitting in a dentist's chair and waiting for the drill to stop. We feel *locked in*, I said, until we feel *burned out*. It wasn't just the contrast between the contemplative life our family had experienced on the Oregon coast and the demands of academic life that bothered me in those years before e-mail and cell phones, Facebook, Twitter, and texting. Although I was struck by how often I met people on campus who had no time to talk, I also heard the echo of something Wendell Berry said to a student one evening. Berry had just finished talking about the destructive impact of industrial agriculture on the Earth and on rural communities. The student asked a little impatiently what he was supposed to do about it. "Think about it," Berry said in his Kentucky drawl, and I was struck by the irony: serious thinking seemed like an unattainable luxury in an academic community trying to live the intellectual life in the fast lane. When a new committee on teaching and learning began its work, I mentioned the irony. In a setting that speaks of mid-country peace, I said, we encourage the finishing kick, the pull-it-out-of-the-fire approach to learning. We try to nurture learning by keeping the student union open all night during finals week and serving free coffee. Instead, we should be slowing things down and encouraging the kind of contemplation that leads to acts of imagination. It was a theme to which I would return many years later, when I had retired from Denison and begun teaching part-time at Dartmouth College.

My stern admonitions surely grew in part from a personal yearning for the life we had in Oregon. In the years after our return, my journal was filled with longing to find a way to live that life again. I was struggling with the death fears that often seem to afflict busy men as they move into middle age, and time seemed somehow out of control. "I feel tyrannized by time," I wrote in my journal, "not living richly in it." As nearly as I can tell, it was E.F. Schumacher's book *Small Is Beautiful: Economics as If People Mattered* (1973) that set me to wondering whether the college where I taught and where I had worked as an administrator was thoughtlessly discarding one of its greatest potential strengths, the community life its size made possible.

Small Is Beautiful is the kind of book that can change a person's life. Schumacher gently and carefully challenges widely accepted views and offers alternatives that have the sound of common sense. He advocates the kind of simple life for whole societies that we aspired to as a family in our Oregon year as hippies. "In the excitement over the unfolding of his scientific and technical powers," Schumacher concludes, "modern man has built a system of production that ravishes nature and a type of society that mutilates man." As his title suggests, Schumacher's solutions have much to do with scale, and he proposes that a rational economic life will

57

apply good work to meeting local needs from local resources, a theme Bill McKibben would develop more fully almost thirty-five years later in *Deep Economy: The Wealth of Communities and the Durable Future* (2007). Schumacher was skeptical of much that we call "high technology," and he makes the case for technologies that match the scale of local community life. He anticipates many of the dislocations that result from our growing dependence on oil. He favors scaling down and conserving resources in a manner sure to change the way we live.

What Schumacher proposed seemed to offer an alternative to the competition, conflict, and expansive growth that lead to war, and it matched the potential strengths in a small liberal arts college in rural Ohio.

I tried *Small Is Beautiful* on my friend Jack Kirby, a historian who was then writing *Black Americans in the Roosevelt Era: Liberalism and Race* (1980), and he agreed that Schumacher's argument offered a cogent critique of Denison. As Jack and I jogged the back roads of Granville Township that fall, we were like two football players whacking each other on their pads, getting ready to kick some ass. We wanted to disagree with the leadership of Joel Smith, a young president we both came to like personally. Under Smith, we seemed to be turning increasingly to large corporate models of accountability and striving for "excellence" that could be standardized and quantified, a trend that seems to have triumphed in higher education. Personnel decisions were influenced by the dubious data used to forecast hard times ahead. Professors were encouraged to compete for merit raises although the winners were kept secret, and despite the fact that Denison claimed to be a teaching college, there was growing pressure to publish. All of these changes, which were taking place elsewhere too, seemed to us to endanger interdisciplinary programs like Black Studies, which had just begun to find its legs.

Buoyed by what was left of the lively spirit of the 1960's and inspired by E.F. Schumacher, Kirby and I collaborated on a memo to the faculty, "'Small is Beautiful': A Conservative View of Change at Denison," in which we argued for the importance of scale in a small liberal arts college. Perhaps because we concluded with controversial proposals, including a standard Denison salary for all faculty members and administrators, our essay stirred up debate, and the faculty devoted two meetings to discussing it. Our critique was presumptuous, but the willingness of busy faculty members to gather and discuss our Schumacherian analysis of the college suggests others shared longings like those I felt after that meditative year in Oregon. In spite of a lively discussion in which several faculty members agreed with much of our analysis, it's fair to say the college, along with many other colleges and universities, moved in a contrary direction, toward a corporate management style that daughter Judy and I would later attack in an online essay in *Higher Ed*. Far from instituting standard salaries, for example, colleges began to distinguish more emphatically the salaries of assistant professors from those of full professors.

Four years later Jack Kirby and I tried again. This time we titled our memo to the faculty "Small is Still Beautiful But a Little Uncertain." It was more hard-hitting and quite a bit longer. I think now it made a stronger case. Almost half of our argument was devoted to examining simulation, elaborate games for allowing students to pretend they are responding to actual problems—for example, a nuclear attack or an economic crisis. The college had devoted large resources to an attempt to become the "simulation center of the Midwest." Simulation games seemed to provide a way of motivating passive students who, according to many professors, lacked basic skills. We argued that simulation might well add to problems we were experiencing in the classroom and that our students lacked *complex* skills, not basic ones—that is, exactly the skills of analysis and expression that a liberal arts college should teach. We pointed out that the faculty was setting out once again to rethink its commitment to general education, the core of shared knowledge that could be said to define liberal arts education, while at the same time we seemed to be encouraging narrow disciplinary specialization. We claimed the faculty was well prepared to teach students who seemed less motivated than the students in our classes a few years earlier, that we were demoralized and overworked by chasing our tails in an effort to simulate a research university. We closed our long essay with a stern invitation: "What we lack is a clear sense of why we are gathered here in Granville. Perhaps it is time for some of us to talk about that—to see if we can frame a sense of purpose that might inform our discussion of general education, our community life, and the nature of excellence in the liberal arts." But we had cried wolf once before, and since then the pace of our college rush hour had quickened. Faculty members were much less willing to talk about it now.

Chapter Eight

The Institute

In 1974 I began to think seriously about becoming a farmer. Twenty years later some of my most thoughtful students would begin to act on a similar dream, except: most of them knew quite a lot about what they were doing, and they had the good sense to sign up for internships on small farms. Although I hadn't shown great promise in our community garden plot, I became an agricultural evangelist, seeking to entice friends who had grown up on farms into going back into farming with me. At least I had enough good sense to know I needed help.

Back in Granville, Nancy, Judy, Annie, and I came together at the end of a day as though from different worlds, and we seemed to be light years away from members of the family in Oregon with whom we'd begun to rebuild ties. Our year in Oregon had suggested the possibility of connecting education, work, and play, living fully in a place and a community, not waiting for the weekend or a vacation or retirement, not hoping to find a better place, but finding meaning and hope here and now. So I began to dream of a communal experiment that might make some of that possible again.

I thought of it as a "castle in the air," and I wrote a proposal in the spring of 1975, almost a year after our return from Oregon, alluding to something Thoreau said in *Walden*: "If you have built castles in the air, your work need not be lost; that is where they should be. Now put the foundations under them." Wanting to entice people into the experiment who might be less given to dreaming than I was, more accustomed to building foundations, I called it an "Institute" and invited my friends to consider the New Alchemy Institute near Falmouth, Massachusetts, a visionary organization that conducted

61

ecological research. Trying to sound hard-headed, I suggested in my proposal that we might think of it "almost as though we were beginning a small business." Although I knew the initial dream had too many hints of the counterculture to interest my brothers, it seemed likely that the more entrepreneurial it looked, the more likely they would be to consider joining if it became a reality. Nancy and I would make the initial investment in a rural house and land, I said in the proposal, and we would develop a formula for taking account of various other kinds of investment, such as a summer spent at the Institute making improvements or time spent writing a proposal for funding. On the question of the Institute's purpose I was fuzzy:

> Its aim, first of all, would be to create some new possibilities in our own lives—allowing us to focus on some things we want to do. Some of us—most of us, perhaps—might maintain our ties with other institutions much of the time, but we might well need to arrange for at least one family to be present at the institute through the whole year. The focus of much of our research and writing would be small-scale efforts to live simply, to reduce waste, to find appropriate technology. . . .
>
> What I am trying to imagine is an alternative that allows us: (1) to ease into it gradually without a sense that we are necessarily burning bridges that connect us with the lives we've been learning to live in the last few years; (2) to find ways to share ourselves more fully with each other than is now possible; (3) to build a place that might embody for our children the possibility of a livable future—that is, it might help them to see that there are ways to take hold of the

craziness that surrounds us so that we don't have to surrender to it; (4) to create for ourselves a place to which we can retreat occasionally in the religious sense of *retreat.*

The mailing list for the proposal was short: two families in Wisconsin, one in California, and another in New York, all friends with whom we'd discussed our interest in communal experiments. All the adults were nearing forty, and all five families had children in elementary school. When I mentioned "the craziness that surrounds us," I had in mind the growing gap between rich and poor, increasing hunger and oppression around the world, the escalating arms race, our degrading environment, our society's wasteful consumption, and the escalating pace of life, even in places as bucolic as Granville. On most of those themes, I thought, the five families agreed.

Two families knew immediately that the idea was not for them. Only one of them provided the kind of critique I had feared. Fred Bruning, a newspaper reporter whose deep love of New York City didn't register fully on my consciousness until years later, when I read articles he wrote after September 11, 2001, began this way:

Essentially my reaction was that you are naïve, perhaps to the point of self-indulgence, and that your idea is functionally irrelevant, if I may coin a phrase, which is to say, that even if the idea is brought to fruition, it will exist somewhere beside the point and not on it, and, further, that whoever named the New Alchemy Institute (of which I had not heard) should be sentenced to a year straining safflower oil in a natural food store, which is probably what he/she is doing already. In short, I was not taken by any of it.

Fearing, perhaps, that he had not made himself clear, Fred went on for several pages without losing his edge, and more than thirty years later, he hasn't softened much on the subject of intentional communities. Still, I've come to believe his impatience with my Institute dream had something to do with ambivalence: not too long after dismissing my proposal, Fred and his family took a year's unpaid leave and went to live on a farm in Vermont. That experience seemed to solidify his conviction that urban life is the only life worth living. Fred, who moves back and forth between an apartment in Brooklyn and a home in Huntington on Long Island, loves New York City in the way Leon Settem loved the Oregon coast.

Still, even today I believe I was onto an idea with promise. A few years later I found a rationale for something like the Institute in a book by classicist D.S. Carne-Ross, *Instaurations* (1979), where he suggests that powerful modern technologies lead to a "dream of absolute dominion," the possibility that technological progress can free us from our contingent role in nature. "It is true," Carne-Ross says, "that the full rigor of necessity still prevails in the experience of great pain or great grief, but these are wordless, incommunicable states that take place in private and hence cause no public scandal." To get beyond our fantasy of total control over nature, Carne-Ross suggests, we must experience directly "the permanent facts of earthly existence." We need projects that put us in touch with natural cycles, the production of food, fuel, clothing, and shelter, and if those are joined with the reading of great classical literature, he says, we can recover the tragic vision required for our species to survive. That, it seems to me, is another way of thinking about what we were up to in dreaming of our Institute. We proposed to raise much of our own food and to take a hand in building and maintaining the place where we lived.

I now believe an important motive for all three of the families who spent many months circulating letters and proposals, traveling, meeting, and trying to bring the Institute into being, was suggested in my phrase "religious sense of *retreat.*" Most of us had moved away from conservative Christian backgrounds, and perhaps for that reason we were uncomfortable with religious language. But as I consider changes in our lives that we didn't discuss in our voluminous correspondence, I think we were seeking to build a place where we could withdraw for meditation, study, and even perhaps *prayer*, although most of us would have been embarrassed to speak that last word aloud. Herm and Ellen had begun to attend a Quaker meeting in Wisconsin, as Nancy and I were doing in Ohio. Terry had begun a quest that would lead him to become a practicing Buddhist, and his wife, Martha, who began as a Catholic, was moving toward evangelical Protestantism.

We corresponded with realtors, and in addition to our correspondence and visits with each other, our three families met for several days on the Oregon coast, acknowledging the irony of traveling thousands of miles and burning much gasoline to dream together of simplicity. We tried to be systematic about the question of location, considering our preferences on matters such as annual rainfall, mountains, wind, humidity, and winter temperatures. Our discussion of location seemed to stall at this rather high level of abstraction, never turning to actual landscapes and communities where we might settle. An ex-student who joined us at our summer meeting in Oregon commented later that we also seemed to avoid discussing our reasons for considering the Institute at all. And years later, Herm, who was by then divorced from Ellen, wrote: "For me the years that included our institute correspondence were a time of extraordinary personal pain and fear, coupled with desperate hopes about what might assuage the pain, diminish the fear, change our lives for the better." It's likely that none of us would have taken the Institute seriously if we hadn't felt some of the same pain and fear and hope, but we didn't talk about it. Years later, when I helped plan a memorial service for Herm in Wisconsin, I remembered how we walked and talked together as often as we could manage while living far apart, how we played guitars and sang together too, but it seems to me the few years we spent trying to imagine our way into community together were the best part of a long, rich friendship.

In the summer of 1976, Nancy and I decided to make a move to end our group's paralysis. Since our year in Oregon we'd saved $8,000, and because we'd bought our house in Ohio for $9,800 a few years earlier, we thought we might have enough money for a down payment on farm property. We'd come to love Oregon's Coast Range, the land surrounding Saddle Mountain, so we decided to look for property on the eastern side of the mountains in the Willamette Valley. Even in 1976, as it turned out, $8,000 was not a realistic sum to put down on farm property in the Willamette Valley. The only place we found that we could afford was a ten-acre hillside farm on a logging road. The profoundly rustic farmhouse tilted eastward, as though it had been caught in a mudslide. The septic system, above ground, was a series of 100-gallon drums linked by lengths of garden hose. The owner had dreamed of building a new house beside the old one, and a bulldozer scar was the remnant of that dream, so recent that nothing was yet growing in it. When Nancy realized this was the only farm we could afford, her agrarian enthusiasm cooled.

We had given up on our search for land and joined my parents in Portland when a call came from friends in Cannon Beach, telling us of a cabin in the woods that we could almost afford. Owned by a physician and his wife who wanted to build a house on an ocean front lot nearby, the cabin was one large octagonal room perched atop two bedrooms and a bathroom arranged in a square. In the octagonal upper story, wooden beams angled down from a round metal plate at the top, giving the ceiling the appearance of a partially flattened wigwam. Large windows on the northern and western angles of the octagon looked toward the Pacific and into second-growth spruce trees that stretched out into thousands of acres of forest, owned then by the Crown Zellerbach Corporation. A second-story deck swept around the octagon beneath the windows, so close to the spruce tree's branches that the deck felt like a tree-house. The downstairs bedrooms had six metal and canvas bunks that swung down from the walls like hammocks on a ship. With additional beds in those rooms and cots upstairs, the cabin could accommodate lots of visitors. Hidden in the trees at the end of a narrow dirt road, this place was not a farm, but it felt like a retreat, and it was no more than a quarter of a mile from Heavenly Daze, where we lived in 1973-74. We borrowed an additional $1,000 on an insurance policy to add to our $8,000 and made an offer.

There were complications, but a few months later, when we were living for six months in Chicago while I taught at the Newberry Library, we became owners of the cabin. Now I think our purchase of the cabin ended the possibility of our actually building the Institute although that wasn't apparent at the time. Terry and Martha came to stay with us in Oregon, and Herm and Ellen lived there with their sons for a year. But during the next few years, as our communal dreaming lost momentum, both couples approached divorce reluctantly yet inexorably. Terry was struggling with depression. He worked with a psychiatrist and tried lithium before he began to use illegal drugs to medicate his despair. At the time, I assumed he was simply listening to wily dealers who convinced him the drugs would enrich his intellectual and spiritual life, and perhaps I was partly right. In the summer of 1978, Terry and Martha visited us in Oregon, and Nancy and I concluded they were medicating the pain of their dissolving marriage, as well as Terry's depression, with illegal drugs. Their shifting moods and firm insistence on the wisdom of insights that made no sense to us seemed chemically induced, but they were gentle and loving with their daughters and with ours as well. One day when Terry had spent several hours throwing a Frisbee into the wind so that it came back to him like a boomerang, I asked if he had been using LSD. He was indeed "doing acid" at that very moment, he said, and he and Martha had used several drugs while they were with us. Terry seemed puzzled and hurt when I said their clandestine use of consciousness-altering drugs while they were our guests felt dishonest to me. That conversation seemed to mark the end of our communal dreaming, and the beginning of a break in a friendship that went back to the first grade.

Herm and Ellen struggled through several more years of marital uncertainty, and Herm later insisted our failed effort to build a community was not the cause. "From my perspective," he wrote, "it was your friends' marriages that prevented realization of the Institute rather than the other way around." But any marriage ceremony that touches on reality will affirm the fact that the communities surrounding marriages help to hold them together, and to me it seemed the Institute might have made a difference. The pain that preceded and then followed the end of Herm and Ellen's marriage went on for a very long time at a high level of intensity. "To children," Allan Bloom writes in *The Closing of the American Mind* (1987), "the voluntary separation of parents seems worse than their death precisely because it is voluntary." I don't know if that is true, but I am sure parents who believe the loving association and deep

68

intimacy of a marriage are sacred feel its end as a kind of doom. The failure of our attempt to build an intentional community seemed tied to that doom, inseparable from the broken marriages.

Chapter Nine

Chicago

November 8, 1976, was a cold, windy Monday in Chicago as I walked the four blocks from the Newberry Library to our temporary apartment on prosperous Bellevue Avenue. After crossing State Street, I saw a young woman in a small, red Toyota, parked by the Oak Street Bank. She caught my attention because she was pretty and because she seemed to be staring at me. She was definitely making eye contact instead of resorting to the slightly averted, expressionless urban face used by women in the city to ward off encounters with strangers. I assumed the young woman must know me, and I angled across the sidewalk toward her car as I approached it. She wore no coat despite the cold, and as I drew closer, she moved her eyes away from mine and began to unbutton her tight, green sweater, pulling it apart just enough to reveal promising hints of her small, perky breasts. The Chicago police were engaged that November in a much-publicized crackdown on prostitution, and more slowly perhaps than the people walking beside me, I realized her rather enticing performance was an alternative to streetwalking.

On Bellevue Avenue, where doormen helped local residents into limousines and shouted to passersby to "curb" their dogs, we were not living the simple agricultural life I'd been imagining. We entertained guests in a living room that had the look of a slightly shabby dance studio, with a full-length mirror for one wall. Our apartment, provided by the Newberry Library, where I was teaching for the semester, was just around the corner from Rush Street, which featured striptease clubs, singles bars, and prostitutes, a nightlife that percolated noisily until dawn. Nancy and I adapted so quickly to the lively tenderloin sounds that on a brief October visit to our

71

home in Granville after a month in Chicago we both broke into laughter at the silence outside our windows when we went to bed.

A few blocks west of our Bellevue apartment was Cabrini-Green, a public housing development that had become a symbol of urban poverty, despair, and crime. And even on Bellevue there were signs of fear. Hurrying back to my apartment one night from a meeting, I cut across our street in the middle of the block and frightened a woman walking ahead of me. Startled, she looked back at me and immediately turned up the steps of a row house as though it were her own. After I passed, I looked back to see her come down the stairs and continue on her way. And one afternoon a few days after frightening the woman on Bellevue Avenue, I was returning from a jog along Lake Michigan, running through a pedestrian tunnel under Michigan Avenue, when I noticed two young men stopped ahead of me, one of them poised as though to throw a punch. I stopped several feet from them and slowly realized the echoing sounds of my running had startled them as I moved toward them. After staring uncertainly at each other for a few long seconds, we sheepishly apologized for frightening each other and continued on our way.

Our family lived in Chicago that fall so I could teach an interdisciplinary seminar on "Art and Commerce" with historian Robert Shimp. Our seminar set out to understand the influence of economics on the kind of artistic and cultural resurgence we call a "renaissance." Our students were drawn from liberal arts colleges around the Midwest, and the work they did in our course earned them a full semester's academic credit. Although they were undergraduates, each student wrote a major research essay using the rich holdings of the Newberry Library, and some of their essays might have qualified as master's theses. The students, serious and lively, were a delight to teach, and I had learned from

E.F. Schumacher's *Small is Beautiful: Economics as if People Mattered* (1973) that I could sometimes understand economics. The discipline that had fascinated my father but only mystified me as an undergraduate now seemed almost to make sense, especially when joined with other fields, including the creative arts. The Newberry Library is a treasure house of collections in the humanities that attract scholars in fields as diverse as cartography, Native American history, the history of music, genealogy, the French Revolution, and the exploration of the American West. Along with its rich holdings, the Newberry has beautiful, well-lit reading rooms and elegant, wood-paneled seminar rooms, nearly every room lined with fine books. The library seemed to offer the essence of scholarly community too, with people meeting to talk about their discoveries in the midst of invaluable collections of books and other documents.

When I went to the Newberry in 1976, I planned to study Nathaniel Hawthorne and Herman Melville, key figures in the mid-nineteenth century period F.O. Matthiessen explored in his book *The American Renaissance: Art and Expression in the Age of Emerson and Whitman* (1941). The lives of both writers raise questions about the connection between economics and creativity. What are we to make, for example, of the fact that both Hawthorne and Melville went to work for a federal government that was rapidly expanding its commercial influence in this period of productivity? How were their creative imaginations influenced by the materialism their writing often challenged? Hawthorne's relationship with the utopian community Brook Farm and the novel that grew out of his experience there, *The Blithedale Romance,* fit nicely into our seminar's concern with "art and commerce," and it connected too with my "Institute" dream so I wrote an essay about it.

But once I glimpsed the library's materials on the Lewis and Clark Expedition, as well as its holdings in

Native American literature and history, I began to feel the scholarly ground shift under my feet just as it had when I found slave narratives and African American folklore. Why, I asked myself, hadn't I encountered any of these materials when I was studying American literature and history? At first I spent my spare moments thumbing through works on display in a reading room devoted to western Americana. By mid-November, however, nineteenth-century descriptions of encounters with Native American societies in the west began to fill my journal, including references to myths and tales collected from small-scale indigenous societies in the Pacific Northwest. My growing interest was partly a result of our family's recent experience in Oregon. It was a way of extending the sense of discovery I found in that wonderful year.

The collections in the Newberry Library were not my first encounter with the Native American cultures of the Pacific Northwest, but the study of those cultures in my early schooling had conveyed a sense of something irretrievably lost. It was as though we were talking about passenger pigeons whose instinctive behavior had not prepared them to defend themselves against the progress of civilization. When I was a second grader at Richmond Elementary School in Portland, my father spent an evening working with grape vines and brown wrapping paper to construct for my class a model of a small, round vessel like the little boats Chinook women sometimes used for gathering food. A businessman with no traditional knowledge could simulate one of these slightly comic, bowl-like boats in an evening although we realized that the beautiful dugout canoes the Chinooks built and used with great skill were another matter. The moral of the exercise seemed to be that Dad had to build the model because the cultures that produced them were gone. A few descendants survived, perhaps, on the Warm Springs Reservation, but the cultures that looked so interesting in retrospect were, sadly, as extinct as dinosaurs. Smallpox and measles were the main villains, we were told. As a boy, I found these accounts of Native American extinction sad, and I didn't think to connect them with the native people I sometimes saw in Portland.

My first encounter with another way of thinking about the Indians I'd studied as a child came at the Newberry. Before I found Native American myths and tales from the region, I found a book by Roy Harvey Pearce, *The Savages of America: A Study of the Indian and the Idea of Civilization* (1953). Pearce claimed belief in the inevitable extinction of indigenous cultures was part of the intellectual armor Europeans wore as they moved across the continent. I found confirmation in documents from the nineteenth and even the twentieth century, including writings of Gustavus Hines, the Methodist missionary. Hines came to the Oregon country in 1840 and published a book about his experience, *Life on the Plains of the Pacific*, in 1852. To begin his missionary work with the Indians, he made a difficult journey by sea from New York City around Cape Horn to Hawaii and on to the Pacific coast, then over the treacherous bar at the mouth of the Columbia River and up the Columbia and Willamette rivers. He was delighted by the landscape: "Surely, thought I, infinite skill has been employed, in fitting up a country which requires nothing more than a population under the influence of the religion of Christ to render it a perfect paradise." But within days he concluded that the present residents would soon be extinct, giving way to "a people more worthy of this beautiful and fertile country." Hines' arduous ministry to the Indians of the Northwest was devoted exclusively to preparing them for the hereafter.

One basis for concluding people are destined for extinction is to assume they lack the intelligence required to survive. (In our own time, a good deal of pessimism about the future of our species grows from the conclusion that we lack adequate intelligence to control the power we've unleashed with our technologies, and this pessimism seems to have grown along with our dawning awareness of climate change.) It wasn't just missionaries who considered the Indians intellectually inferior. James G. Swan, who came to the region in 1852 planning to salt salmon in barrels and sell them in San Francisco, took a view similar to Gustavus Hines'. He hired Chinooks to take him up a small Columbia River tributary because it was late in the season, and fish in the river's lower reaches were beginning to die after spawning. While Swan and his interpreter shot birds, the Indians caught more than 100 salmon on their first afternoon on the river. The next morning the Indians explained that in the night a plover song told them not to fish the river anymore until the next salmon run. "It was our intention," Swan says in *The Northwest Coast* (1857) "to have remained several days, but the Indians, from some superstitious ideas, refused to fish anymore" (42). He tried offering the Indians larger rewards, but they were firm in their refusal. Frustrated and amused, he didn't consider the possibility that they might be protecting the fish runs in that river. Dismissing behavior as superstitious that makes good ecological sense allowed Swan to echo Gustavus Hines: "During the fishing season a good deal of drunkenness may be seen among them, and for the most part they are a miserable, whiskey-drinking set of vagabonds. However, the race of the Chinooks is nearly run."

Lewis and Clark were not inclined to predict extinction for the Indians of the Northwest. Maintaining health and morale in their expeditionary force required knowledge and skills like those exhibited by the Indians of the lower Columbia, and Lewis and Clark recognized the intelligence and resourcefulness of those societies. But the explorers, who had negotiated skillfully with hostile Sioux warriors, grew to be *afraid* of the Chinook and Clatsop people. They came to see these trading societies as the inscrutable offspring of an inhospitable region shrouded in endless rain and fog. Crossing the Great Plains, they found more bison, elk, and bear than they could eat, but when they got to the green conifer forests along the lower Columbia, the land around Saddle Mountain, they found so little game that they were forced to buy dried salmon and roots from the Indians. The people on whom they were dependent for food and information were very different from the societies of the Great Plains with whom they had negotiated brilliantly. These people seemed strangely passive, friendly but canny and unpredictable as traders. Although Lewis and Clark continued to be disciplined ethnographers in their journals, noting the Clatsops' extraordinary skills with canoes and their impressive intelligence, the explorers were increasingly troubled by these mysterious people.

As Asian Americans can attest, to be thought inscrutable is not usually an advantage: people often ascribe malice to those they find mysterious. Such failures of imagination often lead to war. Not long after the explorers built Fort Clatsop on Youngs Bay, fifteen miles northwest of Saddle Mountain, in the winter of 1805-06, Meriwether Lewis's journal, which had fallen into silence as they made their way down the western side of the Rocky Mountains, came alive with a grim new phrase: "the treachery of the aborigines." Not only were they sometimes secretive and furtive, but their openness on sexual matters was shocking. They talked of sex as freely as they talked of food or trade, and among their women, Lewis said, "kindness exceeded the ordinary courtesies of hospitality." Lewis was troubled by the Clatsops' sexual generosity, and he came to see their petty thievery and price-gouging on salmon as tantamount to capital crimes.

A more complex view of the Northwest Indians became available as anthropologists collected stories and songs. Most of the stories are as skeletal as the whale's remains found by William Clark in Cannon Beach, leaving out connections with other narratives, interactions between performer and audience, and knowledge of cultural values and geography. But the sixty-four stories collected by anthropologist Melville Jacobs in 1929-30 from Mrs. Victoria Howard, one of the last two or three speakers of the Clackamas Chinook dialect, reveal much that wasn't visible to outsiders. Not only do they give a larger sense of the people who created and performed the stories, but like slave narratives and African American folklore, they illuminate our own culture. "Clackamas hardly ventured upon a distinction between man and nature," Melville Jacobs points out in a book that brings together eight of Mrs. Howard's narratives with his analysis, *The Content and Style of an Oral Literature*. In contrast with *Walden*, where Henry Thoreau strives for intimacy with the natural world, struggling through the falsities of society to the primeval reality that underlies civilization, these stories assume the primacy of nature. We can forget that our separation from nature is an illusion, that even people who live eighty floors above ground in Chicago's John Hancock Building are not cut off from natural cycles, including death and decay. The Clackamas coyote stories show even the god-like trickster figure to be powerless in the face of nature, but they also show how people live with dignity and patience in a world they can't control. As I became acquainted with these oral traditions, collected by Melville Jacobs near the junction of the Clackamas and Willamette rivers, not far from where my parents retired, I wondered how things might have been different if Lewis and Clark, Gustavus Hines, James Swan and others in the nineteenth century had been able to join the winter story-telling that helped to hold these indigenous societies together.

Just as my sense of American culture, my ostensible area of expertise, was once again jolted in

Chicago, my view of urban life changed during our time in the city. Encounters with prostitutes and homeless people in a part of the city that catered to people of privilege suggested a level of tolerance, even acceptance, of behaviors that would be considered social disorder in a town like Granville. I was drawn to Richard Sennett's book *The Uses of Disorder: Personal Identity and City Life* (1972) and to a statement he makes about disorder: "It is because men are uneasy and intolerant with ambiguity and discord in their own lives that they do not know how to deal with painful disorder in a social setting, and instead escalate disorder to the level of life or death struggle." As we walked around Chicago, it seemed to me there was a level of comfort in the face of ambiguity that I began to see as admirable. Even the young prostitute's quickly averted glance when I approached suggested to me a kind of tact, as though she meant to let me make up my mind whether to greet her, once I understood her mission, without the pressure of continued eye contact.

One day we were visited by one of the families I had tried unsuccessfully to entice into our discussions of the Institute. Bob, a philosopher with agricultural skills and training as an auctioneer, had been my roommate in college, and despite his appealing practical skills, I should have known he was too independent to be drawn to a commune, even one billed as a hard-headed business. When their old station wagon broke down near our apartment on a Sunday, the day they planned to leave Chicago, we found the only car parts stores open anywhere near us were in the neighborhoods to our west, where we had been warned not to walk. We were seeking a large hose for the cooling system, and the three stores we found didn't have it. In the third store, as in the others, the customers were mainly African American, the salespeople mainly white. These were crowded, shabby stores that reminded me of working class diners in the early morning, when customers seem to take pleasure in each other's company. There was a rough civility as car parts and money changed hands. In the third store, Bob hinted at desperation, and a salesman helped him assemble a substitute hose from three smaller hoses and gaskets. The improvised hose did the job long enough to get Bob and his family home.

A few days later I recorded a conversation in my journal that reminded me of our visit to the car parts stores. It took place in a shabby used-book store on Halstead Street. A teenage boy walked into the store with a pile of old paperbacks, and the man behind the counter asked, "You planning to sell or trade?"

"Depends," the kid answered.

"Well, I can tell you right now, you'll get more trading." The man looked over the books and offered the kid $1.50, then $1.75 when the kid didn't say anything. The kid walked back to a shelf and took a hardback he must have had in mind when he came in the store and put it on the counter. "Nah, I couldn't trade you that," the man behind the counter said. "Frank would have my ass. On paperbacks I could go $3.50 though. . . . Hey, you interested in Chesterton? I sure didn't pick you for a Chesterton reader. Somebody hip you on Chesterton?"

The kid nodded his head and barely cracked a sheepish smile. He quickly found a couple of paperbacks and left. Like the man behind the counter, I was curious about how a kid who looked like a high school drop-out got interested in a British writer unknown to most of my students. Something about their exchange defied categories that seemed much more elastic in Chicago than in Granville.

The elasticity in urban life was appealing, and our family felt this personally. Daughter Judy was going into the ninth grade when we went to Chicago, and Annie was beginning the fifth grade. Just across the street from the Newberry Library was a widely respected public elementary school where Annie enrolled. But nervous about inner-city high schools, we sent Judy to the Francis W. Parker School, a private school more than a mile north of us. Judy, who is now a writer, teacher, and activist, loved music and poetry and art, but she was not enthusiastic about school. She was very shy, and she considered herself a mediocre student. When she was elected class president in her first week at Francis Parker, we realized there was something unusual about the school. That eager acceptance by her new peers was just the beginning of an experience I came to think of as educational therapy. By the end of a semester with enthusiastic teachers and more diverse and lively schoolmates than she had ever known, Judy realized she was a good student and a feminist, maybe even a poet. It would be several more years before she knew for sure she was a lesbian.

Although our semester in Chicago was a rich, transforming, time for our family and especially for Judy, we hadn't surrendered our dream of rural community when we returned to Granville in January. We signed the papers for our purchase of the cabin on the Oregon coast while we were in Chicago, and I began work on an essay, "Lewis and Clark Probe the Heart of Darkness," that appeared in *The American Scholar* and led me to write the novel *York's Journal*, an attempt to bring together what I'd learned about slave narratives, Native American oral tradition, and the imperialistic temptations faced by explorers. Still more than ten years away from seeking the Fox Creek forest with my brother Dave, I'd begun to uncover some of the connections among place, violence, and imagination.

Chapter Ten

Going to Court on the Hound

In January of 1980 I set out from Ohio on a fifteen-day, $202 Greyhound bus pass to attend a court appearance in Astoria, Oregon. Hoping to defend our newly purchased property near Cannon Beach and save money by riding the bus, I was also looking for stories. I remembered my bus ride through northern California and Oregon in the spring of 1974, listening most of the night to stories told by a man called Rusty, who claimed he had just been released from prison. The pallor of his rugged features, the unstylish newness of his clothes, and his lack of luggage gave his claim authority, although the fact that he was crossing a state line while on probation made me wonder if he'd decided to resume a life of crime immediately. His seatmate, a slender, high-strung woman with a wavy mane of country singer hair, was from a farm town in northeastern California. She was returning from a weekend with her husband at Camp Pendleton, and she was pretty good with a story herself. Both of them played to those of us in adjoining seats as they traded stories about rattlesnakes and domestic violence.

With his deep, smoky voice, Rusty was the more skilled raconteur. When we arrived in Redding, California, a college student who had perched on my armrest to listen stood up and interrupted one of the stories to say goodbye. "Here now, son, I'd like to get your name before you go," Rusty yelled as the boy started down the aisle. The boy answered politely, and as he backed down the aisle toward the door, Rusty's voice rose: "Here now, George, try to remember old Rusty and be good to your fellow man. If you find a man in trouble, just naturally try to help him. If he gets on your ass, don't be in no hurry to fight him. But here now, George, if he gets on there and just won't get off—kill him."

The boy waved as he started out the door, but he looked startled, and before Rusty could get back to his story-in-progress, his seatmate gave him a brief, stern lecture. Her husband liked to fight in bars, she said, and as far as she could tell, nothing good ever came of it.

When I boarded a bus in Columbus to head for Oregon, I was ready for stories like Rusty's, and in Dayton an attractive woman whose dark hair had begun to show signs of gray joined me. She wore soft jeans and a vinyl jacket, and after settling herself beside me and pulling the tab on a can of diet soda, she began to talk. She gave me a brief account of her life as a divorced, working mother of three daughters. She was a nurse in a General Motors plant, and her work was sometimes frustrating, she said, because people on assembly lines were less concerned with protecting their health than with holding onto a job they'd learned to do without thinking much about it. She understood the problem: a new place on the line could mean months of stress while you got up to speed. When she tried to move workers to another place in the plant for the good of their health, they often filed grievances with the union. Still, she was sympathetic. She saw them saving for years to buy an RV when they retired, only to find they couldn't afford to travel. But hers was a frustrating job.

The Dayton singles scene was difficult too, she told me. Men bought you a drink and thought they owned you. So she often headed off to Indianapolis, as she was this weekend, to visit old friends. And raising adolescent daughters was no picnic either. She told the girls they were unlikely ever again to live as comfortably as they did now, but they didn't believe her. The whole economy was falling apart, as far as she could tell, including General Motors. "Middle people," folks like her family, were going to be hurt by the collapsing economy. Poor folks and wealthy ones weren't likely to notice the change.

She asked me how I made a living, and when I told her I taught English, she gasped. She'd just finished a night course in English at the University of Dayton, and she couldn't write a lick. Her professor told her the problem was she didn't think straight. Having confessed to this shortcoming, she talked breathtaking circles around me on subjects as diverse as Dayton singles bars and the Soviet invasion of Afghanistan. Her stories were freighted with woe, but when we reached the outskirts of Indianapolis, she seemed to want to leave me with a glimpse of hope. She told me about an interview she'd watched recently on television with the writer Henry Miller. "I haven't read a thing he wrote," she said, "but that guy knows how to grow old with style." This seemed to be a kind of benediction as she prepared to leave the bus. She laughed aloud, remembering Miller's humor. Gathering her large leather purse and overnight case, she told me the best way to deal with the hard times ahead might be to laugh like Henry Miller.

Later, on a bus going out of Chicago toward Minneapolis, I talked through the pre-dawn hours with Bill, a slender, dark-haired young man who was looking around for a graduate school that would prepare him to save the world. He'd dropped out of college and joined the Navy, where he learned filmmaking. Now, in his late twenties, he wanted to become an agricultural scientist and help farmers develop sustainable agricultural methods. Oh, he knew American farmers weren't ready to consider scaling back their operations and using fewer chemicals as long as oil was cheap. But someday they'd have to listen, and in the meantime he planned to work with Third World farmers. Bill was happy to meet somebody familiar with E.F. Schumacher and the Kentucky farmer and writer Wendell Berry, whose book *The Unsettling of America* makes a case for affirming

85

smallness and strengthening rural communities. But he let me know he was impatient with Schumacher and Berry. We need more radical political reforms than anything they've proposed, he insisted. It was tempting to tell Bill about our Institute idea and the cabin we'd bought in Oregon, but his impatience with Schumacher and Berry made me think he might share my friend Fred's skepticism. I was sorry to see Bill go in the morning when we both got off the bus to visit friends near St. Paul.

Boarding a bus headed west out of Minneapolis two days later, I noticed several passengers who looked exhausted. A blizzard had blown into Minnesota, stopping bus travel, and they had just spent the night in the Greyhound station. We were about to trace the last two-thirds of Lewis and Clark's route, through North Dakota, Montana, the Idaho panhandle, Washington, and Oregon, and the roads would be slippery most of the way. As we neared the Pacific, there would be a crescendo of spectacular winter weather, with power lines down, ice and snow closing most highways, and big trucks moving like snails on the roads that were open. My companions were the most convivial bus riders I've met in more than thirty years of bus travel, and I have no doubt their sociability had something to do with the snowy, windswept landscape outside our windows. Not only did everyone know we would have to depend on each other if the bus went into a ditch along the frozen road, but we felt the human presence of the drivers, who were not the disembodied voices of airline pilots, but people whose care and skill we could judge pretty knowledgably.

Bus riders now do much of their talking into cell phones, but the sociable passengers I met in 1980 seemed eager to talk with each other. A seventeen-year-old couple set the mood on our westward journey. Separately, they moved around the bus, telling their stories to anyone who would listen and returning occasionally to their seats to nuzzle each other affectionately before taking off again. They were headed for Bozeman, Montana, to start a new life, they said, and they borrowed my road atlas to check the lay of the land. The boy had visited Bozeman briefly while hitchhiking across the country the previous summer, but their chief authority for choosing Bozeman was Robert Pirsig's novel *Zen and the Art of Motorcycle Maintenance* (1974), still popular among young people in 1980. Both of them seemed to be ardent readers, but even though they'd chosen a college town, they had no plans to seek formal education.

Two teen-aged sisters joined us in North Dakota, headed for Coeur d'Alene, Idaho, where they planned to live with relatives and look for work. They had grown up on a farm in South Dakota, and they were so excited by the possibilities they imagined in Idaho that they talked through much of the night. Sometime before dawn one of them changed seats to provide a cowboy with her shoulder for his weary head, but in the morning she returned to sit with her sister.

In eastern Montana a young father and mother got on the bus with their son, who was probably ten. Both the mother and son had black eyes, and the father seemed to be a moody man. Several people speculated quietly that the father had beaten his wife and son, but his apparent tendency to throw punches didn't isolate the family. Passengers went out of their way to befriend them, and before long both parents were asking what we knew about Olympia, Washington, where they were headed for work.

Along with those black eyes, I found another reminder that people who ride the buses are often less insulated from violence than those who ride above them in airliners. These are people, I imagine, unlikely to remain in their seats if someone tried to take over the bus. I met a shy, quiet man who had just returned to

87

Montana from Alaska. He'd worked three years as a heavy equipment operator on the Alaskan pipeline, he told me. After that he prospected for gold. He showed me a snapshot he'd taken of a wolf that visited the remote site where he prospected. He'd come to like the wolf so much, he said, that he fed it, but he was terrified of grizzly bears. When he mentioned later that he carried a .38 pistol while he was prospecting, I asked him skeptically if he thought a pistol would stop a grizzly. He looked sideways at me and spoke with an embarrassed smile. "People still jump claims up there," he said.

Another man I talked with on our way west didn't approve of packing a gun. He was a student of Mahatma Gandhi. He worked summers for the Forest Service, and during the rest of the year he lived in rural villages in India and Latin America. He told of learning from the people in those villages how to live on very little, but what interested him most of all, he said, was their music. He was hoping to become an *ethnomusicologist*, although he seemed uncomfortable with the fancy word, and he was on his way to Seattle to join a friend and study at the University of Washington. He was a shy man, seemingly accustomed to spending time alone, but as the roads grew increasingly icy, he offered me a place to stay in Seattle.

As it turned out, I didn't need to stop in Seattle. On noisy, jarring chains a bus went south from Seattle, through Olympia, where the family with black eyes got off in the middle of the night. In Portland I caught a local bus to the coast with a driver who had never made the trip before, and just as I was nearing 72 hours on the road, not counting the stopover in Minnesota, we arrived in Seaside, where a lawyer, Steve Campbell, was preparing to help me defend our property from a bulldozer hired by people who planned to be our neighbors.

On our first day at the octagonal cabin near Cannon Beach in the summer of 1977, our family had eaten lunch outside on the second story deck, nestled among spruce trees. We watched a deer come down the dirt road that ended at the cabin, and even when she noticed us and bounded into the trees, her presence made us feel welcome in the forest. On the Oregon coast, where deer and elk habitat survive in vast stretches of logging company land, we learned it was unusual to see a deer so close to a house. That first summer in Oregon was a delightful blend of writing, building simple furniture, hiking, and entertaining family and friends, including the two families with whom we'd been discussing the Institute. Much of the forest was second-growth spruce, mature enough that the under-story was relatively clear of undergrowth, and we could easily walk back into the woods to look for morel mushrooms. On a clear day in the afternoon the sunlight angled into the trees from over the ocean, making a warm, golden light. When the sun came over the top of the Coast Range in the morning, shining through droplets on the trees, the forest canopy we saw from our windows sparkled magically. We could hardly believe our good fortune.

But when we returned in the summer of 1978, we found a large spruce tree in pieces on the ground below our cabin. Soil from the lower part of our lot had been scraped downhill to provide fill for a building site. Cleared by a bulldozer, that site was a gaping wound in the temperate rainforest that stretched out from the sides of our cabin. All this damage had been done in the two days just before our arrival, after the departure of a woman who lived in our cabin through the winter and spring. When we talked with the people who had helped us buy the cabin, we learned the damage might be just a beginning. The people who owned the lot below us claimed to be "landlocked," with no access to their building site. They also claimed to have an easement across our property, allowing them to build a road, which explained the downed spruce. The easement made a lot of sense, but if they actually had the right to cut down our tree and build a road across our land, I wondered why they had done it surreptitiously. Why hadn't they discussed it with us? Friends pointed out that the bulldozer had damaged the root systems of spruce trees still standing on our property, increasing the likelihood that they would blow down in a winter storm. Erosion might cause our cabin to slip down the hill, they said, and I remembered Leon Settem's tilted house, destroyed in a mudslide.

The contractor and landowner came a day or two later to look over the site and tell me about their easement. I expressed considerable skepticism, and they climbed in their car and disappeared. When they refused to answer phone calls and letters, I did what many do in our litigious society: I threatened to sue. And when my threats failed to move them, we hired a lawyer.

The scale of our lawsuit was not impressive. My family in Portland favored an attorney who specialized in property law, a man who would probably have raised the stakes, but we chose Steve Campbell, a local man known for his honesty and for running well in the annual Seaside Marathon. Campbell put the case together quickly, but the Clatsop County Courthouse in Astoria was busy, and our day in court was set for January 10, 1980, well over a year after the damage was done. Campbell suggested that we seek $12,500 in damages from the owner, the contractor, and the bulldozer operator, and we were prepared to settle for much less out of court. But the defendants seemed unwilling to communicate with each other, let alone with Steve Campbell, and it soon became apparent that I would have to make the trip to the county courthouse in Astoria.

The first news Steve Campbell gave me when I arrived on the coast, as sleepy as I've ever been, was that our day in court would have to be delayed. One of the defendants had hired an attorney from Portland who specialized in property disputes, and he was not willing to drive over the mountains to Astoria in such wild weather. When I suggested that the property law specialist might drive instead along the Columbia River, thereby avoiding the mountains, Campbell mentioned there were several feet of snow on the Columbia River Highway. I'd been considering the adversarial system we would rely on for justice in the courthouse, and sleepy as I was, I countered that I had just come by bus from Ohio through blizzards and ice storms: the high-powered Portland attorney could save time and money by emulating me. Besides which, I added, I was traveling on a 15-day bus pass and didn't want to get stuck in Kansas or Iowa on my return. Campbell said the attorney couldn't get out of his driveway in Portland, and I would need to take up residence in the Seaside Center Motel. As consolation, he offered me dinner and a chance to join his wife, a delightful local radio personality, their sociable little daughter, and Campbell himself in an after-dinner hot tub. It was a memorable evening, and when I got back to the motel, I slept like a man with a spotless conscience.

After a one-day delay, the judge told the defendants and their attorneys to find their way to Astoria by dogsled, if necessary, and I felt word of my heroic bus ride west had gotten around Astoria. The Portland lawyer was not pleased. Talking with Steve Campbell, he relied less on the kind of counter argument I anticipated and more on *ad hominem* and moral exhortation. Nancy and I claimed in a deposition, he pointed out, that bulldozer damage to our lot made it unsafe for children to play there, and now I asked him to drive over dangerous, icy mountain roads. Did my high moral standards apply only to children? I would be sorry, he said, if he ended up in a ditch and sorrier still if he made it safely to the courtroom in Astoria.

He arrived at the courthouse with time to spare and proved to be so affable that when his little sports car failed to start at the end of a very rainy day, Steve Campbell and I pushed it on foot through heavy rain to a service station near the courthouse and talked amiably with him about a detective novel he was writing.

The trial itself was a disappointment. The courtroom conversation seemed abstract and tedious after the interesting talk aboard the buses. I was mainly impressed by the judge's ability to remain alert through hours of testimony and cross-examination, all of which, including my own participation, seemed beside the point. When we introduced photographs of the damage taken by my father, one of the three defense lawyers methodically led me to admit that Dad could not have taken some of the photographs without straddling the property line and thereby trespassing. This shrewd piece of lawyering probably did no damage to our case, but it made me feel like an idiot because I failed to point out the difference between trespassing in shoes and on a bulldozer.

My reluctant confession on behalf of my father was the dramatic high point of a trial that dragged on interminably through a Friday morning without ever revealing what seemed to me the lesson of the day: neighbors should consult with each other before using chainsaws and bulldozers on each other's land. The adversarial process, by which we hoped to reach a fair and lawful resolution by making the best case for extreme positions consistent with the facts, didn't seem to allow for common sense. Our side had hired an expert forester to talk about the doom likely to follow when the root systems of spruce trees are disturbed. And we asked a realtor to explain how precipitously property values slide when trees are lost and soil begins to move downhill. The defense made persuasive arguments for the essential stability of hillsides that have been subjected to wind and rain for centuries without changing their shape. The talk seemed cut off from the actual soil, the real trees, and the failure of civility. Even our photographs, frozen in time, seemed disconnected from the landscape. They could have been pictures of many places.

When the Portland lawyer requested a "site visit," I was delighted. As we drove south on Highway 101, I began to wonder if the damaged land as a setting might inspire me to a level of eloquence I'd failed to achieve on the stand. Freed from the constraints of the courtroom and the powerless language of our suit—*loss of lateral support, negligent trespass, wrongful and negligent excavation, lessened market value*—I might, like a good poet, fuse the change in our land and the failure of civility with the sensory experience of the place itself. Something brief and slightly ironic might do the job. But it seemed to me instead I saw the judge's eyes glaze over with the boredom I had expected to see in the courtroom; the landscape revealed little evidence of visible damage. Ample rainfall, moderate temperatures, and seeds and spores from surrounding flora had caused impressive healing in the several months since the bulldozer and chainsaw had changed the land. Even the building site, which had been scraped down to naked soil, was alive with ferns, seedlings, and blackberry vines. I was almost speechless as we stood on the property, and lawyer Campbell was left to point lamely at unconvincing evidence that we hadn't made the whole thing up.

Because it was a Friday, the judge excused me from the second day of the trial, scheduled for the following Monday. Breathing a sigh of relief, I took a bus into Portland to visit my brother Dave and my parents, who were still dealing with a power outage and roads closed by fallen trees. There was a woodstove in my parents' mobile home, and they had invited several neighbors to join them until heat was restored to their homes once again. We sat around the stove talking about the lawsuit, and I encountered great sympathy, unmixed with the usual suspicion of my views on politics and religion. Then I hopped a bus south to Eugene for a short visit with brother John and farther south to Chico, California, for an even briefer time with old friend Terry, to talk about the dying dream of our Institute.

The weather was growing warmer. Pools of water stood along the roads in northern California, and ski towns in the Sierras were covered with mud instead of snow. When my bus started east through Nevada, I noticed a mood among my fellow travelers that seemed to differ from that of the passengers coming west, most of whom had seemed to be leaving home and dreaming of new possibilities. Going east, people seemed to be returning.

Mandy came aboard in Reno, and she was going home reluctantly. She was seventeen, she said, but she looked younger despite her bleached hair, and she'd just been released from a juvenile center in Reno. She was returning to her mother, a widow in Butte, Montana. "Life," Mandy repeated in a kind of mantra, "is the shits." And Mandy, she admitted, was not her real name. She chain-smoked through the long January night, asking those of us around her persistent questions about where we were going and where we had been. She dominated a lively group near the back of the bus, a group in which I was a sleepy, increasingly silent member. At a casino rest stop in Nevada, Mandy helped a frightened older woman find a ride to her home in a nearby town, and before the night was over she began necking playfully with a handsome young Hispanic who had just left his girlfriend.

There are many legends about sexual activity aboard long distance buses, but my impression is that innocent cuddling between new acquaintances is more common than anything approaching sexual intercourse,

94

especially since the introduction of the on-board toilet brought an end to the long back seat. To share a double seat through the night without touching one's seat partner can be uncomfortable. To relax enough to drop one's head on another's shoulder can be a great comfort when one's neck muscles begin to tire. Add to that physical need, the loneliness of many long distance travelers, and it is no wonder that strangers sometimes sleep in each other's arms. But more than cuddling requires considerable ingenuity.

The young man nuzzling Mandy had been living in Sacramento, but his girlfriend came home late from a party and they quarreled. Within hours, he said, he quit his job, loaned his car to a friend, and bought a one-way ticket across the country. He had visited old Army buddies at Fort Bragg, and now he was on his way to see his family in Florida. Someday he'd come back for his car.

A young African American couple was part of our lively group. They had not found what they were seeking in Chico, California, and they were on their way back to New York City. They had just ten dollars for food on the trip, and the tall, quiet man nearly missed the bus when we stopped in Iowa City and he took too long to find a grocery store. The bus erupted in a wonderful uproar when the driver closed the door and began to pull away, and there was much cheering and laughter when the tall black figure in a flapping overcoat came running down the street.

The friendliest member of our group, a balding man in his thirties with shoulder-length strands of blond hair, had given up on San Francisco and was going home to Rochester, New York. He'd lived for years by selling marijuana, he said, but changes in the price structure were cutting disastrously into his profits. He spoke reverently of the most beautiful time in his life, when he made a lot of money smuggling large amounts of marijuana into Aspen. Charming and tough, he was so sociable he barely slept from California to Chicago, where we caught different buses. Outside the Nevada casino where Mandy helped the woman find her way home, the retired dealer asked me, "Do you get high?" He pointed to an alley beside the casino, where we could share a joint. Well into middle age, bespectacled like my father, I had not been an active participant in our group at the back of the bus, and I was surprised and honored that he saw me as a potential smoking companion. I wanted to say something friendly and grateful, but all I could think to say was the truth: I was exhausted, and I planned to move into an empty seat near the front of the bus when we started riding again.

The bankrupt marijuana dealer and other members of the group didn't hold my move against me. They joined me at rest stops to talk, seeming to understand that I lacked the stamina to party with them. Mandy changed buses in Salt Lake City, but the rest of the group stuck together all the way to Chicago. They set the mood aboard the bus with their joking and boisterous laughter, and they seemed to make the drivers nervous. Beneath their humor, I heard despair, but I was impressed that their failed dreams hadn't driven them into brooding insularity. They were generous in their noisy way, and a number of young people attached themselves to the group, off and on, during the two nights and two days it took to get to Chicago.

My ride from Chicago back into Ohio seemed quiet, partly because I was too tired to ask questions. It gave me time to think about the resilience and humor I found in life aboard the buses, the ease in the face of mortality and failure that I'd noticed among my parents' old friends, a strength I wanted to cultivate in our Institute. I don't mean to sentimentalize busculture, however. I remember a beautiful morning in eastern Oregon on a Trailways bus trip a few months later, when a driver turned a comment about landscape made by an older woman seated behind him into a quiet diatribe. "If they ever decide to give Glass Butte to somebody," he said, "they'll give it to minorities. Why, they're letting eighty thousand Orientals a week into the country. Why, them coons, some of 'em, demonstrated a while back because they was only having ham and eggs for breakfast. They give 'em mushroom sauce." As minorities came to be a large proportion of the passengers aboard long distance buses, that kind of talk probably became uncommon, but the attitude survived of an abused white underclass that resents both minorities and the privileged people who fly overhead in the big silver birds.

Still, the bus riders, and the drivers too, seemed accustomed to dealing resourcefully with an uncertain, imperfect world. When the usual route to Chicago's bus station was blocked, the driver asked for advice on his loudspeaker, and two passengers collaborated on an alternate route to the station. Arriving on the Oregon coast with a driver new to the route, I had offered sound advice for finding the bus station in Seaside. On the icy night when we were riding over Snoqualmie Pass to Seattle, the driver took our bus off the main highway and down a snow-covered road to a man's house so his wife wouldn't have to drive on the slippery roads to pick him up. Passengers often provided childcare so mothers could use the bathroom or grab something to eat at a rest stop. A sense of contingency seemed to inform busculture. Later that year a Trailways driver about to be relieved in Grand Junction, Colorado, said goodbye this way: "For those of you who enjoyed traveling with me, I wish you much happiness and joy in the future. For those of you who didn't, I wish you intense chest pain." His farewell speech was greeted with laughter and applause. Such exchanges are unlikely to take place aboard American Airlines.

When I got off the bus in Columbus, Nancy told me we'd won a minor victory in the Astoria courtroom: $4,554.03. It wouldn't fix the chain-sawed spruce, but our neighbors might think twice before they cut another down. As of 2013, there was still no building on that lot, and the question of the easement remained a legal mystery.

Chapter Eleven

Our Family Goes Nuclear

On a clear day, the office of William Lindblad, Portland General Electric Company's president in 1981, looked out on Mt. St. Helens and Mt. Hood. His view reminded me a little of the vista from the summit of Saddle Mountain. In mid-April of 1981, when I interviewed Lindblad after several months of unanswered letters and phone calls to PGE, the plume from the Trojan Nuclear Plant's cooling tower was visible as it drifted toward Portland. The president's office might almost have been a tastefully appointed chapel, the furniture elegantly simple and the view through the window as colorful as stained glass. Lindblad, tall and severe in a dark suit, might have been a Puritan minister, his faith in nuclear technology angry and deep. He had, as it turned out, no intention of telling me much about the Trojan plant, but he meant to convince me that my inevitably flawed effort to tell the nuke's story might be an unpardonable sin.

By seeking to write about the Trojan plant I made myself Lindblad's enemy in Oregon's Trojan War, which shouldn't have surprised me. Commercial nuclear power, after all, grew out of the Manhattan Project, which was such a big secret that Vice President Truman didn't learn about it until after President Roosevelt died. More recently, the Bush and Obama administrations have encouraged domestic utilities to start building nuclear plants again after several years during which commercial nuclear power in the United States wasn't considered a good investment. Our leaders were also hinting at the possibility of going to war if Iran persisted in enriching its own nuclear fuel because it is a relatively short step from mastering the nuclear fuel cycle to building nuclear weapons, and many people believed an Iran armed with nuclear weapons might be the last straw in an unstable Middle East. Commercial nuclear power was blessed at its birth with the hope-filled metaphor of beating swords into plowshares, but it was soon apparent to people who thought about safeguards that nuclear technology couldn't be completely separated from its military origins.

Technology's effects on our culture interested me well before the chainsaw and bulldozer transformed our landscape in Oregon. I was influenced by Leo Marx's book *The Machine in the Garden: Technology and the Pastoral Ideal in America* (1964), which explored the tension between our society's pastoral dreaming and our growing dependence on powerful technologies. The dream of the Institute grew partly out of an impulse to live with appropriate technologies, and my long bus rides were partly experiments to determine how it would feel to rely on a means of public transportation less energy-intensive than airplanes. In the 1970's, buses got about six times more passenger-miles per gallon than a typical airliner.

If you thought much about technology in the 1970's, it was nearly impossible to ignore nuclear power, especially after Jimmy Carter, a Navy-trained nuclear engineer, became our president in 1977 and there was a major nuclear accident at Three Mile Island in 1979. As I read about commercial nuclear power, I realized its cultural impact was more pronounced in England and France than in the United States. And that discovery offered a perfect excuse to do what Nancy and I had long wanted to do, live on the other side of the Atlantic. Nancy had been teaching French for years, and I had been in love with nineteenth-century British literature since I was in high school. We began to plan a sabbatical leave in England and France, and we arranged to rent a cottage southwest of London. Then, just a few weeks after I returned from the Astoria courthouse, Mom suffered a stroke that left her with partial paralysis and loss of language. We decided to spend 1980-81 in Oregon.

Thus simply did an English professor in Ohio decide to write about Oregon's only nuke. My first encounter with the Trojan Nuclear Plant had taken place in 1972, three years before it began to operate and eight years before I began my project. Nancy and I were riding a train from Seattle to Portland with our daughters, Judy and Annie, when the great hyperbolic curves of the cooling tower's silhouette appeared across the Columbia River. I had seen photographs of cooling towers before, but I was speechless when Judy pointed to the real thing and asked me about this intrusive new part of the landscape. Now I know the tower was gray and elegant in its massive simplicity, but in my memory of that first glimpse it is brick red, and it dwarfs the Oregon hills behind it. It seemed so out of place and proportion that I didn't really see it at all. In 1972 the tower rose so gigantically in my mind over a familiar, bucolic landscape that I chose to ignore it, and during our first sabbatical year in Oregon, 1973-74, despite making many trips from Cannon Beach inland to Portland, we didn't once drive along the Columbia River on Highway 30, a route that would have taken us past the rising Trojan plant.

In the summer of 1980, having faced up to the nuclear plant's reality, I gingerly approached Oregon's Trojan plant by way of Bethesda, Maryland, and the offices of the Nuclear Regulatory Commission (NRC), where I interviewed Charles Trammell, who was then the NRC's Project Manager for the Trojan. Trammell, a pleasant, laconic man in his thirties, coordinated the federal government's regulation of the plant. To my delight, he seemed unfazed by the prospect of an English professor who wanted to study a nuclear plant. He had just returned from a trip to the Pacific Northwest to assess the possible effects on the Trojan of Mt. St. Helen's recent spectacular eruption some forty miles northeast of the nuclear plant. In the years after 1967, when Portland General Electric (PGE) announced its plans to build the plant, there was considerable discussion in hearings and public debates of how a cataclysmic geological event might injure the plant and release high-level radioactivity. So after Mt. St. Helens blew, Trammell flew over the volcano and the plant to snap pictures, and he seemed to think my interest in the Trojan was perfectly natural.

In several months of talking with anyone connected with the Trojan who would sit still for an interview, from PGE's president to some of Oregon's antinuclear activists, Charles Trammell gave me the most balanced analysis of the plant's history. Still, the image of Trammell flying over the steaming remains of Mt. St. Helens and the plume of water vapor that drifted upriver from the cooling tower while trying to assess the likelihood of a destructive relationship between the mountain and the machine, seemed to me an embodiment of humanity's relationship with nuclear technology. We must assess our most powerful technologies from a distance, and much about their influence on the earth and on our lives remains a mystery until it happens.

Initially the people at PGE seemed to welcome my interest. Charles Trammell told them about my project, and a few days after we arrived at our octagonal cabin in Oregon, Bill Babcock, who was then PGE's nuclear information specialist, called from their office of public relations to say he would set up interviews at the plant. The people I began to interview seemed eager to tell me about their work. Then as winter arrived in November, PGE's upper management in Portland heard about the Ohio English professor talking with people at the Trojan, and my welcome suddenly turned cold. I had just finished a two-hour, taped interview with a psychologist who contracted to work with control room operators at the plant when word came down from PGE management in Portland that it was time to show me the door. For five months, PGE showed me several doors, all of them closed.

One day stands out from the months of talking with anti-nuclear activists and waiting to talk with people at PGE. It was a cool, sunny day on the Oregon coast, and I decided to celebrate the arrival of spring by running along the beach at low tide from Tolovana Park to Hug Point and back, a round trip of seven miles, in scarlet silk longjohns, bright green running shorts, a green sweat shirt, and a green baseball hat with golden wings protruding to the side and back. Northern Oregon beaches were seldom crowded in the spring, and on the day I made that run, more spectacularly attired than I have been before or since, they seemed deserted. I can't remember seeing—or, more important, being seen by—a single person. The solitary sign that I was making an important fashion statement came as I turned at Hug Point to head back home: for the only time in my life I was attacked by a gull. While it followed me, diving and screeching, I couldn't tell if it was more troubled by my winged hat or my red tights.

If I had run north from Tolovana Park in the spring of 1981 instead of south toward Hug Point, my chances of meeting appreciative observers would have increased exponentially. I would have been running toward the town of Cannon Beach, and on the southwest end of town is Haystack Rock, a large monolith that attracts a lot of attention. I once counted seventeen postcard versions of Haystack Rock, including a fog-shrouded monster, a massive gravestone, and a green-haired sphinx with a dazzling blue sky above it. On almost any day without rain there are likely to be people gathered by this huge rock at low tide to observe the sea birds that nest on it, as well as the many fascinating creatures in its tidal pools. Past Haystack Rock, almost to Ecola Creek on the north side of Cannon Beach, is a stretch of sand to which William Clark led a party of eleven, including the Shoshone woman, Sacajawea, and Clark's slave, York, on a two-day journey from Fort Clatsop, hoping to find a whale that had washed ashore. They found the whale's remains, but local Indians had already harvested its oil and blubber, as I would explain in some detail in the novel *York's Journal* (2005). Clark recorded his estimate that the whale had measured 105 feet in its happier days at sea. To some this estimate has seemed an exaggeration, but as one who has never seen a whale except from a great distance, I imagine it to be about right.

I ran south that day in 1981, away from the town, the rock, and thoughts of Clark's failed whaling expedition, partly because I was fed up with civilization. This was not my customary way of thinking. A few months earlier, jogging at low tide on a moonless night along the same beaches, glimpsing just a hint of white froth in the hissing surf far out to my left but unable to see the rocky cliffs to my right, I came around a point feeling disoriented and found great comfort in the distant lights of the town. By the spring of 1981, I must have been fleeing the Trojan Nuclear Plant's cooling tower, which stood beside the Columbia River some 50 miles northeast of the beach where I was running. Built from 40,500 cubic yards of concrete, the tower rose 499 feet above the riverbank. Ironically, I had come to see such cooling towers as the most sensible thing about commercial nuclear power. But an accident two years earlier at Three Mile Island in Pennsylvania had temporarily put cooling towers up there with mushroom clouds as symbols of nuclear danger. And as I thought about the difficulties I'd encountered trying to talk with people at PGE, this particular tower had come to seem a personal affront, a giant middle finger waved my way. The people at PGE who had come to see me as an enemy in Oregon's "Trojan War."

Unsatisfactory relations with nuclear bureaucracies have been a family affliction, as I mentioned in the Prologue. After World War II ended, punctuated by the two nuclear explosions in Japan, my father left his job in the Swan Island shipyard on the Willamette River and took the job at the Hanford Nuclear Reservation in Washington. He kept records on construction projects, probably working with some of the people involved in making plutonium for the atomic bomb we dropped on Nagasaki in August of 1945. The rest of our family stayed in Portland, planning to join him later in Richland, a bedroom community for Hanford. Sometime in the winter of 1947, when I took an adventuresome train ride from Portland to visit Dad for a weekend, I remember the heavily chlorinated water and the stark landscape, as well as the guards and the high wire fences, the feel of a military base. I felt a sense of being watched on the afternoon before I returned to Portland, when Dad and I went fishing in the Columbia River, where we got not even a nibble. That stretch of the river, I learned many years later, had been polluted with high-level radioactive waste. When Mom had begun to pack for our planned move to Richland, Dad suddenly resigned and came home.

He was out of work for more than a year, and he spent much of his time at Portland's main public library, writing essays about business. Although he had majored in journalism at the University of Colorado, his essays weren't published, and I can't find them. They surely revealed no secrets although he might have known a few, but they probably expressed his conviction that the sloppy workmanship and irresponsibility he found at Hanford were inevitable when private business gets mixed up with big government. When he talked with friends about his decision to resign and come home, he told stories of engineers who questioned designs or the quality of materials and were promptly fired or transferred. Now I realize he was talking about carelessness and arrogance and corporate greed blanketed in governmental secrecy, a theme as timely as our increasingly privatized and unending "war on terror." He was explaining too, in his indirect way, that if the bosses wouldn't listen to engineers, they certainly wouldn't listen to him.

In the summer of 1961, when I was working for a construction company in Portland, my boss took me aside one day to talk about my father. Maybe I had said something that hinted at my growing skepticism about his politics because my boss looked me in the eye, as though daring me to show some sign of youthful, cocksure certitude, and said Al Nichols was a man committed to doing things right. He claimed he'd seen my quiet, cautious father get very angry when he ran into careless work. This one-sided conversation made me wonder, when I thought about it later, if Dad said something to people at the nuclear reservation when he resigned.

My father died in 1986, before the public learned much about the leaks at Hanford from underground storage tanks for high level radioactive waste or the possibility of explosions in those tanks or the intentional releases of radioactive iodine from Hanford that got into the local milk supply or the massive radioactive contamination of the Columbia River or the dangerous radiation exposures of workers. But he might not have been surprised by those revelations. He might have acknowledged what I've come to believe is true, that such tragedies are probably inevitable in the making of modern war, but he would have emphasized the dangers in carelessness too. When I was growing up, he seemed obsessed with good workmanship and thrift, neither of which was a particular strength of the Atomic Energy

Commission, which would be replaced in 1975 by the Nuclear Regulatory Commission and an organization that was later absorbed by the Department of Energy. Reflecting on the wastefulness and irresponsibility he saw at Hanford seemed to drive him to the right politically during the years after he left Hanford.

During our year in Oregon, while I sought the cooperation of PGE, my mother struggled to overcome the disabilities left by her stroke, and we tried to help. Mom had been a voracious reader all her life, and she'd written long, description-filled letters. The loss of language was a heavy burden. Still, she fought to get strength back in her right arm and leg, sometimes shouting like a karate competitor. But her speech therapy was so frustrating it often made her cry. When she didn't make progress with language, she seemed weighed down by a depression darker than anything she'd ever experienced, and she had struggled with depression as long as I can remember.

At my urging, Mom and Dad reluctantly agreed to visit a psychologist who specialized in working with older people. Her office was decorated in elegant Danish modern, and the four of us sat in a circle, the psychologist seated with her shoes off in a modified lotus position. She tried briefly to talk with Mom and then turned to ask Dad if he'd reflect on *his* life. With her gently probing questions, he told a life story that included traumatic events I'd never heard. At the end of the hour, the psychologist proposed that my mother take an intelligence test to reveal just what mental functions had survived the stroke. Mom refused, and neither of my parents would consider returning to see the psychologist again.

The more I thought about their refusal, the better I felt about it. Our session seemed unrelated to Mom's deep depression. The psychologist hadn't even mentioned it. I admired Mom's determined effort to hold onto her dignity. They had expected no help from the psychologist, I realized, and they probably agreed to see her to comfort me.

Dad's vision had been failing for several years, and his efforts to preserve its remnants were painful. As the pressure from glaucoma grew, he used medications that made him depressed, a condition new to him. A few days after our visit to the psychologist, in October, as he drove Mom home from a physical therapy session, an artery burst in the middle of the retina in his good eye. He was suddenly blind. His first response sounded to me like panic: watching for shadowy landmarks barely visible with his surviving peripheral vision, he somehow drove several miles back to their mobile home. Once safely home, however, he acted as though he'd been in training for blindness all his life. Within days, he qualified to borrow talking books from the state library, and he used them steadily for the rest of his life. He continued to run their home, still baking bread and building fires in their woodstove.

It was a year quite different from 1973-74, when our Oregon family seemed to rebuild itself after the fractures that came with the Vietnam War. Judy was now a freshman at Earlham College in Indiana, Annie a ninth grader at Seaside High School, seven miles north of our cabin. I spent much of my time eighty miles inland from Cannon Beach with my parents, traveling back and forth between Portland and the coast by bus, and Nancy and Annie sometimes came to Portland on weekends.

In the late spring, when Mom was able to visit our cabin at the coast, she sat outside for hours on our second-story deck, gazing toward the ocean and watching the wrens that moved about in the lower branches of the spruce trees. One evening we pushed her wheelchair down a black-topped trail through ancient trees to Short Sands, a cove protected by Cape Falcon to the north and the northwestern flank of Neahkahnie

Mountain to the south. She watched intently while fishing boats came in to anchor for the night, and as she sat there with the sun going down, a light breeze blowing in her face, she looked relaxed and happy, as though she could live with the loss of language.

We didn't take Mom to Saddle Mountain that spring, and that was probably a mistake. Five miles up the winding road that leads from Highway 26 to a parking lot at the base of Saddle's steep southern face is the Lewis and Clark Mainline, a logging road that was important to her. A few hundred yards east of the road to Saddle Mountain State Park, on that memorably named logging road is a rock outcropping from the Miocene epoch that reveals a lot about local forms of life in prehistoric times. My mother loved to visit that spot and look for marine fossils from a period between five and twenty-six million years ago, when the Coast Range was just beginning to form. The fossils Mom found on Saddle Mountain seemed to speak to her conservative Baptist mind and heart long after she began to attend other churches. I thought she went to Saddle Mountain to test her faith, hoping to understand how the world came into being, believing it could somehow be consistent with her reading of the Bible.

Mom's interest in fossils seemed courageous to me, given her desire to believe in the Bible's "objective, absolute truth," as her guru, Francis Schaeffer, put it. I'm not sure why we didn't think of taking Mom to Saddle Mountain because Nancy and I walked there as often as we could during that difficult year. Guests who came to see our cabin on the coast had to appeal to advanced pregnancy or high winds and heavy rain to avoid paying homage to our mountain.

From the summit of Saddle Mountain on a very clear day it seemed we should see the plume of water vapor from the Trojan's cooling tower some thirty miles to the east, but we never did. Then the plant was shut down on January 4, 1993. The cloud no longer drifts southeast along the Columbia River toward Portland. By 1993, at a plant that had once employed as many as 1300 people, there were only 140 workers. It was a quiet end to Oregon's Trojan war, although PGE would try to give it a sense of dramatic finality in 2006 with its highly publicized dynamiting of the cooling tower.

When PGE management had reluctantly opened the company's doors to me in the late spring of 1981, Bart Withers, the vice president of their Nuclear Division, told me I reminded them of their bad experience with Michael Douglas, whose film about a nuclear accident, *China Syndrome,* opened on March 16, 1979, just a few days before the reactor at Three Mile Island lost its coolant. When Douglas asked to film in control rooms, he was turned away from several nuclear plants, according to Withers, but the director and his film crews were made welcome at the Trojan. "They were going to do a very factual thing," Withers said sadly, "and we opened our hearts and our doors, and they were taken up and allowed to photograph and do all sorts of things. We sure didn't get any good out of that." The portrayal of the nuclear industry as brutally irresponsible in *China Syndrome* made PGE management very suspicious of people who claimed to be interested in nuclear power.

I found it difficult to identify with Michael Douglas or Jane Fonda, his co-star in *China Syndrome* and felt wronged when the people at PGE refused to talk with me about their nuke. But now I see their public relations instincts were good. From their point-of-view I really had become a critic. If I began with a healthy skepticism about commercial nuclear power, my two-hour interview in November with Dr. Larry Mathae, the psychologist who worked with the control room operators, made a serious doubter out of me.

Mathae, a large, intense man, was concerned about the capacity of people faced with great tedium day after day to respond to complex technical crises. "There isn't sufficient demand on the people to maintain a state of vigilance," he said, "and that's deadly. That is hypnotic. There is an incredible amount of monotony here. . . but at the same time they have to go from that standby mode into full operation within just an incredibly short time." Mathae had been hired by PGE to study what they called "the alertness issue" in the Trojan control room, and he proposed that operators be given frequent breaks, with opportunities for physical exercise.

Talking with Mathae, I began to think about soldiers who face the challenge of securing a position that *might* be attacked. The possibility of danger isn't enough to keep soldiers alert over long periods of time, and officers use radio checks, briefings, frequent guard changes, and equipment inspections to avoid the sleep-inducing power of boredom. The comparison reveals the difficulty faced by supervisors in the control room who must devise ways to keep operators' attention on systems that are increasingly automated, and they must do this for long shifts, over months and years. Besides the tedium, operators faced difficulty with their biological clocks, a problem that accompanies shift work. They had six days on the day shift followed by two off, then seven on the swing shift with two off, then seven days on mid shift and five off. In addition to the stress that goes with interrupted sleep patterns, shift work often disrupts family life, and Mathae was asked to provide family counseling. The spouses and children of Trojan staff reported painful encounters, too, with anti-nuclear opinion in their communities. They came to believe Oregon was an especially hostile climate for nuclear power, and one result, according to Mathae was a "siege mentality."

PGE management quickly rejected Mathae's proposals for nurturing alertness in the control room, and when I asked vice president Withers why, he said it was a matter of supervision. "Maybe I'm too old," he said, "but

I think the answer is making the eight hours on the job as meaningful and satisfying as you can, and if you've got boredom, you've probably got some poor supervision. There are shifts where not a whole lot goes on, and you can get by without doing a whole lot. But [on] that same shift, there's a whole lot that could be done. So if you've got good supervision, you don't have a boredom problem." By the time I talked with Bart Withers, on May 6, 1981, I'd seen a document that made me wonder if he was really in touch with life in the control room. Three weeks before the accident at Three Mile Island, a member of the Trojan operations staff had submitted an anonymous memo to PGE management, describing the behavior of operators: "At the present time, the majority of operators do not give their full attention to operating the plant. A visit to any shift will reveal people reading books, magazines, and newspapers. Doing crossword puzzles, playing games, tying flies, making knives from files, doing study courses, drawing pictures, and many other non-productive things." Although the writer of the memo was clearly affronted by the operators' behavior, it sounded to me as though they were doing their level best to battle boredom.

Psychologist Mathae's point was that boredom, a factor in many kinds of work, is dangerous when people with great responsibility suddenly have to react quickly to complex problems. Project manager Charles Trammell put it this way in describing his own experience as a reactor operator: "As long as the gauges are all straight across, you have very little to do. But when you get a problem, or when you're shutting down or starting up, things can get a little hairy." The operators at Three Mile Island and Chernobyl and, most recently, the Fukushima Nuclear Plant could probably explain just how "hairy" it can get. They were unable to make the quick transition from battling boredom to performing the complex actions required to keep their plants safe in a crisis. PGE management seemed unwilling to acknowledge this possibility.

Although I was reluctant to think of myself as PGE's enemy, by the time I was allowed back into the plant in the spring of 1981, I had begun to see a kind foolishness at work that I compared with the slovenly imprudence Dad found at Hanford after World War II. Dad was more willing to talk about the Trojan plant than about Hanford, but it was clear we'd found an area of fundamental agreement.

Still, the winter of PGE's silence was a time of self-doubt for me, even a little anxiety. Teachers are accustomed to rejection, but in the classroom it is likely to come with silence, an occasional snore, rolled eyes, or a muffled groan. I wasn't prepared for months of unanswered letters and telephone calls. Worse, I read the story of Karen Silkwood and her mysterious death in 1974 as she was on her way to give testimony about safety problems in a Kerr-McGee plutonium producing plant in Oklahoma City. Had I learned something more damaging than I knew in my first few interviews at the Trojan? Maybe it was no coincidence that the silence began immediately after I taped the Trojan psychologist. When winter winds blew at night outside our cabin, I occasionally imagined furtive footsteps in the dark, and when our local postmaster said a stranger had been looking for me, I hid my audiotapes.

No harm came to us that winter, and the first hint that PGE's silence might not last forever came in early February, after I sent a draft of a brief essay to the company's board chairman, Robert Short. My essay, "A Closed-Door Policy at PGE," was meant to suggest how my account of the company's apparent policy of concealment would look in print. Nothing came of it immediately, but when I called Bill Babcock, who sometimes picked up his own phone and therefore was obliged to talk with me, he said there might be a change in the wind. "You rattled their cages upstairs," he told me, referring to PGE's seventeenth floor executive suite. He encouraged me to give Robert Short a call, which I did immediately. Chairman Short's secretary had not heard anything about the company's plans to cooperate with me. On the other hand, she thought it unlikely that they would be uncooperative. I could expect to hear from someone soon, she promised.

More than a month later, on the last day of March, a letter arrived from James Durham, PGE's senior vice president and general counsel. "Dear Mr. Nichols," Durham said. "I have been trying to reach you by telephone for some time without success. I would appreciate it if you would give me a call at your convenience concerning your information request on the Trojan plant." The problem, Durham explained when I reached him a few days later, was that the person best prepared to tell the Trojan story as it deserved to be told was the company's new president, William Lindblad. He, unfortunately, was a very busy man, and it was not a story that could be told quickly. I reminded Durham of a list I'd submitted months earlier of several people who appeared to be competent to help me with parts of the Trojan story. Could I, perhaps, talk with a few of them? Durham promised to get back to me soon. After several days of silence, I called to propose a fallback position: would PGE identify *one* person on their technical staff with whom I could check facts? Two days later, Durham called to say I could have some time with William Lindblad.

The president spent most of an afternoon trying to convince me that my version of the Trojan story could only be a disservice to humanity. Convincing someone more than ten months into a writing project to drop it is not very different from suggesting to an avid skier who has carried his skis far up a beautiful slope on foot to shoulder those skis and trudge back down, but Lindblad began by telling me of an experience in California, where he was a manager at the controversial Diablo Canyon Nuclear Plant. A television producer had asked him about doing a show on the Diablo Canyon plant, and Lindblad was too busy to cooperate. A colleague, however, thought it was wrong to send the producer away, and the result was a television show that led to several lawsuits. His colleague, Lindblad said, left the industry, disillusioned because his integrity had been challenged. "I'm deliberately trying to give you nothing quotable," Lindblad said as the afternoon wore on, "but here is something: the accident at Three Mile Island is still going on." This was more than a year after the Pennsylvania reactor had been cooled down, and Lindblad left his statement hanging in the air as a measure of my inability to plumb the mysteries of nuclear power.

William Lindblad was a trained engineer, and I wondered if his certainty that I was not the right person to tell Trojan's story had to do with my background. I reminded him of my virtues, which I'd generously shared with the people in public relations: an undergraduate degree in science, the Lewis and Clark article and another on the debate between science and the humanities, both published in *The American Scholar*, a journal edited in those days by the rather conservative Joseph Epstein. What other proof could they want of my trustworthy scholarship? The proof that I could not be trusted, Lindblad proclaimed, was my choice of a subject: the Trojan Nuclear Plant. Inevitably, I would have an ax to grind because I assumed nuclear power plants were different from other technologies.

Well, the stakes do seem higher for nuclear technology than for most things humans have built, I said. There seems to be a pretty small margin for error, and we tend to make errors, and a nuclear error can lead to catastrophe. Trying to suggest my balanced view of such matters, I added that I was skeptical of claims made for other high technologies as well.

"What is *high* technology?" Lindblad thundered.

I fumbled out something about complexity, dependence on advanced scientific knowledge, initially large capital investment, and expensive maintenance. Peering sternly over his glasses, Lindblad corrected me: for him the cockpit of a DC-10 was high technology, not the control room of a nuclear power plant. High technology, he insisted, is in the eye of the beholder, and if the Trojan plant seemed high tech to me, that was reason enough to write about something else.

When I realized Lindblad was not going to talk with me about the Trojan plant, claiming it was a story only a nuclear engineer could get right, I remembered a statement made by a PGE vice president who claimed opposition to commercial nuclear power in the United States was funded by our country's enemies in the Cold War. And I recalled something Bill Babcock, PGE's nuclear information specialist, said when I first talked with him about my project. "I think it is impossible to inform the public well about nuclear power," he said. "It is totally impossible because to inform the public, you'd have to educate them to a certain level, and I don't think you can do that. The schools can't do it. People will accept nuclear power when they perceive that they understand it. It has nothing to do with really understanding it. It's the way they perceive they understand what dying in a car accident is like and therefore accept that risk." Lindblad seemed to believe it was impossible for me to *understand* nuclear power, let alone explain its significance to anyone else, and I suddenly felt more than a trace of rage. As I rose to leave, however, the president caught me off balance. He'd decided, he said, to give me limited access to the nuclear plant and some of its people.

Lindblad's magnanimous *non sequitur* came late in our year in Oregon, and the limitations he imposed were great. But I had a chance to hear from Bart Withers that PGE compared my interest in Trojan with that of Hollywood's Michael Douglas. And I was able to talk with Leslie Wildfong, an appealing, very serious woman in a line of work that was almost exclusively male in those years. She was called "Shift Technical Adviser" in the Trojan control room, where she sometimes second-guessed male operators, she said. They take it very professionally, she added, and she loved her job. When I asked how she could account for public opposition to the Trojan plant, a technology in which she, like William Lindblad, clearly had deep faith, she mentioned the atomic bombs dropped on Hiroshima and Nagasaki. The people of the United States, she said, have not yet come to grips with their guilt feelings for having dropped those bombs.

In 2005, a graduate student at Portland State University, Gregory Nipper, wrote a fine master's thesis about the Trojan, "Progress and Economy: The Clash of Values over Oregon's Trojan Nuclear Plant." This is Nipper's concluding sentence: "The systematic failure of utilities, contractors, regulatory agencies, and government officials to adequately guard the public interest in the case of Trojan is a salient example of the need for extensive and informed popular involvement in decision making in all arenas and at all levels of politics and society—especially when the consequences involve the health, security, and well-being of the people and the environment." The young historian's Jeffersonian conclusion was a long way from the position of PGE's nuclear information specialist, who reckoned it was "totally impossible to inform the public well about nuclear power."

The story of Oregon's Trojan has yet to be fully told. It can't be finished until the plant has been "decommissioned"—that is, disassembled and entombed in a way likely to be safe for future generations. This process will be far more complex and expensive than anyone imagined when the plant was built.

Chapter Twelve:

Battling Boredom

In January of 1982 I rode a bus from Columbus to Chicago, planning to catch a train west to Portland, where Mom was dying. While I was still in the bus station in Columbus, Dave called to say I might not make it in time unless I caught a plane in Chicago, but a snowstorm was supposed to be approaching, and I stuck with the train. Although there was plenty of snow on the ground when the train left Chicago, I didn't see much falling, and a sign on a bank outside of Milwaukee said 17 degrees below zero, which seemed too cold for a blizzard. But I was committed to land travel by then.

No doubt I was preoccupied, which might help to explain why I didn't find conversations on the train as interesting as the talk I'd heard aboard the buses. In Rugby, North Dakota, sixteen people got on together, headed for a ski vacation somewhere in the Rockies. A loud woman in a fur coat showed them to their seats and told them to call her collect if they weren't having a good time. Most of them settled down to play electronic games instead of talk although a few of the wives began to converse very quietly with each other, no doubt trying not to disturb their husbands' concentration. The electronic games became a subject for banter when their batteries began to falter, and in Havre, Montana, some of the men got off the train to buy gin and ice, which stirred up cocktail chatter. These were people apparently on vacation from serious talk.

My best conversation on the journey came in the dining car as we approached Cut Bank, Montana. I was seated with a soft-spoken farmer from Michigan who introduced himself as Dyk, which he spelled for me. He and his brother and their sons ran an onion and carrot farm near Grand Rapids. Their soil, he said, was wonderful "muck," about 500 acres of it, spread out in plots as far apart as twenty miles. They packed their onions with three computerized machines built in Germany, and they owned nineteen tractors, three eighteen wheelers, and six smaller trucks. They got by with only sixteen full-time workers, three fewer than their tractors. Dyk's wife had died of a brain tumor in 1974, and in the off-season he generally visited a daughter for three weeks on a farm sixty miles north of Pasco, Washington. Then he returned to Grand Rapids and drove to Florida for a month in a motel. He was a lonely, gracious man who loved farming.

A light snow began to fall along the Columbia River south of Pasco after Dyk got off the train, and in the alternating fog, snow, and sunlight at dawn, the Columbia Gorge was stunningly beautiful. The river itself, when it wasn't hidden, was sometimes silver, sometimes dark brown, and the hills across the river were shrouded in dark mystery.

It was mid-morning when I arrived in Portland, and Mom had died at 6 a.m. Dad and my brothers met me, and as the four of us stood together in the echoing old railway station, circled around the beginning of our grief, we might have been a father and sons from an earlier era. The Native American midwife, Mrs. Tinklepaw, who delivered Mom in Hall, Montana, on January 22, 1911, was back-up for a doctor who couldn't get his horse-drawn rig through snow higher than the fence posts. Like the doctor, I hadn't arrived on time, and as the four of us stood around shaking hands but not hugging, we might have been closing a sale on bridles, a horse, or a farm.

We didn't talk about the sadness in Mom's life that began when her friend Dolores was swept from her side as they swam together in the Sandy River just after they graduated from high school. After Dave came out of the vortex that was Vietnam, Mom wrote: "It seemed to me my heart should be light once again." But it wasn't, and her stroke surely added to her sadness. We didn't talk either about the challenge of being a wife and mother with three sons in an era when it seemed okay for the men and boys to settle down with the Sunday paper after church while she fixed dinner. We didn't consider whether things changed for her when the Irish athlete I married, Nancy Shea Nichols, drove us out of the living room and into the kitchen as though she were driving moneychangers out of the temple.

We didn't talk until later about that recent day when a minister asked her if she wanted to die, and she slowly nodded, perhaps reluctant to let Dad know how much her life had come to weigh on her. She pulled off her wedding ring and handed it to Dad. He had cried when she first refused to eat, but now he took the ring, held her hand and whispered gently, "I know." The minister asked if she wanted to take Communion, and she nodded again. She ate bread and sipped wine through a straw, and I wish I'd been there.

We planned a memorial service and a family crypt-side service. Dad asked to have a sheaf of wheat instead of flowers at the memorial service, and we sang "What a Friend We Have in Jesus," "Just a Closer Walk with Thee," and finally "Amazing Grace," a hymn that felt like a powerful pun at a service for Grace Nichols. Afterward, Dad and I drove down to visit our friends Herm and Ellen and their sons at our octagonal cabin, where they were spending a year far from the cornfields Herm knew best. Talking with Herm and Ellen, I could almost believe our dream of the Institute was still alive.

But by August of 1983, more than a year later, my fuzzy dream of agrarian community seemed emphatically unrealistic when I began a term as academic dean at Denison with both of my arms in casts, like a man who has fallen behind on gambling debts. The second-story deck on our octagonal Oregon cabin had collapsed as daughter Annie and I were trying to tear it down to replace it. Judy, who inherited a dark imagination from her father and grandmother, had just stepped out from under the deck to warn us it might fall, and Nancy jumped safely from the top of a stairway left teetering in the air when the deck dropped. Annie, a basketball player, broke an arm too, but somehow three broken arms seemed like minor damage, given what could have happened to Judy and Nancy, and we were giddy about our good fortune as we headed off to the emergency room in Seaside. Annie's main concern, for she had recently become a teenager, was that her father's trousers seemed to have come unbuttoned in the fall.

I had returned to the classroom in Ohio, discouraged by my failure to peer beyond the veils of secrecy at the Trojan Nuclear Plant and make sense of the conflict between those who wanted to shut the plant down and those who believed it was a good answer to our growing energy needs. I was troubled by something Thomas Jefferson said in an 1820 letter to William Charles Jarvis: "I know of no safe depository of the ultimate powers of society but the people themselves, and if we think them not enlightened enough to exercise their control with a wholesome discretion, the remedy is not to take it from them but to inform their discretion by education." A teacher with the rare privilege of devoting a year to studying a single nuclear power plant, I hadn't learned as much as I hoped about how to help my students make the decisions about technology that would protect their lives and those of coming generations.

As I returned to teaching, I was struck again by the corrosive power of boredom and an accompanying sense of helplessness. When I asked students in a folklore course to collect narratives that described successful partying, they often brought back accounts of behavior that seemed to mask great fear of boredom. Like control room operators, students seemed to be fighting tedium. Most of the operators, I had learned, got their initial

122

training in the Navy nuclear program, where they often enlisted because they found high school so boring they couldn't imagine sitting through college classes even though they were often very good students. These men were confident of their technical skills. But according to psychologist Larry Mathae, they knew their ingenious efforts to remain alert in the face of monotony would foster criticism. They knew any mistakes they made would be replayed interminably in public hearings, and they knew engineers and regulatory officials would be watching for their mistakes. They felt powerless to change their high-stress work environment.

When I visited the Trojan plant in April of 1981, shortly after president William Lindblad reluctantly opened a few of the plant's doors to me, I happened upon the immediate aftermath of an event that seemed to reveal why control room operators feared boredom. An electrician's error had caused a short circuit in the plant a day earlier, and that in turn caused the plant's turbine and reactor to shut down automatically within seconds. Ten minutes later, while the shift supervisor in the control room was still trying to figure out what had happened, he received a telephone call from a reporter at ABC News in New York. Someone in the plant had called the network and given the reporter a number so he could dial directly into the control room. Concerned about bad publicity, the shift supervisor couldn't hang up on the reporter, but while he tried to explain what he was still trying to understand himself, he had to organize the search for the cause of the shut-down and approve adjustments in pressure and temperature to maintain equilibrium in the reactor and its cooling system. A day later, having successfully diagnosed the problem and brought the plant back to power, the shift supervisor and others in the control room were not pleased by a news release from PGE's public relations office that claimed the whole problem was handled by automation. Caught between the public's fear of nuclear accidents and the company's desire to emphasize automated safety systems, it seemed as though the control room operators weren't supposed to be in control at all.

The parallels between control room operators and my students occurred to me in a freshman seminar where we read Jonathan Schell's recently published *The Fate of the Earth* (1982), a detailed account of what would happen in a nuclear holocaust. To my surprise, my students claimed they had already considered the grim prospect Schell described although a few of them said they resented his insistence on providing horrific details. The two students who were most eager to discuss the appalling consequences of a nuclear exchange had seemed almost aggressively bored in the weeks leading up to our reading and discussing *The Fate of the Earth*. Now they became active participants, dominating our discussions. It was as though the two of them, both males, had awakened from a trance to find themselves in a group of mentally handicapped companions. They were impatient with the rest of the class. Both of them had already revealed in their essays that they were more thoughtful than their usual classroom demeanor suggested, and now they were intent on showing the rest of us that they were well ahead of Jonathan Schell in their thinking about nuclear holocaust. They did this by repeatedly insisting that Schell's terrifying description of the likely consequences of a nuclear exchange was probably understated. Having presented themselves as nuclear realists, they attacked Schell's proposals for diminishing our nuclear danger. They talked about Cold War psychology and natural human aggression, concluding that we might as well accept the nuclear arms race and its inevitably grim finish. There was something defiant about their unyielding pessimism, but once they had settled *The Fate of the Earth*, both of them returned to their former passivity.

I tried unsuccessfully to bring the two students back into our discussions by reminding them of those shining moments when they had virtually taken over the class. It seemed to me our discussion of Schell's grim book had *taunted* them into talking. It was as though he had treated their worst nightmares casually. That surely wasn't Schell's intent, or mine, but in finding precise language to describe a peril that already troubled them, Schell seemed to challenge them. (Several years later I had a chance to ask Schell about his own response to writing the book. Reading it, I said, made me tremble, and I wondered if writing it bothered him in the same way. No, he said; in fact, there was a kind of comfort in sharing his sense of our danger with others.) Perhaps the two students had broken their silence mainly to convince themselves they weren't afraid. But they probably were, as were others in the class. "What hit me," one woman wrote, "were the long-term effects of a nuclear holocaust on the living: sickness, long drawn-out deaths, mutations, or in other words, the quiet, less violent things. It is not the violence I fear; it is the quiet, the rubble and emptiness." Polls taken in the early 1980's, as the Nuclear Freeze movement gained momentum and nuclear war was discussed in public, revealed that large numbers of young people in many parts of the world, including the United States, expected to die in a nuclear war.

So boredom, fear, and a sense of helplessness seemed interwoven in the lives of control room operators and my students. The operators at the Trojan plant were comfortable with nuclear technology, sure of their own skills, and confident of technological progress, but they feared anti-nuclear hysteria and bureaucratic arrogance. Both students and operators seemed to anticipate a grim future.

The anti-nuclear activists I had interviewed in Oregon seemed much more confident of their ability to make a difference in the world than either my students or the control room operators. Several of the activists had dropped out of college because their classes seemed disconnected from what they took to be the crucial problems facing our society. Carl Freedman, a quiet young man who attended Portland's Reed College in the mid-1970's, decided he needed to study the relationship between physics and economics if he wanted to understand nuclear power. By 1973, two years before the Trojan plant was completed, PGE had announced plans to build *seven* additional nuclear plants in Oregon. Freedman was sure the thinking that led to such sudden nuclear ambition had to be tested. When his undergraduate classes failed to help him make the connections he thought were necessary, Freedman left college and joined another college drop-out, Lloyd Marbet, to oppose PGE's efforts to build additional nukes. Unable to afford legal counsel, Freedman and Marbet studied administrative law and successfully defeated PGE's attorneys in licensing hearings for a second nuclear plant, which the utility planned to build at Pebble Springs. Judging from what happened across the Columbia River in the state of Washington, where the Washington Public Power System's construction of five nuclear plants after 1975 led to financial collapse, it now appears Freedman and Marbet saved PGE and the state of Oregon many millions of dollars.

Thinking about the confident, lively sense of purpose I found in Freedman and Marbet and other young activists who participated skillfully in the political process, I dreamed of a kind of education that would foster such activism when I decided to try my hand as a dean in 1983. Learning of my administrative ambition, an old friend and colleague, Tony Stoneburner, wrote to tell me that *decanal*, a seldom-used word for dean-related matters, was next to *anal* and *banal* in his rhyming dictionary. It was wise counsel, but I claimed my experience as an assistant and associate dean had already taught me one crucial lesson: administrators steer a treacherous course between self-pity and inflated self-regard. I would steer between those dangers and other whirlpools as well, I thought, and although Mom hadn't lived to see me in my new eminence, this was an achievement that looked a lot like a promotion at IBM or General Electric, and Dad and my brothers would recognize my triumph. Wearing a tie again—I'd begun to comply a few years earlier with the casual dress codes introduced in the 1960's—would be a small price to pay for family recognition.

By the time I delivered my decanal inaugural address at Denison's opening convocation in the fall of 1983, my casts had been removed. As I raised my fragile, pale, and hairy forearms to greet incoming students, I began with my grandfather's story about driving a bus in Portland during rush hour, when people standing packed together in the aisle refused to move toward the back of the bus to let more passengers ride. My title was "Beyond Helplessness," and my point was that a liberal education ought to help people find their way beyond a paralyzing sense of helplessness in the face of complex political and technical problems, and we weren't doing very well at that task.

I had a few suggestions. Consider science and technology, I said. If any kind of knowledge is thought to be *empowering*, a very fashionable word in the 1980's, it is scientific knowledge. Sadly, students who aren't science majors, and some who are, find introductory science courses humiliating. (I was speaking from experience here, as a man who had struggled a bit with organic chemistry in my pre-med program.) Far from finding they can learn how to take informed positions on important issues like nuclear power, students often conclude from their introductory science courses that they must defer to experts. The problem hasn't improved much since the 1980's, and it leads young people to believe they can't understand their own local ecosystems, let alone climate change. So they depend on others to make crucial decisions about development and the proper use of resources, even locally. (This scientific humility, even among many college-educated people, has had dire consequences as the Republican Party has tried to politicize science.)

It's not all our fault, I admitted. Many students arrived in college already feeling excluded from scientific knowledge, and they were often suspicious of science itself, as they were of history, but for different reasons. They were enamored of dazzling new technologies, but they didn't expect to understand how the gadgets worked. Students appreciated exotic landscapes like beaches and ski slopes, but they brought little curiosity to most of the natural world. This habit of mind, combined with their fear of mathematics and science, excluded many of them from important political participation.

Having painted this grim picture, I shared my dream. We can be a college, I said, where students majoring in the humanities, the arts, and social sciences study the relations among science, technology, and society. They begin to feel at ease with the physical world. We can be a place where students who arrive fearful of mathematics and science learn they can understand the difficult choices we must make to preserve the earth and ourselves. Our graduates can be prepared to learn about dioxin, weapons systems, nuclear power, the effects of clear-cutting forests, and the side effects of new arthritis drugs. They'll know how to inform themselves about difficult ethical choices. They'll be curious about the environment, eager to know plants and animals. They'll know something about the limits of scientific knowledge, the pleasure of "bafflement," as physician Lewis Thomas put it. "Teach ecology early on," wrote Thomas in *Late Night Thoughts on Listening to*

Mahler's Ninth Symphony (1983). "Let it be understood that the earth's life is a system of interliving, interdependent creatures, and that we do not understand at all how it works." Such humility, I explained, is not the same as feeling excluded from scientific knowledge. It includes all of us, even the experts. Such humility simply acknowledges our human limitations.

This dream of revitalized science education is part of a something larger, I concluded. In the 1980's colleges all over the country were rethinking "general education," searching for that irreducible core of knowledge that we hoped to agree upon and share with every student. It was a good time to move away from fragmentation and specialization, a time to find coherence in our courses. Oh, it was an exciting time to become an academic dean.

Deaning felt more like teamwork to me than teaching did, and Denison's administrative team in 1983 was uncommonly visionary. Our college president was Robert Good, who had been the U.S. ambassador to Zambia during the Kennedy years. His wife, Nancy Good, reminded me of Eleanor Roosevelt. She took on crusades that would have gotten her husband into trouble with a very conservative Board of Trustees. Both of the Goods were passionately committed to bringing cultural diversity to the college. The Provost, Lou Brakeman, was a man with whom I'd worked when I was an assistant and associate dean, and we had become good friends. Like the Goods, Brakeman was committed to making the college a place of multi-cultural understanding. In working with faculty, he offered encouragement and openness to new ideas. Good and Brakeman promoted Denison as an orientation center for black South African students coming to study in the United States. Brakeman worked hard for the adoption of a general education requirement in minority/women's studies that survived much longer than I expected. At a time when faculties at selective colleges around the country were calling for students with higher SAT scores, Good and Brakeman urged the Denison faculty to teach the students well who were actually coming to Denison instead of calling for better students. This was the team I had joined.

But within a few weeks of the semester's beginning, Bob Good found he had an inoperable brain tumor. He worked hard in the next few months to assure continuity and to encourage the faculty to find a sense of shared direction. He held a series of working dinners with faculty, where he asked us to think together about the college's future. In spite of increasing difficulty with language, so that writing was a great struggle for him, Good spoke to the community about the importance of fostering civic responsibility and holding to a firm moral center. At the college's 1984 commencement, which honored Stephen J. Gould, who was also struggling with cancer, Bob Good spoke for the last time to the Denison community about his dreams for the college, and then he was gone. It had been a year devoid of the pettiness that sometimes corrodes academic life, but it was not a year for beginning major reforms.

There is a widely held view that institutional reform is best accomplished by "new blood," people with fresh ideas, unencumbered by knowledge of local traditions and personal sensitivities that stand in the way of change. The presidents who followed Bob Good were committed to strengthening the college, but they were like impatient woodcarvers, eager to set to work while still ignorant of the grain in the wood they proposed to shape.

Within six months of Bob Good's departure, there was increasing talk of a new commitment to generic "excellence," the kind of visible merit that gives an organization competitive advantage in attracting customers. This was an era when many colleges were attracted to the managerial strategies proposed by Thomas J. Peters and Robert W. Waterman, Jr., in their best-selling book, *In Search of Excellence: Lessons from*

America's Best-Run Companies (1982). If we had translated Peters and Waterman's analyses of "excellent companies" such as IBM and McDonalds into terms applicable to colleges, the effects of our quest for excellence might have been more helpful. Peters and Waterman put large emphasis on quality of service and attentiveness to the customer, for example. "Many of the innovative companies," they say, "got their best product ideas from customers. That comes from listening intently and regularly." In the 1960's, when students were marching for peace and equality, we listened to them and broadened our curriculum, and in the 1980's we might have been led by Peters and Waterman to pay more attention to the varied ways students learn. We might have worked to identify their strengths, as well as their weaknesses. Instead, we turned to more sophisticated methods of marketing. When we should have been troubled by ever-rising tuition costs and the growing difficulty of making higher education available to the poor, we drew comfort from marketing studies that showed consumers tended to judge colleges like luxury automobiles, partly by price, and we wanted to be seen as a Mercedes. In personnel decisions we increasingly considered whether we might do better given a buyer's job market, and we cultivated a sense of insecurity and competition among new faculty. We joined a virtual arms race with other colleges, trying to outdo each other in attracting very good students with merit scholarships unrelated to need, and we fostered a spirit of rivalry among students. Because good teaching is labor-intensive and difficult to quantify and make visible to the public, we were drawn increasingly to publication as a measure of excellence. At schools like Denison we began to call ourselves "research colleges."

We turned increasingly to the techniques and technology of corporate management, a continuing trend that daughter Judy and I later explored in *Inside Higher*

Ed. Among the many meetings I attended in my first months as a dean, I recall especially my first session with the Information Technology Committee. The director of our Computer Center spoke enthusiastically of "canned, static systems up front" and the importance of introducing "fail-soft services" and "user-friendly administrative software." He sounded to me like a car salesman trying to dazzle a customer with an incomprehensible explanation of electronic fuel injection, but no one laughed or asked for clarification. In fact, the need for expensive administrative software became a settled conviction within the committee as the year wore on, and the man from the Computer Center promised that "senior management" would have centralized control of information on student academic records, financial matters, potential donors, alumni records, course enrollments, and much more. No one seemed interested in considering whether it made sense for a deliberately small college to adopt a kind of centralized data processing developed for large, unwieldy organizations. It had seemed a virtue to me that faculty and administrators talked with each other when they needed to know about something in the other's department. Far from being a waste of time, such conversations were part of what we meant by "academic community." What, I wondered, did we stand to lose from growing reliance on centralized data processing?

When the director of our Computer Center resigned to go into business, we hired someone just as firmly committed to expensive administrative software. And the new director had already decided where we ought to buy it. Within a few months we were installing software designed for a large university, putting much data in the machine that we didn't need because it was required to get the system running properly. This system, which cost hundreds of thousands of dollars, was a long-term headache for nearly every office in the college. And then, in a move that reminded me of generals who retire to work for weapons contractors, our new director left the college to work for the software company from which we had made our ill-advised purchase.

While the college invested heavily in the dream of centralized information control, faculty members yearned for new computers in ways that seemed almost sexual or at least similar to the longing I felt as a teenager for a beautiful car. The college provided interest-free loans for those of us who wanted to buy computers, and many of us did. Soon we had college-owned computers in our offices too. Even as I began to rely increasingly on my own computer, I felt more and more like a Luddite. An administrative assistant captured my ambivalence with a T-shirt that said, "I hate computers" on the front and "just kidding" on the back. Faculty members and administrators, it seemed to me, talked more reasonably about personnel decisions, student judicial cases, and even changes in the curriculum, than about computing. Discussions of computing had an air of theological dispute, and the increasing hope we invested in this technology began to worry me.

Trying to understand the passionate intensity in much discourse about information technology, I reviewed the history of computer-related prophecies. In 1960 Nobel laureate Herbert Simon of Carnegie-Mellon University promised this: "Within the very near future—much less than twenty-five years—we shall have the technical ability of substituting machines for any and all human functions in organizations. Within the same period, we shall have acquired an extensive and empirically tested theory of human cognitive processes and their interaction with human emotions, attitudes, and values." In 1970, Marvin Minsky of the Massachusetts Institute of Technology had even grander dreams: "In from three to eight years, we will have a machine with the general intelligence of an average human being. I mean a machine that will be able to read Shakespeare, grease a car, play office politics, tell a joke, have a fight. At that point, the machine will begin to educate itself with fantastic speed. In a few months, it will be a genius level, and a few months after that, its power will be incalculable." Our local dreams seemed modest by comparison. In addition to the hope and hype of enhanced productivity and our almost primal hunger for the machines themselves, my colleagues had a desperate need to make sense of a world smothered by information. They wanted administrative software, not to interpret information, as Simon and Minsky fantasized, but to make their own decisions wiser because the computer would keep track of information and manipulate it rapidly. The underlying assumption was that the larger quantities of data available to us, along with the ability to process it swiftly, would lead us to make good decisions. It was the kind of thinking that went into targeting for the colossal number of bombs we dropped in Vietnam. It is an assumption about thinking itself that leaves out of account the quality of information and the role of imagination. Like other managerial methods drawn from large corporations, our growing investment in data processing was an attempt to find a shortcut to excellence.

If I had been an aspiring educational reformer when I began my term as academic dean, I became a curmudgeon, dragging my feet as the college moved relentlessly toward technical rationality. Interviewed by students about a new "wellness" program at the college that I now think had considerable promise, I said it sounded like an idea hatched in a southern California hot tub. Within a year I was reading David V. Sheehan's *The Anxiety Disease* (1983). Receiving invitations to seminars, workshops, and institutes on educational management, I began to remind anyone willing to listen that the word *manage* comes from an Italian word for training horses.

In three years and a half as a dean, I found I could push paper, for these were days before email, and I took pleasure in ceremonial occasions that allowed me to talk about my educational dreams. They were not much different, I came to realize, from my dreams for the Institute. Had I come to the dean's office from other jobs in our society, I might not have noticed how unfulfilling the work was. But teaching, when it goes well, is often a joyful enterprise, and I felt the difference daily. Some days I felt as though my job might kill me. My breathing grew labored and my heart pounded when I felt implicated in personnel decisions I judged to be unfair. Talking with a group of faculty about why I was leaving the job so soon, with virtually all my dreams unrealized, I read to them from a letter I imagined writing to the director of a holistic health clinic: "Not only are my mind and body engaged in constant battle as I seek to look alert in meetings that bore me and to look calm in meetings that enrage me, but my days are lived out in disconnected fragments."

If my decanal career was a failure, it corresponded with a time of some success as a citizen. In 1983 I joined a group of Granville citizens in trying to convince our Village Council to pass a resolution that urged the U.S. and the Soviet Union to stop building more nuclear weapons. The Nuclear Freeze Movement of which we were a part emerged at a time when our national government was committed to the policy of Mutually Assured Destruction (MAD), which attempted to keep the peace by announcing that if the Soviet Union attacked us with nuclear weapons, we would obliterate their cities even if the side effects were the end of civilization.

Members of the Village Council wondered, understandably, if nuclear weapons were properly within their jurisdiction. My argument was that politicians should take into account the impact of their actions on future generations. Church leaders from many denominations, politicians at every level of government, and millions of citizens all over the world, including children without the power to vote, were trying to end a nuclear arms race that threatened all our lives. We needed to work together, I argued, to stop winding the spring of our doomsday machine ever tighter.

The discussion with the Village Council reminded me of much talk about endangered species. When people defended Spotted Owls and Snail Darters, they were usually trying to save whole forests and rivers from environmental destruction. But they talked about particular owl and fish species mainly because we have a federal law meant to prevent the extinction of species. We don't have a law to prevent the extinction of civilization so those of us in the Nuclear Freeze Movement talked about things like civil defense planning. People from Columbus planned to come to Granville and share our resources in case of a nuclear strike on Ohio's state capital, we pointed out, so shouldn't our local political leaders have the power to help avoid such a disaster?

The Granville Village Council chose not to pass a nuclear freeze resolution, but our group of citizens organized a petition drive that put the resolution on the ballot. We sent speakers into the community's churches and organized public debates. Because I was co-chair of our group, the Secretary of State, Sherrod Brown, who would later be elected to the U.S. Senate in November of 2006, called me long after I'd gone to sleep on the night of the election to say our resolution had passed. My surprise and delight reminded me of a morning long ago when I arose at dawn and saw the surprising silhouette of a bicycle in front of our Christmas tree.

Chapter Thirteen

Low Intensity War in Nicaragua

Near the end of my term as a dean in 1986, I flew from Ohio to Oregon in the middle of the spring semester. Dad was dying of liver cancer. Since Mom died, he'd been unable to find a retirement home able to provide food that didn't make him sick from allergies he and Mom had learned to cook around. He was allergic to legumes, and just about every kind of processed food imaginable seemed to have a soy product or another legume. So he was living with John and his family in Eugene when he got the prognosis. Dave couldn't face Dad's dying, and I wasn't much better, but our younger brother seemed to know what to do. When Dad found out about his condition, he agreed to stay on with John, insisting he would soon need to be hospitalized so John and Barbara and their two children wouldn't have to deal with the end stage of his dying. But John convinced Dad to stay with them as long as possible in those last days, and by the time I was able to get there, Dad had accepted visiting hospice care.

In the four years after Mom died, Dad and I found issues on which we could agree. Unable to see, he came to appreciate National Public Radio and grew more and more skeptical of President Reagan's efforts to destroy the Sandinista revolution in Nicaragua. One of the things I did in my years as a dean that felt consequential was to stand on a corner in Granville every Thursday morning with many of the same people who had campaigned for a nuclear freeze referendum. We were declaring our solidarity with demonstrators standing in front of the U.S. Embassy in Managua, Nicaragua, on Thursday mornings to protest the "low intensity" war our country was waging there. The Thursday morning vigils began with the U.S.

invasion of Grenada in October of 1983. The ostensible reason for that invasion was the need to protect American citizens, and the Committee of U.S. Citizens Living in Nicaragua (CUSCLIN) began their vigils as a way of saying they'd feel a whole lot safer if they didn't have to worry about a U.S. invasion of Nicaragua. Increasingly, I felt Dad might have joined our Granville vigil if he'd been in town. He might not have approved of my signing a pledge to commit civil disobedience if we invaded Nicaragua, but he was sympathetic with our reasons for standing on the corner.

While I was visiting Dad in Eugene, a search committee from Lewis and Clark College in Portland called to ask if I would interview for a position as their academic dean. If they could set it up while I was still in Oregon, I said I'd be glad to talk with them, but I couldn't imagine getting free to come to Oregon again any time soon. They managed to pull together two days of interviews, a chance for me to consider whether my frustrations with my deanly duties at Denison were specific to the college where I taught or were just an inevitable side effect of work in academic administration. After talking with people on the beautiful Lewis and Clark campus about what they wanted from a dean, I concluded that their faculty, like Denison's, was confused about their institutional purpose. Some of them were drawn to the increased emphasis on publication that accompanies the dream of a "research college." In addition, the existence of their law school with its inflated salaries seemed to have damaged their commitment to smallness and simplicity, important virtues in liberal arts colleges. I decided I wasn't cut out to be a dean even back home in Oregon, and Dad understood.

When we talked on that last visit, Dad was focused on dying, and we spoke little about politics, religion, or education. He didn't want a funeral, and I didn't return to Oregon when he died.

But several months later, I attended a memorial service in Managua, Nicaragua, for Ben Linder, a young man from Oregon. A Contra force supported by our government killed Linder and two of his Nicaraguan companions.

I arrived in Nicaragua by way of France and Costa Rica, a journey that began with Nancy and daughter Annie, a college sophomore, guiding me into Paris on New Year's Day of 1987 because they both spoke French. It was a cold, snowy month in Paris, and labor problems made for uncertain train and Metro schedules, as well as occasional *perturbations* in electricity and telephone service. A friend who came to visit us from Lyon covered the first 300 miles in less than two hours on the TGV train and spent the rest of the day waiting for a Metro, looking for a taxi, and finally walking to our apartment in Boulogne. It was a time of heightened concern about terrorism, and national police with machine guns and assault rifles patrolled the streets, careening through traffic in blue buses, their sirens rising and falling dramatically. It was emphatically not April in Paris, but it was a profound and deeply welcome change from the life of an academic administrator in Ohio.

We spent our first evening in Paris as guests in the apartment of a businessman, a Conservative, who invited his tennis partner, a Socialist, to join us at dinner. They gave us a glimpse of the very civil polarity in French political culture that was embodied then in Conservative Prime Minister Jacques Chirac and Socialist President Francois Mitterand. The conversation swung politely back and forth between French and English, touching lightly and comfortably on political differences in a way that suggested both men were long past trying to convince each other of anything. My efforts to probe their political disagreements went nowhere. Neither the Conservative nor the Socialist had been able to understand, they said, the great fuss over Watergate, and now they were equally bewildered by the clamor over the Iran-Contra affair, which was just beginning to unravel, revealing how the Reagan administration had funded the Contras in Nicaragua despite congressional opposition. Nancy, Annie, and I were unable to convince them it was cause for serious concern when the President secretly armed a Middle Eastern power and pursued a "low intensity war" in Central America, failing to inform Congress. We came away believing their political differences were cushioned by charming cynicism.

As we left their apartment, I had a brief flashback. The high-spirited, friendly evening with good food and wine and the discovery of our political disconnection seemed to be a condensed version of a custom I'd observed in conversations with students at Denison. They often spent a semester or even a year in another country and came to believe they'd uncovered the essential superiority of their own culture. Such conclusions seemed to coexist with longing to return to Paris or London or Madrid and affection for friends encountered there. But their conviction of U.S. superiority might also represent a profound educational failure if it turned out to be a consumer's approach to international studies, as if cultural comparisons were nothing more than a search for a preferred model.

After Annie left Paris to finish her sophomore year at Haverford College, we visited a family that challenged my stereotypes of the French. These people were in-laws of a colleague, and they had an aristocratic *de* in their name. They invited us to a simple meal in the warm, unpretentious kitchen of their large Paris apartment. The husband, a physicist, talked enthusiastically about Sojourners, the progressive, evangelical Christian group in the United States that my parents' pastor had urged upon us. The French physicist and his wife had met Jim Wallis of Sojourners, and they were deeply impressed with him. I mentioned that Nancy and I shared some of

Jim Wallis's concerns about U.S. policy in Nicaragua, and we hoped to go there soon to see for ourselves how our country was responding to the Sandinista revolution. The physicist's wife asked what alternatives there might be to fighting the spread of Communism in Latin America. Monstrous things, she said, happened in Cambodia after France and the United States gave up on saving Vietnam from Communism. I asked if she would agree that U.S. intervention had caused great suffering in Vietnam, and she asked me to write to her after going to Nicaragua. Then she politely changed the subject and spoke movingly of her own fear of death, touched off by her uncertain health and the deaths of friends and relatives. It was a conversation that moved well beyond small talk despite our hosts' reluctance to explore our disagreements.

As it happened, I went to Nicaragua without Nancy because daughter Judy, living that year in Puerto Viejo, Costa Rica, was having a difficult first pregnancy, and Nancy stayed with her in Puerto Viejo to help. My brother Dave had called when we were briefly back in the U.S., to say a trip to Nicaragua was entirely too risky for a responsible husband and father, a man soon to be a grandfather. His own experiences in Vietnam had led him to take a position on gun control that would sadden the hearts of the National Rifle Association, and his thoughts on physical danger carried weight. I promised to seek a trustworthy guide and found Dick Junkin in Costa Rica, who was about to take a group of Presbyterians from North Carolina on a ten-day tour of Nicaragua. He agreed to let me join them.

So I was in the company of Presbyterians in Managua when I attended the memorial mass for Ben Linder, the 27 year-old engineer from Portland, Oregon. As a high school senior, in 1977, Linder had been part of an "occupation" of the Trojan Nuclear Plant, an act of civil disobedience that owed much to Gandhi's philosophy of non-violence. When he was killed ten years later, on April 28, 1987, near San Jose de Bocay, a remote village in northern Nicaragua, Linder was carrying an assault rifle. His decision to carry a weapon must have been difficult for Linder, and people who worked with him on rural electrification projects in Nicaragua said he hoped the rifle would buy him time to hunker down and wait for help if he were ambushed. But when the ambush came, he had no chance to use his rifle. He was knocked down by a grenade or a shotgun blast, maybe both, and then shot once in the head at close range. Two of his six Nicaraguan companions, Sergio Hernandez and Pablo Rosales, were also killed, the first also shot in the head, the second knifed or bayoneted in the chest. Four other workers on their small hydroelectric project just a mile from San Jose de Bocay escaped the Contra patrol's ambush. Contra leaders later claimed they had mistaken Ben Linder for a Cuban, but some people I met in Nicaragua believed his killing signaled an open season on North Americans working with the Sandinista government to build schools, health clinics, bridges, and other infrastructure.

The mass was held in Santa Maria de los Angeles in Managua's Barrio Riguerro. It was for Ben Linder, Pablo Rosales, Sergio Hernandez, and more than 200 other Nicaraguans from the barrio who had died in the war. A Franciscan priest, Father Uriel Molina, officiated in a simple, round church that was less imposing than the smallest of the many churches Nancy and I had recently visited during our two months in Europe. But it was filled with the liveliest music I'd heard in a church even though the Baptists of my childhood could make hymns swing. There were several guitars and powerful vocalists, and a North American fiddler improvised in the breaks. Jugglers commemorated Linder's skills as a clown. Several mothers from the barrio sat in front with flowers and photographs of their dead sons, and when they spoke the names of their sons, the congregation shouted *presente, presente, presente.* During the service individuals occasionally called *Benjamin Linder,* and the congregation responded *presente, presente, presente.*

By the spring of 1987, the Nicaraguan revolution was almost eight years old, and it was in trouble. Inflation was out of control, food was scarce, and *campesino* families were moving into Managua and other cities to escape the havoc of war in the countryside. To discourage urban immigration, the Sandinista government deliberately made shortages worse in the cities. So life in Managua was particularly difficult. But the memorial service in Santa Maria de los Angeles was a celebration of life nevertheless. The murals on the walls of the church, painted by volunteers from Italy, were filled with light and color, and the songs and stories were filled with hope. I was reminded of the sheaf of wheat Dad had chosen for Mom's funeral, suggesting life and hope springing from death.

In his brief homily, Father Molina said the recent history of Barrio Riguerro was a tale of hope. During the 1979 insurrection, he reminded the congregation, they had built barricades in their barrio, expecting an attack from Anastasio Somoza's National Guard because the people of Barrio Riguerro had been a thorn in the dictator's side. Father Molina told of an evening in June of 1979 when he walked through the streets of the barrio and heard people crying in their homes. They feared what would happen to their families when fighting began in the streets. Then a North American journalist from ABC News, Bill Stewart, arrived to do a story about their barrio, and a guardsman stopped Stewart, ordered him to his knees then to his stomach and shot him in the head, just as someone had shot Ben Linder. Stewart's cameraman videotaped the killing and escaped, and within hours the casual execution was playing on television all over the United States. Crucial frames appeared as photographs in newspapers and magazines. Although not much was said about the death of Stewart's interpreter, Juan Francisco Espinoza, who was shot off camera, the death of Bill Stewart made a difference. The government of the United States ended its support of dictator Somoza, and without U.S. support he had to flee in less than a month. There was no more bloodshed in Barrio Riguerro, Father Molina said, and he added that Ben Linder's death, like Bill Stewart's, might save many Nicaraguan lives. The people of the United States would come to understand that their support of the Contras brought death and destruction to Nicaragua. Ben Linder would be resurrected and remembered in the months and years to come.

I was moved by the fusion of hope and grief I found in Santa Maria de los Angeles. In the days that followed the memorial service, I heard unassuming eloquence from people in other parts of Nicaragua. A mother stood in a community garden in the tiny town of Esquipulas and released an avalanche of language about the loss of her four sons in the war. (A more famous town called *Esquipulas*, in Guatemala, was the site of a meeting of the five Central American presidents just a few months earlier that led to a peace plan developed by Costa Rican President Oscar Arias.) And I listened to an old farmer at the Norlan Lumby Co-op, a dairy farm that was barely able to produce enough milk for the farmers' own children. He pointed at a milking house under construction, and said, "This is just a seed that is being sown."

When I returned to the United States, troubled by what I'd seen and heard, one scene in the memorial service echoed repeatedly in my memory: Ben Linder's mother, Elisabeth, a very small woman, stood up to talk about her son just five days after his killing. He had great fears as a child, she said. Even when he went to high school, he was afraid to walk across a bridge to school, and when he later rode his unicycle down through Washington, Oregon, and much of California, he told his parents, he never stopped being afraid of the bridges he crossed along the way. He was one of 91 people arrested at the Trojan Nuclear Plant, trying to close it down, and he was afraid then, she said. But he no longer felt any fear when he went to work in the very dangerous part of Nicaragua where he was killed. His mother said she was proud that he was buried in Nicaraguan soil.

My voice broke when I told my old friend Fred Bruning about Linder and his family. Fred, whose response to my Institute dream in 1975 was a triumph of satirical good humor, flew off to San Jose de Bocay, where Linder had died. Fred traveled around Nicaragua interviewing people who had known the young engineer. He visited the Linder family in Oregon, and he wrote a long, powerful essay about Ben Linder for *Newsday.* Daughter Judy wrote "The Killing of the Engineer Who Rode the Unicycle," a poem that appeared in *The Seattle Review,* and her poem led to a correspondence with Ben Linder's mother.

I decided at least I could take a group of students to Nicaragua to see the effects of U.S. policy there. My historian friend Jack Kirby, who taught courses on American culture and Latin America, agreed to collaborate on a course that would include a journey to Nicaragua. We began with a week of reading, and in January 11, 1988, our group of thirteen arrived in Managua. We visited hospitals and cooperative farms and talked with mothers whose sons had been killed in the war. In Ocotal we met a mother who had just lost all of her family except one infant daughter in a Contra attack on her village, and Jack and I stayed overnight in a tiny house with a woman who had recently lost her son. Like my visit to Nicaragua a few months earlier, our stay might have been primarily a seminar in grief, collateral damage, and miraculous hope if we hadn't decided to visit the port town of Rama on the Atlantic coast.

Two years before we took our class to Nicaragua, a Baptist minister and peace activist from Granville, George Williamson, had visited Nicaragua's Atlantic coast and returned to make arrangements for Granville to adopt Rama as a sister city. Our mayor, Thomas Gallant, wrote to Rama's mayor, Samuel Mejia Pena, and the relationship was established. We went there with gifts for their schools from the people of Granville.

I was particularly eager to visit Rama because one of the most interesting people I met in my earlier visit to Managua was Ray Hooker, a representative to the Nicaraguan National Assembly from the Atlantic Coast. A tall, dark-skinned man whose grandmothers were a Miskito Indian and an African, Hooker seemed to be a deeply religious intellectual. He claimed North Americans could understand the difficulty of bringing the Nicaraguan revolution to the Atlantic Coast if we imagined what it would have been like to end slavery in the United States at the same time our country gained its independence from England. Before the revolution of 1979, Hooker said, Nicaragua was really a colony of the United States, and the Atlantic coast was a colony of the colony. "You know," Hooker said, "revolutions are not easy kinds of endeavor, and your revolution in the United States is still incomplete. Despite the language of your Declaration of Independence, it was not until the 1950's that you began to overcome racism. Maybe we are crazy to try to do it all at once, but we don't have 200 years to make the Atlantic coast's Indians and Africans a part of the new Nicaragua."

As we drove toward Rama through remote, hilly cattle country, I thought about Hooker's description of the region and wondered whether the problems he described would be visible in a town of some 48,000, where local people speak Miskito, Chinese, Spanish, and English. In

Juigalpa, still several hours from our destination, a pastor from Rama came to meet us. All was *tranquilo* in Rama, he said, and we could continue our journey. Then we began to see heavily armed Sandinista soldiers dug in along the road, several of them at every bridge, and our guide said the fences around all the power poles enclosed land mines.

Mayra Climaco Aguilar, a young Nicaraguan woman, was our guide. She had fought in the Sandinista army until she developed a heart problem, and before we left Juigalpa she changed into her uniform. She sat beside the bus driver, looking very alert as we drove past heavily armed soldiers and dodged potholes that were said sometimes to hide landmines. Although I had convinced myself that the last thing the Contras would want to do was blow up a bus of North American college students because it could threaten the continued support of the Reagan administration, Mayra's change of clothing and demeanor made me nervous. I began to think of my brother's warning, and I wasn't comforted when a Methodist missionary traveling with us, Peggy Heiner, told me more about Mayra, whose parents had posed as merchants during the overthrow of Somoza and brought guns across the border from Costa Rica. As a little girl, Mayra would sometimes sleep on top of a blanket used to cover the guns. When she was eight, Mayra was caught carrying Sandinista pamphlets, and she was taken to a room and placed in a chair across from a boy she knew who was being tortured. The torturers turned away from the boy and pulled out all her toenails, Peggy said, and she didn't cry or give them any names. But Somoza's people identified her family, and her father fled to Costa Rica, where they followed and killed him. Her mother was killed soon afterward, and Mayra's husband had recently been killed in the war.

We arrived in Rama just as darkness was about to settle. The mayor had planned to meet us, but he'd been called away. Empty trucks standing on the unpaved streets were the only evidence that this was a port, and when we saw the hotel where we were staying, a dirty place with tiny cubicles and cots, Jack and I decided to take the students for a walk around town while Mayra made arrangements for our supper. As we gathered in the lobby, which doubled as a bar, Jack and I compounded an earlier error. One of our students had taken to dressing like Rambo, sporting a headband, a muscle shirt, and a three-day beard. He asked good questions of people we met along the way, especially in a meeting with a Christian-based community in Ocotal, and we were reluctant to say anything about his costume. But as we waited for other students to gather in the lobby, Rambo got in a staring match with a very drunk young man who claimed to be an ex-Contra fighter seeking sanctuary. One of us should have taken Rambo outside, but we didn't.

When we did go outside as a group, the drunk man came with us, still staring at Rambo. Dressed nattily in dark blue slacks, a light blue shirt, and cowboy boots, he stumbled occasionally, but he could also move with surprising grace. He walked beside our group, at the edge of the road, and at first he was silent. After we had moved out of sight of the hotel, he began to speak rapidly and angrily in Spanish, addressing people passing by who ignored him as he ranted about North Americans and mercenary whores. Then he tried to get Rambo to fight. When Rambo refused and no one else responded to his insults, he dropped into a crouch and pretended to spray us all with machine gun fire. It was a terrifying piece of play-acting because guns seemed to be everywhere in Nicaragua, but inhabitants of Rama going past only stared, trance-like and passive, at the surprisingly graceful drunk and the frightened *gringos*. The citizens of Rama seemed like zombies who had seen too much violence to be moved or even amused by the well-acted simulation.

We returned to the hotel with the ex-Contra following, and the children gathered outside told us Contras had recently been spotted just twelve kilometers outside of town. Rambo went upstairs to lock himself in his little cubicle, and the woman who ran the hotel called the police. After a bit the ex-Contra went upstairs, apparently looking for Rambo. I went upstairs too and stood in the hallway affecting the shambling innocence of an adult who knows where Easter eggs are hidden but is determined not to give the hiding place away to the kids. Just what I would do if the ex-Contra found Rambo's cubicle was not at all clear to me, and when he passed me and our eyes met, his stare was as menacing as any gaze I've encountered. After a few minutes, he went back downstairs, and he was talking with Peggy Heiner and a student when the police came for him.

The students were not comforted. They wanted to leave immediately and return to Managua. I explained that it would be far more dangerous to travel at night on the road out of Rama than to stay in town, but they weren't convinced. Only when several young Sandinista soldiers joined us at dinner to tell us the ex-Contra would remain in custody until we were well on our way out of town did the students agree to retire to their cubicles.

The next evening, safely back in Juigalpa, I improvised a song, borrowed a guitar from Julieta Martinez, a Nicaraguan Denison alum who accompanied us, and we sang it to the students:

The Rama Trauma

On a bus bound for Rama from the heart of Managua
We drove on a hot, muggy day.
We were scared of the fighting and mosquitoes biting

149

So we didn't have too much to say.
We listened to Dylan and thought of the killin'
That's happened along Rama road,
But with Antonio steering and Santoni cheering
We found our sweet Rama abode.

In a hotel called Amy, that's Amy, not Jamie.
We stopped for the night near the shore
When a drunk "freedom fighter" inflamed like a lighter
Shouted out mercenary bore!
We got our best wisha when they called the militia
To put him away for the night
While Mayra found quiet to enhance our bean diet
And we all thought we'd had quite a fright.

The next morning in Rama we found the real trauma
When we talked with the people in town,
As they told of dead preachers and the killing of teachers
And small children lost and not found.
We met Samuel Mejia, whose work as the mayor
Could easily cost him his life.
We met folks from the mountains in an asentiamento
And we knew they had seen the real strife.
Yes, the next morning in Rama we saw the real trauma,
The folks who were feeling the USA knife.

The students were not diverted. Our reading and discussions had prepared them for encounters with the grief and collateral damage caused by our policy of low-intensity conflict, but the Rama trauma was something else. They felt—we all felt—a hint of the fear civilians must feel when caught up in a war, maybe something like the terror we have tried to resist since September 11, 2001. Momentarily at least, all trust broke down, and it felt as though we'd stepped into the middle of madness. Although no one said so, it was clear: the students had seen enough. On our way back to Managua, we visited a hospital in Juigalpa, a sister hospital to one in Ann Arbor, Michigan, and most of the students chose not to come inside and meet soldiers and civilians wounded in the war. Two students from our class went on to work fulltime in the peace movement, and several of them became activists in the months and years that followed our trip to Nicaragua, but for a few days after our experience in Rama, they seemed paralyzed. Until we flew out of Managua, most of them spent their spare time and more money than some of them could afford drinking at the most non-Nicaraguan place they could find, the Intercontinental Hotel. We met people living in grim circumstances throughout Nicaragua who were somehow filled with hope. And we even found such people in Rama, but it was hard to sustain hope ourselves as we headed for home.

Chapter Fourteen

Walking in a Tropical Rainforest

Someone looking for hope in the 1980's could do worse than visit the La Selva Biological Station some 50 miles northeast of San Jose in Costa Rica. At the edge of a beautiful tropical rainforest there was an educational community of environmental scientists engaged in activities very different from the violence occurring in Nicaragua, where Contras, aided by the Reagan administration, were fighting the Sandinista government of Daniel Ortega. I visited La Selva on my way to Nicaragua in the spring of 1987, and in 1989 I returned to walk and talk with scientists. It was part of my attempt to understand something I'd come to think of as "the environmental imagination," which would be the title of a book by Lawrence Buell, published in 1995.

Although I was drawn to the tropical rainforest's magnificent complexity, I was also afraid of it. It's ironic that someone who calls himself an environmentalist can be afraid of tropical rainforests or "jungles," as we called them when I was young, but I can testify to the enduring power of that fear. When I first visited La Selva, I'd begun to teach environmental studies courses with Juliana Mulroy, a biologist who had done research in tropical rainforests, and I'd read quite a lot about their strange, vulnerable beauty, the unimaginably rich diversity of their life forms, and their rapid destruction. I was eager to walk in the famous lowland forest at La Selva and talk with people who studied it. But in 1987, when Nancy and I set out to enter the forest on our first night in Puerto Viejo, I thought of a sentence in Nathaniel Hawthorne's short story "Young Goodman Brown": "The whole forest was peopled with frightful sounds; the creaking of trees, the howling of wild beasts, and the yell of Indians; while, sometimes, the wind tolled like a distant church-bell, and sometimes gave a broad roar around the traveler, as if all nature were laughing him to scorn." The forest at La Selva that night was quiet, with barely a breeze. But I'd brought my own internal howling from the Tarzan movies of my youth and a lifetime of knowing the jungle as a metaphor for nature beyond human control.

Our guide was reassuring. Over the years, as daughter and poet, Judy has shown good sense. Never drawn to motorcycle racing, skydiving, or other unnecessary risks, she is quite brave, but her poems are filled with dark imagining. It was Judy who realized our deck in Oregon was in trouble before it dropped. So her eagerness to show us the forest on our first night in town suggested she had found no good reason to be afraid of it.

As it turned out, most of the excitement that night came before we reached the forest. When we crossed a footbridge over the Puerto Viejo River, we saw a sloth feeding high in a tree above the water. It seemed to be vaguely disturbed by our flashlights, but its comic, slow-motion, upside-down movements made the animal an unthreatening representative of nocturnal wildlife. Still approaching the forest, we came upon a line of leaf-cutter ants at work on a carambola tree. They carried pieces of leaf raised like sails above them, tacking and jibing along their way, seemingly oblivious to us and to our flashlights. Then, at the edge of the forest, two bright green eyes peered at us from beneath another tree. They turned out to be a click beetle with two luminescent spots on its back. After that, our first taste of the climax forest was anti-climactic. It was very dark, but it was quieter by far than an Ohio woods in May, when spring peepers are calling.

The next morning we returned to La Selva, and before we reached the forest we stopped to identify several birds Nancy and I had never seen before:

Oropendola, Snowy Katinga, Great Tyrant Flycatcher, Shining Honey Creeper, Yellow-crowned Euphonia, Chesnut-mandible Toucan, Red-rumped Tanager, Blue-gray Tanager, Blue Dacnis, Collared Aracari, Squirrel Cuckoo, Rufus Motmot, Baird's Trogon, and Orange-bellied Trogon. When we pulled ourselves past the boundary so rich in birdlife and into the shade of the forest itself, we saw more birds. The understory allowed longer vistas than I'd imagined, but the birds moved elusively in and out of the thick canopy and through patches of light. Even the birds with brilliant colors often disappeared before we could get a good look at them. And then we saw our first Blue Morpho, an iridescent blue butterfly with a six-inch wingspread that moved through sunlight and shadows like a messenger from a mystical land. By the time we spotted a small anteater with brown fur and a very dark vest, I was already awestruck by the forest. We must have startled the anteater as we stepped into a clearing that had begun to reforest itself, and it began to climb a small tree. The tree leaned with the animal's weight, and the anteater seemed to realize this was not a sensible escape route. So it took advantage of the bending trunk and transferred to an even smaller tree, which it followed back to earth. With its feet on solid ground, the animal moved sedately away from us until, still in full view, it stopped to search for ants. Like the sloth, the anteater was apparently not altogether pleased to meet humans, but neither did it take us entirely seriously.

My growing wonder in the forest didn't diminish my fear. In fact, my journal entries from that first visit to La Selva seem to be a systematic effort to justify my worries. There are large bala ants in my journal, said to sting as painfully as scorpions. Not a bala ant touched me, but it seemed important to mention their ominous presence. And the fer-de-lance and bushmaster slithered through my journal although I didn't see a single poisonous snake on that first visit. When I talked with a biologist who had worked in the rainforest for several years, I asked him if he ever thought about snakes on his daily jogs along the forest trails. "I think of little else," he said, and I carefully recorded his statement because it seemed to justify my fear. My only encounter with a snake might almost have taken place in an Ohio farmyard. It was a green vine snake, perhaps three feet long and very thin, and it was trying to swallow a large frog. The drama went on for several minutes, as the snake held the frog in a mouth-to-mouth position while the frog blew itself up like a balloon to avoid being swallowed. Finally, the snake gave up and moved gracefully into the vines, quickly becoming invisible, and the frog sat still for several minutes, seemingly exhausted. I felt relief, as though I were fortunate to have come through the encounter unscathed.

One of the things I learned when I returned to talk with scientists at La Selva in 1989 was that fear was not limited to tenderfeet like me. Nancy Greig, then a graduate student working on the reproduction of piper, a shrub common in Costa Rican rainforests, seemed more at home in the forest than anyone else I met there. Other scientists said she was the best naturalist working at La Selva at the time, by which they seemed to mean she was more familiar with the whole ecosystem than anyone else. One day I went with Greig as she checked the shrubs she'd marked in the forest's understory. She seemed relaxed even though much of the time we walked off the trails, and only once did I see her refer to a map she carried. But when I asked her whether she worried about poisonous snakes, she said she carried a battery-powered stun gun because there was some evidence that repeated shocks to a snakebite can reduce its effects, and she was afraid she couldn't administer an injection of anti-venom to herself or to someone else. When she decided to do research in the tropics, Greig said, she made her will.

Another young scientist, Brian Brown, did much of his fieldwork at night, collecting tiny flies that parasitize leafcutter ants. One night at dinner Brown invited several of us to go with him to see a bushmaster, a poisonous snake for which anti-venom was thought to be ineffective. A photographer had found this snake coiled beside a trail two or three nights earlier, and it was likely to return to the same hunting spot for several nights in a row. Those of us at the table had come to dinner without the knee-high rubber boots we wore in the forest to protect ourselves from snakebites, but we went with Brown anyway, and his memory of the snake's position was unerring. The sight of the large, muscular bushmaster coiled beside the trail, seemingly unbothered by our flashlights and flashbulbs, was unforgettably beautiful. My own photographs, taken from a deeply respectful distance, don't begin to capture the latent power I felt in the coiled snake.

In a dinner conversation the following evening with several biologists, I waited for a lull in the talk to bring up the bushmaster. Our snake veneration group, I said, sure had trusted Brian Brown when we accompanied him at night without wearing our boots. Nancy Greig pointed out that we also seemed to trust the snake to return to exactly the same place. Had it chosen a spot fifteen meters nearer the dining hall, she suggested, one of us might have stepped on it and been bitten. Our bootless expedition to see the snake, in short, was foolish.

Feeling chastised, I turned the conversation to my own fear and told of finding comfort in a passage from E.O. Wilson's *Biophilia* (1984), where he tells of handling poisonous snakes as a boy in the Florida panhandle and Alabama, then finding as an adult that he became more fearful. He sometimes dreams, he says in *Biophilia*, of a serpent that is "life-promising and life-threatening, seductive and treacherous." Wilson's book explores our species' "urge to affiliate with other life forms," but he

157

also offers an evolutionary explanation for the mixture of aversion and fascination most humans and other primates feel for snakes. The biologists weren't put off by my fear or my fascination with it. All of them knew at least one person who had been literally snake-bitten. They told of a biologist who panicked and couldn't bring himself to inject anti-venom when a companion was snake-bitten. John Kress from the Smithsonian Institution, who worked in tropical rainforests all over the world, confessed that he was terrified of the fer-de-lance. Someone told a story of a Costa Rican field assistant who waited for a fer-de-lance to move slowly through his legs as he was working on his knees in an experimental plot. He reported that it was a religious experience.

The complex attitudes La Selva scientists brought to the forest came to represent, for me, one of the virtues I find in ecology. Not only were they willing to consider their own fear, but they paid attention to nearby Puerto Viejo, and they were concerned about La Selva's influence on the lives of local people. They were specialists, but far from being limited by the divide-and-conquer methods of modern science, they seemed comfortable with the uncertainty and inclusiveness that characterize ecology. They were eager to find unexpected connections among life forms and habitat. They approached the forest with the kind of eagerness that must have marked nineteenth-century naturalists who hoped to find a new species every time they went into the field. There are still many unidentified life forms to be found in tropical rainforests, but what excited these scientists was the possibility of understanding how species interact with each other and with changes in their habitat. And unlike eco-fundamentalists, who view humans as aliens in "nature," these scientists included our species in their thinking. As they walked the trails of La Selva, weighed down by umbrellas, cameras, binoculars, and other equipment, they appeared to be seeking knowledge more comprehensive and whole than is typical of our intellectually fragmented age.

Was it possible, I wondered, that these young scientists were finding their way back toward a kind of knowledge characteristic of small-scale societies? I thought of Colin Turnbull's descriptions of the BaMbuti Pygmies in *The Forest People* (1961). The BaMbuti moved playfully through the forest, hunting and gathering and dancing and singing, and yet they considered it a death sentence to be cast out of the community to live alone. They understood fear of the forest so well they could cultivate it among neighboring African villagers as a way of discouraging them from trespassing on the BaMbuti's sacred environment. In a letter, anthropologist Dell Hymes describes similar attitudes among the native people who inhabited the land around Fox Creek on Oregon's Saddle Mountain: "It's my impression that Oregon Indians were afraid of the environmental surround. At least in terms of being alone. Villages were centers and safe. Further out, there might be danger that could empower (guardian spirit), and certainly trails with which one was acquainted, but dangers too." The scientists at La Selva seemed to be recovering a way of imagining nature that arises from deep intimacy with landscapes industrial societies often sentimentalize and often destroy.

I found a community of learning at La Selva, where people set out to explore, among other things, an idea proposed by Wendell Berry in *The Unsettling of America: Culture and Agriculture* (1977): "it is impossible to care for each other more or differently than we care for the earth." This was a community, I thought, that was accomplishing much of what I'd tried to imagine for the Institute.

The La Selva Biological Station began as a rustic field station in the Sarapaqui region of Costa Rica when the Organization of Tropical Studies, a consortium of

159

universities, bought the land in 1968. If it had become a community of learning, it had also become an institution with air-conditioned laboratories, a library, lodging for scientists and other visitors, a dining hall, and miles of trails. (La Selva's annual budget in 1989 was $500,000. By 2006 it had grown to $1.2 million and by 2013 to $1.67 million.) More than half of La Selva's 3700 acres are "old growth" or primary tropical rainforest, and the rest are in various stages of reforestation. The Costa Rican government extended the large Braulio Carrillo National Park northwest to meet La Selva's southern boundary, and unbroken forest extends in a 128,500 acre corridor from cloud forest at 9500 feet in Braulio Carrillo to hot rainforest at just above sea level in La Selva. Scientists come to La Selva to study insect and animal behavior, plant distribution, soil chemistry, the giant trees that dominate the forest canopy, the gaps created when great trees fall, archeological evidence left by indigenous people who once lived in the forest, and much else. In recent years scientists have paid increasing attention to reforestation and agro-economy.

The pace of development in the region quickened at just about the same time scientists began to come to La Selva, and the price of progress was visible in Puerto Viejo, less than two miles from the entrance to the biological station. Huge logs were hauled through town nearly every day from unprotected forests in the region. Along the road between Puerto Viejo and La Selva in 1989 I saw heavily loaded log trucks parked, waiting for the checkpoint in town to close. Logging had damaged nearby watersheds while bringing little wealth or employment to Puerto Viejo. Most of the land close to town had already been cleared for cattle ranches, banana plantations and other agriculture, and the town's drinking water made children sick. The economy in Puerto Viejo was not robust, and few young people went beyond the sixth grade before they had to leave school to work.

The scientists at La Selva knew their work was dependent on the shifting winds of political change, and some of them were in Costa Rica as much because of its political stability as because of the forests. Some had worked in Panama, Peru, and Nicaragua, and they knew war was a greater threat to their work than poisonous snakes would ever be. Funding priorities and the detachment required by science can breed caution and conservatism in politics, but in 1989 the scientists at La Selva were both well informed and skeptical about the Reagan administration's policies in Latin America. When they talked politics, they focused on more than the politics of science.

Our low-intensity war in Nicaragua was a looming presence at the La Selva dinner tables. There was an internment camp for Nicaraguan refugees on the road between La Selva and the cloud forest at Monte Verde, where scientists from La Selva often did research. A National Guard camp on the road from La Selva to Puerto Viejo gave a sense of military presence even though Costa Rica had no army. And there were Nicaraguan refugees living around Puerto Viejo.

Perhaps inevitably, La Selva scientists talked about progress and war, a conjunction of themes that haunt science, just as they mark the rest of our history. Nineteenth-century naturalist Thomas Belt linked war and social progress explicitly in A Naturalist in Nicaragua (1874) when he tried to explain what had happened to the indigenous people of Central America:

Will these Indians ever again attain to that pitch of civilisation at which they had arrived before the conquest? I fear not. The whip that kept them to the mark in the old days was the continual warfare between the different tribes, and this has ceased forever.

161

War is not always a curse. . . . Those in which the tribal instinct was strongest, who stood shoulder to shoulder with their fellows, reverenced and obeyed their chiefs, and excelled in feats of strength and agility, would annihilate or subjugate the weaker and less warlike races.

Unlike Gustavus Hines, who arrived on the Oregon coast about twenty years before the publication of Darwin's *The Origin of Species* (1859) and immediately concluded it was God's will that indigenous people go extinct to make room for the immigration of Christians like himself, Belt had a "scientific" explanation, social Darwinism, for what he saw as a loss of cultural vitality among indigenous people. Neither the missionary nor the scientist considered the possibility that brutal imperial expansion was responsible for what they saw happening to the natives, and Belt ignored evidence of indigenous environmental destruction that preceded the conquest.

I was impressed when the scientists at La Selva expressed their concern about the influence of their own "exotic" culture on the human inhabitants of the ecosystem they had come to study. Even very perceptive observers of nature and culture have sometimes failed to take into account the impact of "progress" on cultures rooted in particular ecosytems. In John Muir's *My First Summer in the Sierra Nevada* (1911), for example, the naturalist describes the devastating impact of gold miners on the land in California: "roads blasted in solid rock, wild streams dammed and turned out of their channels to work in the mines like slaves." But when Muir meets an impoverished Native American, he is so put off by her grime that he appears to blame the victim:

In every way she seemed sadly unlike nature's neat well-dressed animals, though living like them on the bounty of the wilderness. Strange that mankind alone is dirty. Had she been clad in fur, or cloth woven of grass or shredded bark, like the juniper and libocedrus mats, she might then have seemed a rightful part of the wilderness; like a good wolf, or bear. But from no point of view that I have found are such debased fellow beings a whit more natural than the blaring tailored tourists we saw that frightened birds and squirrels.

To think of the woman in this way, Muir had to abstract her from history and from the damaged ecosystem where she lived. Such a view allowed him to accept the term *Digger Indian* used by California settlers to distinguish "debased" native people from noble Indians.

Anthropologist Colin Turnbull makes a similar intellectual move in his troubling book *The Mountain People* (1972). His study of the Ik, a hunting and gathering society evicted from their traditional hunting territory in East Africa, leaves out of account the connection between their cultural identity and the ecosystem in which their culture developed. Like Native American societies in the United States that were moved onto reservation land very different from the ecosystems in which their cultures were rooted, the Ik were moved out of their home, the Kidepo Valley, and into mountains separating Uganda, Sudan, and Kenya, where they were told to become farmers. Under pressures of starvation, corrupt welfare, and the loss of dignity that accompanies the sudden devaluation of traditional skills, Ik society disintegrated as Turnbull watched. Surprisingly, Turnbull, who had explored with great sensitivity the relationship between BaMbuti culture and the Ituri Forest in *The Forest People*, concluded from the disintegration of Ik society that he had uncovered a grim truth about human nature. "The Ik teach us," he says, "that our much vaunted human values are not inherent in humanity at all, but are associated only with a particular form of survival called society, and that all, even society itself, are luxuries than can be dispensed with."

If John Muir could ignore the devastating impact on indigenous people of gold miners' greed and violence and Colin Turnbull could account only at the highest level of abstraction for the cultural catastrophe caused by uprooting the Ik from their native land, I wondered whether the people at La Selva would be sufficiently attentive to the influence of "progress," including their biological station, on the human inhabitants of the ecosystem they were studying.

They were concerned about such matters, as I've said, but the station's relationships with local Costa Ricans seemed to involve a delicate balancing act. By 1989, the field station provided almost fifty jobs to the people of Puerto Viejo and outlying communities, and Costa Ricans were doing much of the fieldwork, maintaining trails, building new laboratories, cooking, cleaning, handling finances, and guiding visitors. One of the tensions between local Costa Ricans and the scientists is suggested by a personnel decision made while I was there. A worker who was maintaining a trail came upon a fer-de-lance and killed it with his machete. He was immediately fired. It was a violation of the rules at La Selva, but it must have been an instinctive act of self-protection for someone who had grown up in the region. Local people had been accustomed to hunting and fishing and taking firewood from the forest, as well as protecting themselves from poisonous snakes, and now those uses of the land were against the rules.

I spent an evening with Danilo, a field assistant then in his mid-twenties, and I asked him if the presence of the biological station had encouraged people in communities around La Selva to appreciate the forest in new ways. No, he said, because the scientists at La Selva see local *campesinos* as destroyers of the forest, and no one has taught them how to make a living other than by cutting and burning and farming. The people at La Selva brought school children to walk in the forest, he admitted, and perhaps that would help some of them learn to love the trees and the animals. But many poor people say, "The forest cannot bring me money."

The scientists should teach local people about sustainable agricultural practices, Danilo said, because they face an impossible choice between poverty and deforestation. And some of this was beginning to happen. Researchers in a program funded by the MacArthur Foundation had been identifying native tree species that would grow in the high light environment of cleared land. They were studying the effects of reforestation on damaged soils, and trying to help local farmers improve their economic condition by planting trees. Already, they had found a native species that could grow over twenty feet in three years under the right conditions.

When I arrived at the little house Danilo built from beautiful native hardwoods, he showed me the trees, fruits, and flowers he had planted on the land where he lived with his wife and one year-old daughter. He was bringing the forest back to the farmland. When he first began to work at La Selva, Danilo said, he knew *nada* about the forest. *Nada*, he repeated. Now he was learning the plants, and he owned several books about the forest. I talked with scientists who said Danilo, who was still attending night classes in Puerto Viejo to complete his high school equivalency, was already able teach them things about the forest.

But the impulse toward technical rationality that worried me when I was a dean at Denison University had begun to influence La Selva as well. As the biological station attracted funding, a large share of the money went for research facilities and sophisticated equipment, and fees for working at La Selva had begun to rise, partly to pay for expensive maintenance of equipment used mainly by North American scientists. Despite a fee structure intended to encourage the work of Costa Rican scientists, several Costa Ricans told me the field station was less and less accessible to them financially unless they were part of a well-funded research team. I wondered if people who came to the forest without much funding but with passionate interest in a research question were an endangered species at La Selva. Behind the leisurely conversations at meals, I glimpsed hints of a frenetic pace. In 1989 the co-directors of La Selva, for example, Deborah and David Clark, were unable to find much time to talk about the station's intellectual life. They were too busy writing proposals, pursuing their own research, and administering an increasingly complex institution. As I watched them rush from one task to another, I was reminded of my manic years as an academic dean.

In a 1983 doctoral dissertation based on research done at La Selva, I found a telling portent of technical rationality. *Access methods* is the key phrase in the title of Donald Ray Perry's "Access Methods, Observations, Pollination Biology, Bee Foraging Behavior, and Bee Community Structure Within a Neotropical Wet Forest Canopy." Perry was a pioneer in developing techniques for getting people into the canopy of the rainforest, where much of the forest's biodiversity is found. His techniques, a triumph of intermediate technology, included the placement of climbing lines with a crossbow and the use of sophisticated rock-climbing equipment. But in a section of the dissertation devoted to imagining more advanced methods of working in the canopy there is a proposal that suggests Perry's frustration with heat, insects, snakes, thorns, and perhaps even labor problems. He imagines a web system that would make possible automated

166

research almost anywhere in the canopy of a plot as large as 40 acres:

A final system, still in the conceptual stages of development, would employ an automated web that would carry a remote sensing module. The module would contain video cameras, directional microphones and speakers, a mechanical arm for specimen collection, infrared lights for nocturnal work, and camera mounts for still and motion picture photography. The module would be driven from a ground level building having a full assortment of sound and video recording and playback equipment. The many uses for such a system need no elaboration.

What began as a search for methods to bring human observers into the richly populated forest canopy, which had been almost inaccessible, becomes a quest for technology that can replace humans. The ultimate goal would seem to be robots rolling along the trails and through the canopy, sending data back to universities in the temperate zone, where tropical biologists sit in front of consoles to do their work. In such a fantasy the connections between tropical rainforest biology and human communities, between "local soil and local culture," as Wendell Berry puts it, seem to disappear.

But such dreams run counter to the complex reality I observed at La Selva in 1989. It was a community of learning in which teaching and research seemed inseparable, and both were tied to concrete experience in the forest. Walking the trails with scientists, I understood why field seminars in tropical biology offered by the Organization for Tropical Studies have influenced the careers of many biologists. Knowing the world in a way that grounds theory and feeling in concrete experience fosters imagination. Ecology as it seemed to be practiced at La Selva in 1989 called people back to that capacity to find connections among things that differ from each other: organisms and their surroundings, knowledge and feeling, ideas and physical experience. Such thinking, it seems to me, produces more than good science. At its best, it is likely to avoid the simplicities and abstractions we use to justify destructive forms of violence.

Chapter Fifteen

Presidential Aspirations

In the fall of 1945, when I was walking home from the second grade at Richmond Elementary School in Portland, Oregon, stepping carefully over the cracks so as not to break my mother's back, I heard a grandmotherly woman speak across her fence to a woman somewhat younger. Pointing at me and smiling, she said, "That young man may someday be our president." The other woman looked across at me and didn't laugh. Although I knew even then they were thinking of more than a college presidency, I came to the humble belief that they simply recognized the likelihood of executive leadership in my destiny. (Only briefly, in the months and years immediately following September 11, 2001, did I come to believe I could fill our nation's presidency more capably than the incumbent.)

Five years after hearing the presidential prophecy, I was elected president of Richmond Elementary School's 4-H club. My peers perceived hidden strength in me: they also nominated me to represent them in a statewide health contest, ignoring the fact that I was very thin and a little pasty-faced. My co-nominee, Mary Ellen Adams, was just my age, but she was three inches taller, ruddy-faced and athletic. Richmond's school nurse gently informed our club that my muscle tone was not likely to carry me far in the contest, and they quietly replaced me with Holly Hutchins, whose biceps became visible when he flexed them. Mary Ellen and Holly moved easily through the regional qualifiers, and in August of 1951 Mary Ellen's picture appeared on the front page of the *Oregonian* beside that of a smiling, robust farm boy from downstate. She had won the whole thing at the Oregon State Fair.

My resounding defeat in the politics of health did not diminish my executive influence, however, and no one seemed surprised when I was elected captain of Richmond's Safety Patrol in the eighth grade. The captaincy was my first truly serious executive responsibility. The power in our Safety Patrol's white military belts and red flags could be abused. Young officers would occasionally swing red flags whimsically into the street, thereby halting traffic unnecessarily and causing complaints with the potential to undercut local support for public education. My main task was to encourage flag discipline. But my most dramatic moment as captain came one day in the spring of 1952, when several classes from Richmond Elementary School marched more than a mile east to Franklin High School to hear the Portland Symphony. Our walk included crossings of three busy streets, and on this day I carried a flag in spite of my administrative eminence. At the corner of Division Street and 50th Avenue, I stopped a bus driven by William Martin Watson, my grandfather. It was a proud moment for both of us as we waved to each other although I knew enough about the tyranny of city bus schedules to understand that I had dropped a wrench in the machinery of my grandfather's day. But for three years after that, until he died, he told the story of my stopping his bus to let the Richmond Elementary legions cross. He said he stood up and pointed me out to his passengers.

Politically, my four years at Franklin High were difficult. Before the word itself gained wide currency, I was perhaps beginning to be a *nerd* at just about the time the Nerd first appeared in Dr. Seuss's *If I Ran the Zoo* (1950). It wasn't that I exhibited unstylish enthusiasm for physics or the violin, but I was slow to mature. Neither socially nor athletically adept, I found it difficult to build a power base for a presidential campaign despite my ambition. Mom reminded me gently more than once that

170

my father's Aunt Maude had told her early in her marriage to my father that Nichols men were known for achieving full adulthood slowly. Our maturity was well worth waiting for, she had promised. My own patience ran out in my senior year, and I cobbled together a desperate campaign for the class presidency. My only clear memory of the campaign is an image from the senior class movie: in slacks that end midway down my shins, revealing white socks, and wearing my father's sport coat, which droops from my shoulders, I gangle across the stage to a very large microphone and deliver a brief, rather pleasant speech. My voice doesn't break at all. Phil Schnabel, a high hurdler who played offensive end on the football team and pulled down rebounds for our state championship basketball team, edged me out at the polls.

Park College in Missouri, my next educational stop, was very small, and although I didn't star in soccer, basketball, and tennis, as a campaign brochure might put it, I was allowed to play. Given my athletic participation and my presidential aspirations, it would have been shocking if I hadn't been elected president of our tiny senior class, and I was. But it was an office with few responsibilities, and the only thing my administration accomplished was the disbanding of a senior honorary society that had reproduced itself year after without a clear fix on the virtues it meant to honor.

During my years in graduate school, I laid low. This was the time when I was moving leftward, away from my conservative Republican roots. It was a time of new fatherhood and my growing interest in Henry Thoreau, whose transcendental politics were so radical I couldn't quite digest them. It was a period of political latency.

The fall of 1966, when I took a job at Denison University, was an exciting time politically. Denison was not a hotbed of radical politics, but I soon found that, despite my gradual move leftward, I remained well to the right of the students I found most interesting. My conservative roots were still visible in my suit and tie, my clean-shaven face and neatly trimmed hair. I listened politely to increasingly polarized faculty debates that often touched on the Vietnam War, and my slightly schizoid political profile led me to be tactful in my battle with local management at Kaiser Aluminum & Chemical Corporation over the engineer they fired after he refused to buy U.S. savings bonds and wore a Black Power button. My delicacy in the matter of Kaiser, joined with my reassuring personal appearance, led to my appointment as an assistant dean or, as some faculty called me, "dean of dissent." In an era of demonstrations and boycotts, a time of student and faculty unrest, my ambiguous political profile must have seemed just the ticket for buffering political collisions and mediating conflicts. And that, in turn, led to my nomination for a Danforth fellowship to spend 1969-70 at Yale University, studying the developing field of Afro-American Studies.

During my year in New Haven, livelier dissent came to Denison at just about the same time a new president arrived. As Dean of Students at Stanford University, Joel P. Smith had been the California institution's man with a bullhorn at student demonstrations. That history, combined with his background as an attorney and pressure from a conservative board of trustees, led Smith to respond very sternly to a set of demands from Denison's black students. One result was a boycott of classes that further polarized the faculty. Another result was the new president's decision to replace me with someone less inclined to see both sides of the difficult political issues dividing the college. My year as Denison's dissent specialist had been emotionally exhausting, and I was eager to get back into the classroom with the slave narratives I'd found at Yale. So the thought of returning to fulltime teaching was very appealing, but Smith's decision, made without consulting me, felt too much like being fired, and I decided to fight it. As in my Kaiser crusade, I moved with tact, writing politely to Smith and the seven members of his personnel committee to say my dismissal from an administrative position that had been, so very briefly, an important part of my duties seemed to put my whole career in jeopardy. My chances to earn tenure, I said poignantly, seemed greatly diminished. At the very least, I deserved an evaluation of my work. Within a week, the besieged president called me in New Haven to restore a position I would happily have surrendered voluntarily.

Following my restoration as a junior administrator, my own presidential aspirations fell into a decade of dormancy and then were briefly inflamed in 1983, when I accepted a position as academic dean. My ambition was then drenched in the kind of administrative disappointments that are often part of life in middle management. It sputtered to life again in the spring of 1988, with the resignation of Andrew de Rocco from Denison's presidency. The elaborate machinery of a presidential search, I soon realized, could not be assembled in time to find a replacement by the fall. The provost and dean were both new to their jobs, and it was not long before my name came up as a likely interim president. Then, just as the trustees were about to meet and choose the interim president, I was asked to give Denison's commencement address. Anglican Bishop Trevor Huddleston had been scheduled to speak, but the day before he was to fly from London, he was injured in a fall. Given just a few hours to prepare my pinch-hitting address, I crafted what amounted to a campaign speech based on Bishop Huddleston's important work opposing South African apartheid. I told my audience about the work of a ninety seven year old Quaker, Mildred Scott Olmstead, who had spoken a few days earlier at my daughter's Haverford College commencement. Olmstead told stories of her life as an internationalist, conveying a sense of the great joy to be found in toiling for peace and justice. My commencement address echoed Olmstead's, emphasizing the injustice I saw in our low-intensity war in Nicaragua. Somewhere along the way, as I neared the end, my voice broke, just as I thought it would years earlier in my campaign speech at Franklin High.

What I didn't know as I swept my arms skyward on that beautiful commencement day in May of 1988, sending sonorous sentences sweeping over the graduating class, their parents, the faculty, and various honored guests was that Michael Eisner, a Denison alumnus, at that time the celebrated CEO of the Walt Disney Company, would speak from the same podium just one year later. Would that knowledge have influenced my behavior? I think so. Had I known, for instance, that Eisner would distribute Mickey Mouse hats to members of the 1989 graduating class, I might have led off with Groucho Marx mustaches and spectacles. Had I been informed that Eisner's address, "The Skills of Freedom," would be quite upbeat, I might have snipped a few of the grimmer sentences from my own remarks, titled "Fear, Joy and Justice." In spite of having sandwiched *Joy* between *Fear* and *Justice*, I took too long to cut to the gladness. I talked about my fear of the bushmaster and fer-de-lance, for example, and if my snake stories weren't enough to give graduates the heebie-jeebies as they headed out of Granville, I talked, too, about Ben Linder, whose memorial service I had recently attended in Managua. My point was that Linder had known for some time that he and his co-workers in Nicaragua were considered enemies in our war, but he found a sense of purpose, a belief in the importance of his work, that helped him overcome his fear.

Michael Eisner, as it turned out, had something to say about fear, too. He recalled the speaker at his own

174

Denison commencement in 1964, two years before I arrived. This was a Dartmouth College professor who, according to Eisner, worried aloud that Denison would not survive the next two or three decades without vigilant leadership. "I am happy to report," Eisner said, "that Professor Stewart's fears were greatly exaggerated." So much for commencement speakers who try to give you the heebie-jeebies, he seemed to say, although he didn't claim the college actually had vigilant leadership.

Had I known my own approach to commencementeering would come under attack from a man whose monthly take home pay probably exceeded my lifetime earnings, I might have said a thing or two about Mickey Mouse. I might have appealed to Stephen Jay Gould, the Harvard evolutionary biologist who had spoken at Denison's commencement in 1984. *Just remember*, I might have said, *what Professor Gould wrote about Mickey Mouse: far from maturing over the years, Mickey evolved from adulthood into infancy. That charming little mouse began in the 1920's as a disreputable rat-like adult, but his head and eyes have slowly gotten larger so that now he looks like an innocent child. Is that any model for life after graduation?* Gould didn't actually indict Mickey in his Denison commencement speech. He made the point in an earlier essay, "A Biological Homage to Mickey Mouse," but it's an important point, and I might have repeated it.

Graduates, I might have said, once I established precedent for an attack on the lovable little cartoon character, *our consumer culture will try to call you back to a Mickey Mouse childhood. But resist those sirens. Life is not Disneyworld. It is not even a planned community like Disney's Celebration, a town where company executives resolve political disagreements. Oh, life is good in Celebration, good here in Granville too, but it is better for some of us than for others. Here in Granville we can barely see across the growing chasm that*

175

separates us from the poor and powerless. My fondest hope for you is that you will celebrate the gift of your education by finding ways to bring food, housing, health care, education, and justice to the millions of people all over the world who need your help. It was probably fortunate that I didn't know I was a warm-up act for Michael Eisner.

As it turned out, Eisner had some interesting things to say once he got Mickey out of the way. He told of a ritual among executives at Disney, for example. "We get together in a room," he said, "and everybody puts out ideas for scripts or projects, knowing they'll probably be gonged." He was telling the graduates not to be afraid of failure. As he put it, "most of the world's truly successful people fail many times over the course of a lifetime." Failure was a theme I could have explored with some authority.

But as I spoke in the spring of 1988, I hadn't yet tasted the bitter failure that would hit me two weeks later, when Denison's chairman of the board called to tell me I hadn't been chosen for the interim presidency. The truth was I'd already started to make plans. First, there would be a presidential trip to Nicaragua with students, faculty, and trustees to visit one of our most distinguished alumni, Gustavo Parajon, who worked with the Nicaraguan poor and sought to end hostilities there.

In May of 1987, when he was in town for his son's graduation from Denison, Parajon had spoken at the First Baptist Church in Granville. "We have been confronted in the last seven or eight years with an experience we had never imagined in our lives," he told the Baptists:

> That is the naked aggression of the United States in our country. And having lived here in the United States myself for thirteen years and having been inspired by the great ideals of the American founding fathers, what we have seen and

176

experienced has been so devastating and shocking that the concern and Christian commitment of many Americans have been a great comfort to us.

The visit I imagined with Parajon would be partly ceremonial, partly educational, and I planned more symbolic acts to stir up political debate on campus as an alternative to an intense, dysfunctional social life, fueled by alcohol. I planned to involve local public school teachers in conversations with our faculty about education. Oh, I had very large plans for using the interim presidency as a bully pulpit.

The chairman's announcement felt like a punch in the stomach, and I may have sounded a little angry when I asked what went wrong. A successful investment manager, the chairman had surely broken bad news to clients about investments gone sour, but he seemed to be thrown off-stride by my question. He hesitated, began a circuitous sentence, and broke it off to say that, of course, nothing had gone wrong. They simply chose someone who seemed a stronger candidate. The intensity of my disappointment surprised me. I hadn't thought an adult could feel such naked longing, so powerful an impulse to ask for another chance. But by the time the chairman hung up, my candidacy for the real presidency was beginning.

The last leg of my presidential campaign began with my nomination by Charles P. Henry, who was then chairman of the board for Amnesty International in the United States. An African American alumnus of Denison and a tenured member of the faculty at the University of California, Henry was the student who resolved the boycott in our first Black Studies course back in 1968. After completing a doctorate at the University of Chicago and teaching at Howard University, he returned for a few years to teach at Denison, where the Political Science department judged him to lack the attributes they expected from politically scientific colleagues. So he left for a distinguished career at the University of California at Berkeley. His work with Amnesty International and his books on politics embodied values I wanted to emphasize in my campaign, and in a long letter to the presidential search committee, I built my platform on my nomination by Charles Henry. Campaigns for college presidencies generally take place behind the scenes until two or three finalists are chosen, but I had a long, congenial interview with the faculty, students, and trustees of the search committee. Aware that the likelihood of my being chosen was roughly the same as the probability of my election to national office, I spoke with candor about my view of the college's strengths and weaknesses. I argued that taking my candidacy seriously and making a Denison professor a finalist would build the confidence of our faculty. And a president who knew the institution well, I said, could build on the college's strengths, working with the grain.

We met in the large living room of a mansion used in those days as the college's guesthouse, and as I walked across the beautiful grounds to my car afterward, I experienced a pleasant moment of self-congratulation. My answers to the committee's questions had verged on eloquence, it seemed to me, and I wondered fleetingly if the guesthouse might someday become my presidential palace.

Had I been persuasive? Apparently not. When the finalists were announced, my name was not among them. The bank president who chaired the search committee told me they were afraid I couldn't raise money. And perhaps they were right.

Chapter Sixteen

The First Fox Creek Expedition (1991)

While I dabbled unsuccessfully in college politics, my brother Dave bought an old building in southeast Portland, not far from where we grew up. He planned to make it the new home for his small wholesale business, Fox Lamp and Fixture. The two-story building, which many years earlier had been a local post office, was so dilapidated I thought at first the project might be a mistake. Nancy and I visited the building in the early stages of its renovation, providing an afternoon of manual labor as we shoveled dirt to make room for new floor joists and hauled away pieces of the foundation Dave had to replace. While he was renovating the old post office from the ground up, carefully preserving its historic exterior, Fox Lamp and Fixture was doing business a few blocks away with Dave's wife, Karen, behind the counter. In the meantime the engine blew in Dave's battered delivery van, and he rebuilt that too. While we recycled newspapers, cans, and bottles, Dave recycled cars and buildings, and it occurred to me that his thrifty, independent effort to make a new home for their family business was as authentically conservative as Dad's decision to leave the Hanford Nuclear Reservation when he decided they were doing slovenly work. Maybe my admiration for Dave's work made it possible for us to talk about politics as we shoveled. But we didn't agree about much.

A few months later, however, in mid-February of 1991, just a month after our government had begun the massive aerial attacks on targets in Iraq and Kuwait we called "Desert Storm," Dave called me in Ohio to ask what I thought of the news. By this time I'd learned quite a lot about the effort to save the old growth in the Fox

Creek forest on Saddle Mountain, and I was focused on the possibility that Dave might lead us into the forest. The last thing I wanted to do was talk about something on which we were as sure to disagree as "Desert Storm" so I was noncommittal. Then Nancy joined our conversation, and Dave asked what she thought about events in the Persian Gulf. She said she was troubled about the bombing, which was sure to kill innocent civilians, and she worried about the likelihood of a land war. With that, I confessed that I'd helped organize a teach-in at the college on the Persian Gulf, and I added my own opinion that we should have given sanctions more time to work before we started bombing.

To my astonishment, Dave agreed. His closest friend from the Marine Corps was in the region, working on logistics in the desert, and Dave was worried about him. He believed our risks were out of proportion to our real interests in the Persian Gulf. Even more surprisingly, he said his reservations about our policy in the Middle East were leading him to wonder about our invasions of Grenada in 1983 and Panama in 1989. The last time we had agreed on U.S. foreign policy was in April of 1980, when President Carter made a desperate effort to free hostages in Iran militarily, and Dave thought it was a mistake. I hadn't taken Dave's assessment altogether seriously then because he was generally critical of Democrats. But his doubts about "Desert Storm" and our supposed victories in Grenada and Panama, implicit criticisms of President Reagan and the first President Bush, suggested something new in our longstanding debates on American politics.

A week later, as the ground war was about to begin in Kuwait and Iraq, I called Dave. Nancy was in New York, helping with our newborn granddaughter Ana, and it was not a good time to tell my wife I thought our nation was so hungry for victory we might roll across Kuwait and Iraq at great cost to our troops and the people and land we claimed to be protecting. The move from "Desert Shield" to "Desert Storm" to "Desert Sabre," the name for the ground assault, sounded to me like something proposed by a public relations specialist in movie titles. And there had been way too much talk, I thought, about making up for our failure in Vietnam. So I launched into a diatribe. "I'm tired," I said, "of all the stories about soldiers returning from Vietnam drenched in the spittle of anti-war protesters. It didn't happen."

Dave said he had definitely heard of Vietnam veterans who were spat upon, and he added that when he took graduate courses at Portland State University in the early 1970's, he learned it was best to keep silent about his time in Vietnam. He said these things gently and added that the ground war might not be the horror I imagined. Without saying a word about it, he reminded me that he'd seen bodies lined up along the streets of Hue after the Tet Offensive, and he'd called in napalm close to his own position to protect his men. Once again, I wondered if I could ever imagine my way into the reality he knew. And I doubted Dave would ever lead us to the Fox Creek forest.

My reasons for wanting to find Fox Creek were both therapeutic and political. My wildest therapeutic imagining probably owed a lot to Leslie Marmon Silko's novel *Ceremony* (1977) about Tayo, a Laguna Pueblo Indian. Tayo returns from fighting in World War II and watching his cousin Rocky die on the Bataan Death March, suffering in part from what we have come to call post-traumatic shock disorder. I longed to play the role of Silko's Navajo shaman, Betonie, who works out a complex ceremony in the mountains of New Mexico that begins Tayo's healing. My hunch was that if I could persuade Dave to return to the woods after more than twenty years of forest avoidance, the ceremony would happen on its own. It might be something like psychoanalysis, I thought, dredging up and purifying dark

181

memories of the war and reminding Dave of how the woods can be a place of peace and beauty.

Another ex-Marine figured in my political motives. Doug Ray had served in El Salvador during the years when the Reagan administration made fighting Communism in Central America the cornerstone of our foreign policy. Now, in 1991, Ray was trying to keep Cavenham Forest Industries from logging a piece of land at the edge of the Fox Creek forest. His fear, shared by several local citizens and a biologist from Oregon's Department of Fish and Wildlife, was that clear-cutting near Fox Creek would make the ancient forest there vulnerable to winter storms coming in off the Pacific and damage biological diversity in adjoining wetlands. Although Ray and his allies could have based their crusade on two endangered species, the Marbled Murrelet, and the Cope's salamander, they chose instead to make the broader case for protecting biological diversity on Saddle Mountain. A local biology teacher, Neal Maine, who had been Doug Ray's mentor in high school and our daughter Annie's biology teacher in 1980-81, influenced their choice. Law suits aimed at preserving old growth forest in the Pacific Northwest often relied on the Endangered Species Act, claiming old trees are necessary habitat for the Northern Spotted Owl, but those suits could be warped into debates that seemed to pit owls against logging communities. Neal Maine urged Doug Ray and his allies "not to default to the rhetoric of single-critter protection," as he put it, and they didn't.

When I first met Doug Ray, he was a young entrepreneur who owned three clothing stores in Seaside and Cannon Beach. He wore a tee shirt and jeans, and with his close-cropped hair, ruddy complexion, and solid build, he had the look of someone who might spend a lot of time hunting and fishing, as he did. He grew up in Seaside, where his father was a logger. After graduating from Seaside High School in 1975, he worked in town for three years and then joined the Marines. During his five years in the Marines, he married a woman from Denmark, and they returned to Seaside in 1983 to go into the retail clothing business. If this doesn't fit the profile of a man who would take the lead in defending a small forest against a powerful corporation, using a rather complex argument for biological diversity, it's because I haven't told about Neal Maine.

For Doug Ray, Neal Maine seems to have been a teacher whose influence rests like a dormant seed, waiting for the right circumstance to germinate. One of Maine's primary teaching techniques was to send the young Doug out of the classroom, where he was bored, to Saddle Mountain. When he found the kid was interested in fossils, he encouraged him to search for marine fossils in the same Miocene outcropping on Saddle Mountain that interested my mother. Ray became a passionate fossil hunter, but the effect of his field experience wasn't apparent as promptly as educational evaluators and standardized tests demand. It took about fifteen years.

Maine knew how to find the Fox Creek forest by driving on a web of logging roads northwest of Saddle Mountain, and that knowledge led Doug Ray to get back in touch with his old biology teacher in 1989. Ray had been reading about ancient forests, and one of his father's old friends, a logger, told him of a forest on Saddle Mountain that could give a person the feel for what the Coast Range was like when Lewis and Clark arrived in the nineteenth century. People driving through second-growth trees along Highway 26 from Portland might think they knew what ancient forests were, he said, but this was the real thing. Doug Ray had been thinking about why he was drawn back to the north coast of Oregon with his Danish wife, and he knew it had a lot to do with the land. In fact, he had begun to give mini-lectures to customers at the espresso bar in one of his stores, telling them about inter-tidal zones, hiking trails, hidden coves, and surprising vistas. They spent time shopping in the midst of so much natural beauty, Ray guessed, because they knew so little about the land and the ocean. Sometimes they came back to the store just to thank him for encouraging them to look around. He didn't tell them about the Fox Creek forest because he thought of it as a place Neal Maine was trying to protect from the designs of progress.

But Ray made frequent visits to Fox Creek after Neal Maine told him how to find it. Sometimes he took friends; more often he went there alone. Then in early April of 1991 he took friends from Denmark and Australia and found tags on second-growth hemlocks and several older trees, right up to the edge of the ancient forest. "My dad was a logger," Ray reminded me, "and I knew what those tags meant." They meant Cavenham Forest Industries would soon cut all those trees unless someone intervened, and Ray's reading in forest ecology had convinced him the 100-acre patch of old growth would be endangered by clear-cutting to its very edge. So he went home and called Oregon's Parks department and several other agencies, asking what could be done to provide a buffer zone for the old growth, especially to protect the habitat along an unnamed tributary to Fox Creek. People in several offices told him the matter was out of their hands.

A few days later, Ray went alone to Fox Creek and on his way found loggers clear-cutting just a mile and a half from the edge of the forest he wanted to save. He saw two Hairy Woodpeckers trying to find their way into a nesting cavity that had come down with a fallen tree. At Fox Creek, sitting with his back against a huge tree, he fell asleep, and like Rip Van Winkle when he awakened, Ray thought the world had changed as he opened his eyes. A black-tail doe—characteristically very shy—was standing within a few feet of him, and Ray took it as a sign that he was destined to protect the Fox Creek forest.

He made more phone calls. He talked with people in Oregon's Department of Forestry, the Parks Department, and the Department of Fish and Wildlife. He called the Governor's office. He asked a Cavenham executive for a delay in logging the parcel near Fox Creek. He sought advice from the Forest Conservation Council, the Audubon Society, the Nature Conservancy, the Oregon Coast Range Association, the Wilderness Society, and Oregon's Natural Resources Council. Most of the people "shined him off," as Ray put it. There was nothing they could do. Then he invited a reporter from the *Oregonian* to come to visit Fox Creek, and he made more phone calls. Sometimes he made several calls in one day to individuals slow to get back to him, and he stirred up anger among potential allies. It was his first attempt at environmental activism, and he made mistakes.

While he waged his telephone campaign and tried to get the *Oregonian* interested, Ray sought the help of a local environmental organization, the North Coast Land Conservancy. Founded in 1986, the local conservancy had already bought endangered wetlands in Seaside and a nesting site for Bald Eagles along the Columbia River near Astoria. The organization was working to protect other endangered habitat in the area, and its president, not surprisingly, was local biology teacher Neal Maine. The conservancy's board agreed to have Maine and Ray develop a proposal for a land swap to submit to Cavenham Forest Industries and Oregon's Parks Department. The idea was for the state to trade land from Saddle Mountain State Park for the parcel of land near Fox Creek. They based their proposal, "Fox Creek: Habitat Diversity Worth Saving," on the importance of protecting both genetic diversity within species found at Fox Creek and the rare species that need such habitat to survive.

In the meantime, on July 1, 1991, reporter Kathie Durbin published "Battle Over the Mountain" in the *Oregonian*, a well-researched article about Doug Ray's attempt to keep Cavenham from logging up to the edge of the Fox Creek old growth. Durbin mentioned the Cope's salamander, the Marbled Murrelet, and even the Spotted Owl, but the thrust of her article was to explain the broader concern for biological diversity. "Ecologically," Durbin wrote, "this pocket of old growth and wetlands belongs to Saddle Mountain, a botanically rich island of virgin, coastal forest and wildflower-carpeted bluffs in a sea of clear-cuts." It was the "sea of clear-cuts" that worried Doug Ray and his allies, some 800 acres logged since 1988 on land surrounding Saddle Mountain.

The "Battle Over the Mountain" had heated up by late August, when Nancy and I set out to find our way into the old growth. Rather than use the web of logging roads that leads to the northwestern edge of the Fox Creek forest, we planned to park our car in Saddle Mountain State Park as though we were about to climb the trail to the summit. But instead of walking east through the campground and up the trail, we proposed to go west through a small picnic ground and then north on elk trails to find Fox Creek on foot. We planned to sleep among the giant trees. To do that, we needed help from a reconnaissance specialist who knew how to use a topographic map and a compass.

Dave never seems to have doubted that we'd go to Fox Creek, but when Nancy and I arrived in Oregon in August, we had to change our plans a bit. Initially, we intended to take food for three days and two nights, enough for Nancy, Dave and his seventeen-year-old son, Chris, and me. We hoped to sleep our first night next to Fox Creek and spend the next two days circling the mountain, trying to find an unnamed, smaller stand of old growth on the southeast flank of the mountain, identifiable in aerial photographs. Maps suggested that we'd be able to find plenty of water along the way.

A few days before we were set to go, Dave's wife, Karen, and their eleven-year-old daughter, Kate, asked if they could join the expedition. Owners of small family businesses generally find it hard to carve three days out of their schedules for something as frivolous as a backpacking trip, and as it became clear that Dave was actually going to do this, our expedition began to look exciting. Neither Karen nor Kate had ever backpacked, and when I mentioned our expanding party to local friends, they suggested that we sleep in the campground at night and take day hikes to find the Fox Creek forest. But Karen and Kate were outraged by that suggestion. They had borrowed backpacks, and they weren't signing up for two nights in a Saddle Mountain suburb. We settled on a compromise: we would backpack out to Fox Creek and spend our first night there, hoping to find our way back to the campground for the second night.

So we set out through the Saddle Mountain picnic grounds on the morning of August 24, a day on which all the instruments agreed rain was likely. On the ocean side of Saddle Mountain a prediction of rain carries with it the sense of inevitability that accompanies tidal charts, but our spirits were high nevertheless. After walking through the picnic grounds and into a thicket dominated by alder we turned north on an elk trail. Kate and Chris seemed determined not to act like tenderfeet, and they wrestled their packs through heavy underbrush without complaining. Dave led the way with the topographic map enclosed in plastic, and I was in the rear. Within minutes we found ourselves in a forest without much undergrowth, grazed back by deer and elk, and the alder trees got larger and farther apart. Open spaces were blanketed with fern and moss, and the grass looked almost as though it had been mowed. Occasional rays of sunlight made bright patches on the smooth, light-skinned alder trunks.

When I walked up to join Dave so I could look at the map, he flashed a hand signal at me without looking back, and then he turned around with a sheepish grin and said he'd forgotten there was no reason to maintain noise discipline. A few minutes later, when the two of us climbed out on a rock outcropping to check ridge lines against the map, Dave showed me where he would have had me stop to cover him as he moved out into the open. That was the last echo of Vietnam. Increasingly, Dave seemed wholly focused on finding Fox Creek and pointing out changes in the landscape. Occasionally, he left his pack with us and went ahead to find a way over difficult terrain. He seemed, Nancy whispered to me, "quietly ecstatic."

We began in alder, light-colored hardwood trees that grow quickly in logged-over areas. If we'd been on Cavenham land, the alders would have been killed with herbicides to make room for more saleable conifers, although within a few years alder became too valuable to kill. It makes beautiful furniture, and in a few years we would buy a table made from Oregon alder. We had been advised to follow elk trails around the west side of Saddle Mountain, but Dave soon realized that not all elk trails lead toward Fox Creek, and the rest of us understood that even though a full-grown elk can stand five feet at the shoulder and weigh 1000 pounds, they sometimes travel in places where people with backpacks are hard-pressed to go. For two hours we moved mainly north through underbrush and alder on land that had once been logged over, seeing an occasional Sitka spruce. Then we began to get glimpses of large trees ahead, jutting far above the alder canopy, and after that we encountered an ancient red cedar, its trunk twenty feet around at the base and sinewy, as though it were fused from many smaller trees. Gray-green moss covered fallen trees and limbs, and large-leafed clover carpeted small clearings. Beside the elk trails in spongy clearings, we saw water standing in hoof-prints. Even though it had been an unusually dry August in Clatsop County, there were small springs and seeps on the steep ground. Dave kept us close to the cliffs on the west side of the mountain, but even there the ground was sometimes marshy, and we saw elk wallows so trampled they had the look of cattle pens. I wondered if clear-cutting on the land around Saddle Mountain had driven more elk into the old growth than the steep terrain could support. But though we saw elk droppings and hoof-prints all around us, we saw no elk. We found burrows made by mountain beaver, a brown rodent the size of a small house cat, but we saw no wildlife as we came into the old growth.

Without underbrush to obscure my vision, I watched Dave check the map and circle like a shaman, one hand pointing in the direction he hoped was due north, nodding toward the cliffs as though reassuring himself it all made good sense. By mid-afternoon the light began to change, as though we'd entered a room with a very high ceiling and an indeterminate light source. The only sound we could hear might have been wind in the distant canopy or falling water. It probably wasn't water because when we found the Fox Creek streambed, it was dry. We carried just a quart of water for each of us so the silent, dry streambed made me a little nervous. But we followed it downhill, through ravines made by huge nurse logs, some of them sprouting hemlocks that might have been seedlings when Lewis and Clark arrived on the Columbia River in 1806. Huge, fallen trees were everywhere on the steep terrain, making movement here at least as difficult as finding our way through undergrowth. Sometimes our best route was along the trunk of a giant log even when it led only approximately in the direction we wanted to travel. Kate, who had more trouble climbing onto the logs and over them with her pack than the rest of us, began to tire. Slender, bespectacled, shy with her aunt and uncle from Ohio, she seemed to be quietly struggling to keep her spirits from collapsing as we moved downhill, looking for water and a level place to sleep.

The water was audible before we saw it, a sound like wind in the trees. It gathered quickly in the creek bed as we moved down its course through terrain so steep there were falls and pools every few feet. We soon stopped beside the creek, and Dave left his pack with us while he looked downstream for level ground. He was gone for half an hour, and the five of us sat talking quietly beneath a giant cedar. We could see hemlock and spruce around us too, but we hadn't yet found a Douglas fir, the tree that grows largest of all in Oregon's old growth stands west of the Cascade Mountains. It was evening now, the light beginning to fade, and Dave's return was a little haunting. Sometimes we could hear his movements as though he might step around the next tree, and then there was silence, except for the falling water, as though he were hiding. This uncanny alternation, like a radio station that comes in clearly and then fades away, happened several times as Dave moved back and forth between high and low ground on his return. The ground, he said, got no more level anywhere within reach of our tired legs. He suggested that we move a hundred yards uphill and across Fox Creek to a spot near a small tributary, marked by the feathered remains of a Blue Jay.

Nancy and I pitched our mountain tent with care because of the weather predictions, and Dave used two blue tarps to make a shelter for his family that looked as though it could withstand a violent winter squall. We ate hard rolls with macaroni and cheese for supper, and the food restored Kate's strength so fully that when Dave and I proposed to look around before it got dark, she asked to go along. We headed north, wondering if we might find Cavenham's new clear-cut, but instead we saw our first Douglas firs, foreshortened by wind and lightning but with trunks over thirty feet around. It was growing dark as we turned back, and I heard a call that sounded like a sea bird. It was almost surely not a Marbled Murrelet because it was long past their nesting season, but I told Dave and Kate how Murrelet males and females change places on their nests in old growth at dawn, taking turns in their search for food at sea. Our return was like a replay of Dave's, as we alternately heard Nancy, Chris, and Karen's talk and laughter clearly and then had no sense that they were even nearby.

The blue flame of our propane stove as we walked into our camp in the falling dark was a comforting reminder of the benefits of civilization. I remembered the reassuring lights of Cannon Beach years ago as I came around Silver Point on a very dark night and our recent train ride through the western suburbs of Minneapolis, where cars parked on the streets glistened almost colorlessly in the glare of yellow vapor lights, and blue security lamps gave yards and buildings a harsh, disreputable glow. But minutes later, as we rolled through darkness beyond the city, a pair of red lights on a radio tower seemed as beautiful as rubies. I recalled too my descent into Costa Rica at night, when tiny lights tracing a mountain village could have been a string of diamonds, and I think now of the young Ben Linder's effort to generate enough hydroelectric power to light a single bulb in each house in the Nicaraguan village of San Jose de Bocay. The farther one gets from the Las Vegas excesses of our culture, the easier it is to appreciate the importance, the beauty, of electricity and fire.

Our tent was no more than twenty feet from the shelter Dave built for his family, but a giant cedar log between us made Dave, Karen, Chris, and Kate seem far away. Nancy and I talked for a while, and then their laughter began to drift over the log. It grew in volume and continued for more than an hour—joyous, riotous laughter. We talked of calling the State Police to break up the party next door, and I thought of Nathaniel Hawthorne, who would have been fascinated by such laughter ringing through a forest in New England. I wondered how Hawthorne might have understood Karen's beautifully musical laughter because she was so often silent. Her work as a psychiatric nurse in a VA hospital while Dave was in Vietnam seemed to end her love of nursing. Since his return, she had done many things to add to their income in difficult times, answering telephones and cleaning houses before she began to run their office, but she hadn't returned to the profession for which she was trained. Safe with her family in the Fox Creek forest, maybe she felt the war was completely behind them, or so I imagined.

The rain never came. It was a warm, dry night with a nearly full moon that reflected blue light through openings in the forest canopy. In the marshy, temperate rainforest there was not a drop of dew on our tent in the morning. The only moisture was inside, from our respiration. As it grew light, we heard birds in the distance that we couldn't identify, and when I stepped outside, I saw two gray squirrels. The deep quiet of the forest struck me again, and of course no one could tell me the source of the night's wonderful, cascading laughter.

We planned to walk west, away from the mountain, to see more of the old growth, and then Dave figured we could cover new ground on our way back to the campground and our cars. When we neared the edge of the old growth, where we stopped for lunch, we found a stainless steel cup and a very old beer bottle, the first signs of civilization that we weren't carrying since we walked out of the picnic ground. Before we turned back, we glimpsed a large clear-cut through the trees and a plantation that appeared to be all hemlock. Despite our compass and topographic map and Dave's determination to keep us moving west, we realized as we started back that the lay of the land had taken us farther north than we intended. Our return trip would be longer than we expected. Dave and I developed a contingency plan: if our expedition members began to tire, we'd walk directly west to a logging road, and Chris and I, youthful baseball player and aging jogger, would leave our packs to follow logging roads to our cars. Our plan began to look very good when we came to the edge of the Fox Creek forest and crossed into Cavenham land, where logging had left the land nearly impassable with slash and undergrowth. But Dave found a way through the brushy "clear-cut" and back into Saddle Mountain State Park, where we were soon walking through the most beautiful alder forest I've ever seen. The trees were widely spaced in grassy meadows, and the golden light reminded me of a sunny autumn day in an Ohio hardwood forest. We moved up a ridge beside a powerful stream, unnamed on the map, probably flowing southwest into the Lewis and Clark River.

Dave was determined not to miss the parking lot on its southern side, in which case we would strike the paved road that leads to Saddle Mountain. If we had to slog back to the campground on pavement, he feared insurrection. So he led us east instead, back into steep terrain beneath the mountain's western cliffs. It was difficult going, but our expedition team's morale was shored up by coincidence: although we weren't retracing our steps from the day before, we crossed paths with our outbound route and found a pair of sneakers that had been hanging on Karen's pack as we made our way to Fox Creek. Not long after this surprising recovery, I heard Nancy, who was walking in front with Dave, say, "Macadam! Macadam!" This was her New England way of announcing she had spotted the parking lot below us.

Resisting the mountain's tendency to make us drift downhill, Dave brought us back well above the campground, as though we were pioneering a new path to Saddle Mountain's summit.

We slept that night in the campground without putting up the tent or the shelter, and sometime after midnight Nancy and I were awakened by the wild laughter of coyotes that seemed to be coming from where we'd just been. Nancy reminded me of an early morning on Oregon's Paulina Lake in the summer of 1961, when we might as well have been on our honeymoon because our first year together in Baltimore at Johns Hopkins University had gone by so quickly. That morning Nancy wakened me to ask about the barking laughter outside our tent, and I told her it was nothing to worry about, just hyenas. Now we both knew what we were hearing, and we considered waking Dave, Karen, Chris, and Kate. But the coyote laughter and its promise of resilient wildness were no more wonderful than their laughter of the night before with its promise of healing. So we lay awake in moonlight bright enough to read by and listened.

Chapter Seventeen

Wars, Words and Pictures

All bloody principles and practices, we, as to our own particulars, do utterly deny, with all outward wars and strife and fightings with outward weapons, for any end or under any pretence whatsoever. And this is our testimony to the whole world.
—-From Friends Peace Testimony, 1661

On the overcast Sunday morning of May 21, 2006, the Trojan Nuclear Plant's 499-foot cooling tower sank into rubble, imploded by 2,800 pounds of skillfully deployed dynamite. Depending on their perspectives, people seemed to view the tower's fall as the triumphant or tragic end of Oregon's "Trojan War." Lloyd Marbet, one of the activists who had opposed nuclear power in Oregon, told *The Oregonian*: "I hate to see it go. It's a monument to the failure of that technology and to the arrogance of the people promoting it." When a helicopter flew over the tower in the hour before it was demolished, another observer recalled how Ken Lay, the late, convicted chief of Enron, which had swallowed Portland General Electric in 1997, flew in to visit the plant shortly before cutting off the workers' 401(k) plans.

Three weeks after the Trojan tower was demolished, the man billed as "America's deadliest enemy in Iraq," Musab al-Zarqawi, was blasted into history with five companions by two 500-pound bombs. President Bush celebrated this victory in the "war on terror" by making a quick trip to Baghdad. But I wondered what difference it might have made to consider Zarqawi an international criminal, as he was, instead of an enemy combatant in the "war on terror." Collateral damage, taken for granted in war, is unacceptable in fighting crime. When police kill innocent civilians, they can lose

195

their jobs and sometimes go to prison. But dead noncombatants are an acceptable side effect in war. Would the mother and her child who died with Zarqawi have been treated as hostages worthy of protection if Zarqawi had been considered a criminal? And how many missiles and 500-pound bombs, I wondered in that time before drones, have we used to kill innocent people and destroy the wrong houses in Iraq, Afghanistan, and Pakistan because someone thought a deadly enemy was there?

Much of my thinking in recent years, including my ambivalent response to the demolition of the Trojan Nuclear Plant's cooling tower, has probably been influenced by our "war on terror." The "successful" bombing of Zarqawi seemed to be a sign of things to come. We have a history of being suckers for technical fixes, and it's not hard to imagine that even critics of the wars in Iraq and Afghanistan could be drawn to a strategy that increases the amount of bombing while reducing the number of troops on the ground and pulling back those who remain into military enclaves to reduce casualties. "Precision bombing" and "targeted assassinations" and drone strikes have become important parts of our approach to foreign policy. After September 11, 2001, when terrorists turned airliners into bombs, President Bush's instinct was to rely increasingly on the machines of air war, and President Obama's foreign policy has been even more dependent on drones. When Al Qaeda fighters hid in deep caves in the mountains of Afghanistan, President Bush called for a new kind of nuclear bomb that would tunnel into the earth before it exploded. Our increasing use of drones seems to be a variation of this kind of thinking.

Maybe someone will force us to look at the horrific results of air war, as the photographer Nick Ut did when we napalmed the village of Trang Bang in Vietnam. He gave us the famous picture of nine-year-old Kim Phuc

Phan Thi as she ran naked toward the camera, her clothes and her body burned. I wonder how the American public's response to our increasing use of drones might change if the aerial photographs used to document "kills" were made available. The buoyant optimism so crucial to our American character is partly a result of our distance from the horrors of war.

But photographs can be used to make a case for the justice of our "war on terror," as I learned when I wrote a column for a local Ohio paper, *The Granville Sentinel,* criticizing our leaders for trying to make torture a legitimate part of our tactics. A reader responded by saying my column made him ashamed of his town, adding that what our soldiers did at the Abu Ghraib prison was nothing more than "fraternity pranks."

"Because of the secrecy," I wrote back, "it's hard to know what 'fraternity pranks' mean at Abu Ghraib, Guantanamo Bay, and several other bases around the world where suspected terrorists are being interrogated. But it seems clear that people have died as a result and international trust in the United States has diminished." Then I sent the reader a rather long statement from the Friends Committee on National Legislation that makes the case for taking torture very seriously.

As an answer, the reader sent me a series of five photographs. In the first several naked men are piled in a collapsing pyramid in Abu Ghraib, their genitals airbrushed out, a clothed man and woman smiling in the background. The caption is: "You call this an atrocity." In the second photo five hooded terrorists stand behind a bound prisoner, and the caption is: "THIS IS an atrocity." In the third and fourth photos a figure holds a severed head, and the caption reads: "So was this." Finally, there is a photo of the Twin Towers enveloped in smoke and a question: "WHICH PART DON'T YOU GET?"

The loaded question implied in the gathering of photographs might go something like this: "If young

American soldiers, traumatized by what happened to the U.S. on September 11, 2001, have a little fun with terrorist suspects because they know of the horrible things such people do to their prisoners, who can blame them?" But the late Susan Sontag described the shortcoming of such pictorial thinking in her book *On Photography* (1977) when she pointed out that the frozen moment captured in a photograph can oversimplify and sometimes sentimentalize the subject. The feelings evoked by frozen images are often disconnected from a complex story that can be fully expressed only in words.

With some background, the questions raised by the photographs the reader sent are likely to become more complicated. Does the picture taken at Abu Ghraib, for example, offer only a hint of what happens when our political culture embraces the techniques of "dirty war"? What kind of leadership makes young soldiers want to be photographed as they humiliate prisoners? If we teach young soldiers to be proud of torturing others, what have we done to the soldiers? If we justify torture by saying our enemies commit atrocities, what have we done to ourselves, and where does it end?

We need words to get at the truth behind photographs, and the words we choose are crucial. When we get serious about eradicating a problem in our society, we're drawn to the language of war, to the word *war* itself. We often declare metaphorical war on the problem. Hoping to put an end to destitution, we declared a *war on poverty*, but other concerns led to an unannounced armistice. When the violence and disease linked with addiction began to worry us, we called our response a *war on drugs*, often understood as a part of a larger *war on crime*. Terrified by "terrorism," our leaders declared war on terror. Poverty, drug addiction, crime, and terrorism are problems that cannot be solved by war, but we invest hope in the unrelenting commitment, the use of naked power, suggested by the war metaphor. A nation at war places few restrictions on itself and its leaders, and that fact suggests both the strength of the metaphor and its dangerous weakness.

Our "war on drugs" reveals some of the dangers in the metaphor. We hold in prisons all over our country today people who might be thought of as collateral damage in the war on drugs. Many of them serve long sentences, not because they killed or maimed someone, but because they were caught with illegal drugs, and in thousands of cases the drug is marijuana. My old friend Terry has done time in prisons as a user. He came close to being tried under California's "three strikes" law that could have put him in prison for life, and his situation was not unusual: many drug offenders serving life sentences in our prison system have never been convicted of a violent crime. In some jurisdictions an offender can serve a longer sentence for possessing crack cocaine than for taking a human life. This is one cost of our "war" on drugs.

In 1994 I accompanied a regional American Friends Service Committee group to meet with several lifers at the Gus Harrison Facility in Adrian, Michigan. None of the men who met with us had been convicted of a violent crime. Their life sentences, in most cases, resulted from repeated drug convictions. We had only one hour together, and several inmates wanted to talk about how their lives had been influenced by the changing politics of crime. They deferred to each other, giving the quietest among them opportunities to speak. A musician told of a time in prison when he had been allowed to practice almost every day. In 1994 he was lucky if he was able to spend an hour a week with his guitar. Another man, an artist who had been allowed several shows on the outside while he was in prison, told how he was now forced to give up the art supplies he had collected over several years. In 1994 he was permitted a box of pastel chalks and a small tablet. These changes and others like them, the inmates said, didn't result from broken rules or state-mandated regulations. They were decrees from a warden responding to political pressure. They were part of a national trend away from rehabilitation and toward increasing use of isolation in what critics began to call "the prison-industrial complex." They were victims, I now realize, in our "war on drugs."

No matter how carefully the strategies of a war are planned, its results are usually unpredictable, disorderly, and chaotic. Critics congratulated Steven Spielberg for capturing the horrifying chaos of World War II in his film *Saving Private Ryan*, and we know the B-52 flying several miles above Afghanistan, visible only by its contrail even on the clearest of days, relying on powerful computers to take account of distance, wind speed, the enemy's reported position, and other variables, often rains death and chaos on the innocent.

The usually circumspect *New York Times* allowed itself this headline on November 18, 2001: "Surprise. War Works After All." Eric Schmitt's article under that banner is a celebration of the sudden crumbling of Taliban control in Afghanistan as a result of our bombing and the energized Northern Alliance's advances on the ground. "Just as Americans were staggered nine weeks ago to find their homeland vulnerable to terrorism on a horrifying scale," Schmitt wrote, "now they had reason to question old fears of frustration and quagmire." Those fears returned.

But there are older and darker fears of war than frustration and quagmire, as we learned again in Iraq. In addition to the killing of innocents, there is the uncontrollable momentum of war that leaves political objectives in its dust. In the early years of our war in Iraq we killed tens of thousands of noncombatants, destroyed infrastructure, and fostered the hatred that is the crucial fuel for terrorism.

Chapter Eighteen

Isolation and Imagination

> The northern wing [of New York's Auburn prison] having been nearly finished in 1821, eighty prisoners were placed there, and a separate cell was given to each. This trial, from which so happy a result had been anticipated, was fatal to the greater part of the convicts: in order to reform them, they had been submitted to complete isolation; but this absolute solitude, if nothing interrupt it, is beyond the strength of man; it destroys the criminal without intermission and without pity; it does not reform, it kills.
>
> (Gustave de Beaumont and Alexis de Tocqueville, *The Penitentiary System in the United States*, 1833).

We live in a time when people text or tweet or check their status on Facebook while they drive a potentially lethal car, rendered socially irresponsible by their conviction that life is primarily a performance lived online. People share news of their daily grind or post embarrassing photographs, maybe hoping something will "go viral" and reach well beyond their virtual friends and communities. They might achieve celebrity. Few seem to fear a loss of privacy, perhaps because they fear boredom and isolation more. And at the same time our culture has shifted in the direction of online unreality, virtual communities, we have increasingly used isolation as punishment in our prisons.

My interest in prisons began in 1960, when I visited the federal penitentiary in Leavenworth, Kansas. An English professor, Peter Hilty, invited me to join him at the graduation of that year's Dale Carnegie class in Leavenworth, and initially the evening played into some of my stereotypes of inmates and their world. Architecturally, the prison itself seemed more like a medieval castle than the nondescript high school many modern prisons have become. Halls echoed and gates clanked. The prisoners gave graduation speeches that celebrated the Dale Carnegie method of positive thinking, saying nothing about the fact that they were serving time in a federal prison. I thought they were engaged in elaborate self-delusion, which was more or less what I expected of them.

But seated just to my right was my professor's star pupil in his Leavenworth writing class, a lifer who was interested in my plans for graduate school and my thoughts about the world outside. He seemed interested in just about everything, even the speeches, and he kept up whispered, ironic commentary. When a speaker told proudly of how he made money at the Kentucky Derby by buying programs outside the gates and selling them for more inside, the lifer whispered to me, "Forget Johns Hopkins, try Churchill Downs." Later, as we sat at a table drinking coffee with a few prisoners, my professor said something polite about the graduation exercises, and the lifer responded quietly with what seemed to me the truth: the Dale Carnegie class appeared to be a training program for con men.

For a long time I thought of the Leavenworth lifer as an exception when I thought about inmates at all. Then my oldest friend, Terry, went to prison twice on drug convictions in the late 1980's, and although our friendship had fallen on hard times, I knew he fit none of my assumptions about the people in our prisons. He had never stolen anything, and although he was a skilled boxer when he was young, he was never a violent adult. He'd become a gentle, very loving father. He resorted to illegal drugs, it seemed to me, as a way of medicating depression after prescribed lithium gave him no relief, and later his use of drugs became inseparable from a transcendental faith that in recent years has led him deeply into Buddhism. Terry was never held in isolation, but his experience was difficult enough that when he faced the possibility of a third conviction, he said he planned to leave the country and told a reporter he would choose suicide rather than go to prison again. Thanks perhaps to California's seriously overcrowded prison system, he remained outside the walls.

In 1998, I met a class of long-term prisoners at Green Haven prison in Stormville, New York. On that visit, I accompanied several Vassar College students who were scheduled to teach a class normally taught by the inmates themselves. The students had been attending the class for several weeks, and on this evening some of them led a discussion titled "Communities Under Attack." They invited prisoners to comment on passages from a book by Jerome Miller, *Search and Destroy: African American Males in the Criminal Justice System* (1996). Except for one Latino, all of the inmates in the class were African American. In 1926 our prisons held almost 80% white men, according to Jerome Miller, but by 1993 the proportion was down to 27%. The change was largely a result of the growing numbers of African American men who began to fill our prisons. Young men in the black communities of America stand a very good chance statistically of going to prison, and they are sent there for many reasons, according to Miller, some of them violations that would be likely to earn someone like me, white and middle class, a stern reprimand. Many are serving long terms after being caught in the war on drugs. None of this surprised the men in the class, and they added powerful stories to the ones from Miller's book.

After more than an hour, another Vassar student took over. She lectured the class on environmental justice, pointing out that toxic waste dumps and polluting industries cluster around minority communities. Make a map, she said, of the most dangerously polluted parts of our country and another map of our poorest minority neighborhoods, urban and rural. Now superimpose the maps, and you will find they are almost the same. Again, this was not news to the prisoners. They had noticed sewage treatment plants, toxic waste incinerators, and chemical plants in their own neighborhoods. And they had already dismissed the argument that polluting industries bring jobs to their communities. They spoke of the importance of community organizing to resist such injustice and they talked about ways of holding local politicians accountable.

But the student insisted on another view. The key, she said, is the power of the consumer. Careful, knowledgeable buying, she argued, can bring environmental justice. A mutual respect between the prisoners and the students was apparent in this discussion. The young woman's certainty that careful consumerism is the answer for prisoners whose families and neighbors are unlikely to be big spenders seemed to flow from the innocence of great privilege. The men spoke gently, without sarcasm, as they talked about the need for community activism. Having studied together for years, they were skilled at discussion, comfortable with each other, and seemingly confident of their ability to disagree without causing bad feelings.

By the time I visited Green Haven in the fall of 1998, federal and state funding for education in prisons had dried up. Isolation was the growing trend in criminal justice. But it would have been hard for anyone to sit through the meeting at Michigan's Gus Harrison Facility, the class at New York's Green Haven, or even the conversation that followed the Dale Carnegie class graduation at Leavenworth in 1960 without recognizing the possibility of rehabilitation in that kind of human contact.

In December of 1999 I began to correspond with an inmate I'll call Clark in the Ohio State Penitentiary (OSP), the state's newly built "supermax." He was twenty-nine, and he claimed to be innocent of the crime for which he was convicted at seventeen although one of his attorneys wrote to me of his "heinous" crime. In 1998 Clark had been transferred from the maximum-security prison in Lucasville to the OSP in Youngstown for attacking another prisoner with a knife, which Clark claimed he did in self-defense.

I began writing to Clark as part of a Quaker "pen pal" project that focused on people in isolation. In one of his first letters Clark mentioned that his next-door neighbor in their pod spent much of the day and night shouting and pounding on his door. "I tried to help him out," Clark wrote, "but he disrespected me, I think he is kind of crazy, he seriously need some help." A few weeks later, Clark responded to my suggestion that his neighbor might not mean to be disrespectful but might simply be feeling uncontrollable rage:

> No, my next door neighbor is not doing anything out of anger, he got it in his mind that everybody owes him something in life, not only that I can hear him talking to himself & sometimes it sounds as if he is talking to 3 or 4 people, by how he be laughing and yelling at himself, so I know he's crazy, & and I also know he does not belong in this prison.
>
> Bill, you got to realize I know who is playing crazy and who is crazy.

Within a month of mentioning his loud, crazy neighbor, Clark reported that a woman with the American Friends Service Committee (AFSC) "hooked him up with a pen pal and now he is quiet."

In *Lucasville: The Untold Story of a Prison Uprising* (2004), a book that critiques the thinking that shapes much incarceration, historian Staughton Lynd quotes from an 1890 Supreme Court decision, *In re Medley*, which describes the effects of extended isolation on prisoners in terms that agree with Beaumont and Tocqueville's account:

> A considerable number of the prisoners fell, even after a short confinement, into a semi-fatuous condition, from which it was next to impossible to arouse them, and others became violently insane; others still, committed suicide; while those who stood the ordeal better were not generally reformed, and in most cases did not recover sufficient mental activity to be of any subsequent service to the community.

For almost a century after *Medley* solitary confinement was used mainly as an extraordinary form of punishment within our country's prison system. Then the federal penitentiary in Marion, Illinois, adopted "permanent lock-down" in 1983 as a response to violence and the growing influence of gangs in the prison, and "control units" for isolating inmates began to spring up all over the country. Prisoners in "supermaxes" usually spend at least twenty-three hours a day alone in tiny cells. They eat, exercise, and shower alone, often living in these conditions with no knowledge of how long their punishment will last.

We know more about the psychological effects of isolation now than Gustave de Beaumont and Alexis de

Tocqueville did when they came from France to study our prisons. Psychologists and psychiatrists report that sensory deprivation can cause hallucinations, confusion, and psychotic behavior. Isolation is especially destructive when people experience it as an arbitrary form of punishment with no fixed end. But despite all the evidence of its inhumanity, the practice gained increasing popularity in the U.S. after 1983 and for several years it was the subject of surprisingly little criticism.

In a prison system that puts little emphasis on rehabilitation while housing more and more people who would have been held in asylums for the mentally ill years ago, a sense of isolation seems to be part of inmates' experience even when they're not in solitary confinement. In 2003 I rode a bus with a man who said he'd just been released from Ohio's Pickaway Correctional Institution and was headed home after twenty-three years. I'd noticed him as we waited to board in Columbus. Loud and restless, carrying no luggage, he wore jeans, a plaid flannel shirt, and new work boots. His dark blond hair was combed straight back, and his handsome face had the pinched look of a man who might be younger than he appeared. He was forty-three, he said, and he'd been in prison since he was nineteen. He'd found religion in prison, he told anyone who cared to listen, and that helped him do his time. He planned to sit down and cry with his mother for a while and then take a shower, he said. He wanted to find out what was happening out here in the world, and he needed to get a cell phone right away.

In Springfield, Ohio, a younger man, just released from Ohio's London Correctional Institution, joined the conversation, and the emphasis changed. The older parolee had killed a man twenty-four years ago, he said, and he still believed it was justified. He'd done eleven years in Lucasville and survived the 1993 riot that became the justification for building Ohio's "supermax," the Ohio State Penitentiary. There was anger mixed with joy in his voice now. As we pulled out of Springfield, he shouted that he'd soon be "fucking home." The bus driver, a woman, slowed down and shouted back that he might not get home right away if he used that kind of language. I could hear the anger and the years away from women pent up like dark water behind a dam as the parolee asked the driver what she meant to do about it. She pulled the bus to a stop and turned around to say she would have him removed from the bus, and I assumed the people who took him away would have guns and badges and wouldn't put him up in a motel. The parolee was silent until she set the bus in motion again, and then he asked if she really would have put him off the bus. When the driver said yes, he admitted he believed her. As the two parolees began to talk again, they focused on what helped them do their time in prison, and they spoke of letters. Their correspondents had been mainly inmates in other prisons, they said, people who understood the corrosive power of loneliness, and they both intended to write to their friends still in prison.

Solitude can be a very good thing. After my granddaughter Ana went to camp, she told me of her delight in a "solo" experience, several hours spent alone on a little island in a lake, with time to think and write and listen to the sounds of summer. Most religious traditions affirm the restorative power of solitude when it is chosen, not felt as exclusion from human community. And it seems clear that some people withstand the psychological effects of prolonged, enforced isolation better than others. A few years ago I worked with a man I'll call Harold who spent forty years in prison, four of them in "the hole." Harold was in his mid-sixties when we became acquainted, and we occasionally traveled together from Columbus to meetings in Chicago and Ann Arbor. His years in isolation came more than two decades ago in Arizona. An African-American who had murdered a white drug dealer, Harold claimed white supremacists had put out a contract on him, and the inmate who was supposed to kill him bragged about it. Harold's response was to enter the gang member's cell on his way to breakfast and stab the man several times with a sharpened toothbrush, believing if he survived the fight, he'd be placed in isolation.

Both men survived, and Harold was put in the hole, as he expected. Although isolation is sometimes used to protect inmates from the general population in prisons, Harold wasn't sure he'd be safe. Sometimes, he said, inmates were able to smuggle gasoline into the Hole to douse someone and throw a match in their cell. Harold thought about that possibility when he heard someone walk past his cell. Fear is common response in extended isolation, and Harold claimed he found great comfort in reading. The only shock he remembers from his four years in the Hole had to do with women: his Arizona prison began to hire women as correction officers to work with the general population while he was in isolation. When he came out of the Hole, he said, the presence of women with authority made him feel as though the world had been turned upside down.

Walking in Chicago, Harold seemed fearless. He talked comfortably with people I would have avoided, including drunks and men asking for money. Just once, in an Indianapolis bus station, he seemed nervous when a group of teenage boys he called "gangbangers" roamed restlessly around us, seemingly looking for trouble. He was still on probation then, and I suspect he worried about the possibility of an incident likely to involve the police. A handsome, muscular man, well over six feet tall, Harold usually appeared supremely self-confident, which must be a requirement for holding onto one's sanity through years of isolation.

On February 25, 2002, Federal Judge James S. Gwin issued an opinion that ultimately freed another

African American inmate who seemed able to withstand the effects of isolation. The man I'll call Lawrence, another of my correspondents at Ohio's supermax, should never have been put in solitary confinement. He was apparently a victim of the state's need to fill its most expensive prison. It costs much more to confine someone in a supermax rather than a maximum-security prison. Completed in 1998, the OSP cost $65 million, which amounts to over $129,000 for each of the 502 cells. The penitentiary initially reported a $22 million annual budget, which amounted to almost $44,000 annually for each inmate when the prison was full. Since 2002, when the OSP first came under scrutiny in federal court, the prison hasn't been full in spite of transferring most of the state's death row inmates to the supermax in 2005.

In April of 1993, at the age of 22, Lawrence began serving a sentence of three to fifteen years for armed robbery, a first offense, at Ohio's medium security Orient Correctional Institution. In 1998 he was charged with assaulting a correction officer while intoxicated. A discipline committee at Orient placed him in isolation and recommended that his classification level remain the same and he *not* be transferred to Ohio's supermax. The Orient warden agreed. The local prosecutor's office dismissed a criminal indictment against Lawrence that resulted from the alleged assault. Despite those recommendations and the lack of an indictment, Chief Bernard Ryznar of Ohio's Bureau of Classification raised Lawrence's security classification three levels, from medium to high maximum security, and moved him to the supermax in October of 1998.

Why would a state official ignore a unanimous recommendation from professionals working with an inmate and isolate a first offender in a facility designed for "the worst of the worst"? Judge James Gwin, responding in February of 2002 to a class action suit brought by the American Civil Liberties Union of Ohio and the Center for Constitutional Rights, wrote in his 56-page opinion that the state might be putting people in isolation simply because of its large investment in the Ohio State Penitentiary. "The opening of the OSP has created too much capacity for the highest level of security," Judge Gwin said. "After the huge investment in the OSP, Ohio risks having a 'because we have built it, they will come' mind set." Judge Gwin found, too, that prisoners in the supermax "face an atypical and significant hardship" and that almost 200 men were transferred there in 1998 and early 1999 without an adequate hearing.

While Lawrence was serving time in isolation at Ohio's supermax, according to Judge Gwin, he participated in programs and complied with prison rules. "The only exceptions," the judge writes, "were attempting to share a newspaper with another inmate and being found with an altered radio because a screw had come out of the radio cover." A reclassification committee decided to keep Lawrence at the supermax despite more than a year of good behavior, Judge Gwin reports. After more than two years the committee recommended that he be removed from the supermax with his classification reduced, but they were overruled by Ohio prison administrators. Although parole board guidelines recommended parole after 48 to 60 months for a first-time offender convicted of armed robbery, Lawrence could not be paroled even after he had served over 90 months because he was classified as high maximum security.

A few months after Judge Gwin rendered his opinion in February of 2002, Lawrence was transferred, reclassified, and paroled. As with thousands of men who are punished with years of isolation, one wonders how well his experience prepared him to face life on the outside. After Lawrence had spent three years in Ohio's supermax, I asked for his assessment of isolation's effects on prisoners. "I really do not feel that society knows or even cares about the effects of this type of isolation," he wrote. "The truth is they should be scared to death because many of these men will be in their community one day soon. This place will take all of a man's human qualities and destroy them."

Lawrence believed he eluded the destructive power of isolation. "I have been blessed to remain strong mentally and physically in the Belly of the Beast," he wrote. "I try to look at it as intellectual isolation rather than solitary confinement." Despite his sense of intellectual isolation, Lawrence kept up on current events, and his correspondence revealed considerable knowledge of history. Once, for example, I mentioned my work on a novel about the slave who accompanied the Lewis and Clark Expedition, and Lawrence wrote to tell me several things he had read about York. He asked to read the manuscript, which I was allowed to mail to him in small pieces, and he provided helpful commentary. As for his physical condition, Lawrence once described at length the grueling workout schedule he followed in his cell. "I'm in what I call 'animal shape,'" he concluded. "A few guys have tried to work out with me but [they] only last for the first couple of days and then never call over to me to work out again."

In the summer of 2007 I talked with a young physician who had recently begun to practice in a Michigan prison. His clinic was understaffed, and he sometimes had to cancel all his appointments in a given day just to address emergencies. The prison diet, he said, was adequate but not healthy, and most of the inmates took poor care of themselves on the outside. Hepatitis was common. The result was a prison population much less healthy than most people of similar ages on the outside. But the mutual trust required for good patient care was nearly impossible to cultivate in prison, he said. Not only do prisoners seek painkillers and other drugs to help them do their time, but almost anything doctors typically provide patients can mean a valuable privilege in prison. Crutches, for example, can get an inmate to the front of a food line, and deciding whether a patient seeking crutches truly needs them can be difficult. In a society that fails to provide good healthcare for many millions of its citizens, it would be surprising if more than two million prison inmates were decently cared for, and they are not.

Institutions that imprison people in ways known to induce mental illness don't provide adequate treatment, and predictably, one result can be suicide. In April of 2000 an inmate named Richard Pitts hanged himself at Ohio's supermax, the third suicide since the OSP opened in 1998. Pitts had been transferred to the supermax because he was trained in martial arts. Inmates on Richard Pitts' pod said he appeared to fall quickly into depression from being isolated, and he sought help. When a correction officer found him hanging in his cell, according to inmates, there was a delay while officers formed an "extraction team" to enter his cell together in a wedge and apply leg irons and handcuffs. Although Pitts was dead, OSP procedures required that his body be put in restraints before medical personnel could enter.

The mantra repeated by politicians and correction professionals, that these men are "the worst of the worst," is not always true. In many cases they are not, but people hired to enforce dehumanizing treatment have to try to convince themselves the inmates are less than human, and almost anything they do seems justified. Shortly after inmate Clark exchanged letters with me about his growing interest in the coyotes and wild turkeys he glimpsed in an open field outside his tiny window, a prison administrator at OSP moved him to a cell with a window looking out on a parking lot. It seemed possible the administrator believed it was wrong for an inmate to experience anything resembling joy.

What makes that kind of thinking possible is the assumption that these are dangerous people capable of monstrous acts, and some of them surely are. But in many more cases they are people with whom most of us have much in common, people who might be rehabilitated. As we have withdrawn funds for educational programs in the prisons, they have become, increasingly, universities of crime. If inmates are teaching each other to be more skillful criminals, one obvious solution is to isolate them from each other. This arrangement allows prison administrators to ratchet up punishment in ways largely independent of the courts and gain more control over prisoners without inviting public attention. But because prisons are crowded and the number of prisoners who actually require such high security is relatively small, people are moved into isolation in ways that are sometimes arbitrary and unjust. While our society seems poised to rethink our commitment to capital punishment and maybe even "waterboarding," our increasing use of isolation that "destroys the criminal without intermission and without pity," as Beaumont and Tocqueville put it in 1833, must also be on the agenda.

Chapter Nineteen

Real Estate Realities

The octagonal cabin Nancy and I bought on the Oregon coast as a substitute for the farm we imagined as a home for our Institute increased in value in the 1990's. Large houses rose around us, and the expense of protecting our cabin from the effects of wood rot in a temperate rainforest grew more rapidly than we were willing to raise the rent. We concluded it was time to sell the cabin, and we learned about a federal law, the 1031 Exchange, one of the tax loopholes that help the well-to-do keep on doing well.

Say, for example, you want to sell your private jet and get one with a better sound system, but you'd prefer not to pay taxes on the profit you make: you sell it and put the money in escrow with a 1031 Exchange company that charges a little something for holding the money. Then you're allowed 45 days to identify three new airplanes and 180 days to purchase one of them. Presto! It's a trade, and there's no capital gains tax.

We couldn't buy an executive jet because the law requires that the exchange be for a similar investment property, but this was 1999, with real estate prices rising. We began to look for land closer to our home in Ohio and nearer the eastern side of our family. We considered an ancient farmhouse in the Berkshires, a log chalet on a mountain, and even an island in Ashmere Lake, near Pittsfield, Massachusetts, Nancy's hometown. I was drawn to the idea of a country estate in Granville, Massachusetts, the town that provided pioneers who settled Granville, Ohio. I might have been able to syndicate my newspaper column, "Rambling Around Granville." We found a place in New York's Columbia County, three hours north of New York City—a house

215

that looked a bit like a barn on more than five acres in the rural town of Canaan. I read that a Dutch settler, Lourens Van Alen, bought land west of Canaan from the Mohicans in 1667 for five kettles, three guns, six axes, five cloth garments, six lead bars, 50 pieces of wampum and a few other considerations. If you take inflation into account, our trade for the Oregon cabin seemed to be a good deal.

But of course it wasn't that simple. We had built much of the furniture for the Oregon cabin, and even though it was uncomfortable in its angular simplicity, we hated to give it up, but we couldn't justify trucking it across the country to Canaan. We had built a wall in the octagonal room upstairs and Dave and I laid brick to guard a woodstove. We had won the lawsuit against the neighbors who sent in a bulldozer to knock down our tree and scrape off topsoil for fill on their lot, and we watched our forest lot recover. It was a little like trading an old friend with whom you've shared important memories for someone with whom you might not have much in common.

The house in Canaan was approximately three times as large as the cabin for which we traded it. In addition to its barn-like gambrel roof, an electric garage door opener, and a beautiful brass rooster weather vane, it had a Culligan water softener.

But the most exciting part was the land—5.31 acres. It felt as though we'd finally found our farm. It was almost a right triangle, with a hypotenuse that curved along a dirt road. The curving hypotenuse was somewhat longer than three football fields. One leg stretched more than two football fields, the other just over one, and within that space there were lots of second-growth pine, maple, and oak trees, where someone had worked an upland farm many years earlier. This triangular wilderness, probably abandoned as farmland when people found better topsoil farther west in places like Ohio, started us dreaming agriculturally again. West of Canaan was Roxbury Farm, a large and successful participant in the Community Supported Agriculture movement. Jean-Paul Courtens, a recent Dutch settler, had found a profitable way to grow vegetables for people in Albany and New York City who wanted to know the origins of their food. Kristen Kordet, a Denison graduate who once choreographed and performed a memorable modern dance in the college's Biology Reserve, was an intern on Roxbury Farm when we arrived in the neighborhood, and Kristen could advise us on growing food in Canaan. Just across the Massachusetts border in Pittsfield was my brother-in-law Charlie, who cultivated one of the finest gardens in the area. He could teach us too.

In the meantime urban civilization would bring renters to our door in Canaan. They would come in the summer, real estate people told us, fleeing the City and looking for high culture across the Massachusetts border in the Berkshires, where music, dance, and theatre thrive.

This transcontinental transaction, our real estate trade, was not guilt-free, for we had joined a dubious movement. Internet millionaires and Wall Street moguls from New York City were buying farmland in Columbia County at a terrific pace. Roxbury Farm was an exception to the anti-agricultural rule: it had been twenty years since farmers could afford to buy land in Columbia County. But we had given up on living without self-reproach, and we had no difficulty finding summer renters, just as the real estate people predicted.

When we arrived for our first family Christmas at the Canaan homestead, we were shocked to find evidence of arboreal banditry. There are stories of western men who use helicopters to haul cedar logs out of ancient forests like the one we'd come to love at Fox Creek, and I'd heard of rascals in Kansas who cut down

217

walnut trees on farms while the family is in town shopping, and we had lost a spruce tree to a man deviously building a road across our lot. But when we traded our Oregon cabin for the house and land in Canaan, I thought we were leaving such arboreal outlaws behind. So it was a shock when we found the unmistakable signs of a chainsaw.

This scene differed from the destruction we had found more than twenty years earlier in Oregon. There was no evidence of a bulldozer, and the many oaks and maples cut down were small ones, not much thicker around at the base than my wrist. A few had been cut into stove lengths, but most of them were stretched out where they had fallen. As I piled up trees the size of overgrown fishing poles, I considered the question of motive. We had probably not interrupted a firewood robbery. This was not the kind of wood you choose to stoke a fire, and we had left a cord of seasoned oak under a tarp much closer to the road. Aesthetics seemed a more likely explanation. This chainsaw massacre was done, I guessed, by people who preferred a forest without undergrowth to obstruct the eye. They had in mind something like the beautiful alder forest on Oregon's Saddle Mountain, where elk graze on seedlings and underbrush, giving the woods the appearance of a carefully manicured park. An additional possibility occurred to me: the momentum of technology. If you own a guided missile or a chainsaw, you feel pressure to use it. With a noisy, gas-powered saw you can cut down many little trees in an hour, and you might tell yourself you were doing a favor for the people who owned the land.

My last two hypotheses were close to the truth, as I learned when we returned to Ohio. Our next-door neighbor in Canaan emailed us to explain the fallen trees. They were not felled by bandits but by a legitimate professional working for pay on our new neighbor's land, which I had taken for ours. The crime, if there was one, was my melodramatic building of funeral pyres on land owned by my neighbor, and I apologized.

Yet the ruthless weeding out of the forest was a harbinger of horrors to come. A few months later, machines once again transformed the forest downhill from us. On land I had mistakenly thought we owned, where our grandchildren played in an unnamed creek— or "kill," as they often call creeks in this Dutch-influenced part of New York—a bulldozer, a chainsaw, and a backhoe made a crater large enough to hold our house. This time, however, there would be no work for lawyers. The crater was on our neighbor's property, and unlike the rascals in Oregon who skulked about and refused to discuss what they had done to the land, our New York neighbor, a psychiatrist who sometimes treated writer's block, was happy to talk about the crater. In fact, he made a point of letting us know he had ordered the transformation.

Just two weeks after the machines snorted, wheezed, and screamed the crater into being, even my sadly jaundiced eye could see it was likely to become a beautiful pond within the year. This had once been the site of a farm pond. It was unlikely to give way and cause erosion, as badly constructed ponds sometimes do. The contractor who built it found three underground springs in addition to the little creek, and he lined the outlet with big stones. He knew what he was doing. You could almost say the pond was meant to be there.

But if I had been asked to recommend a name for the new body of water adjoining our land, I would have suggested "Forbidden Pond." It would be off-limits for our grandchildren, our neighbor explained, even if responsible adults accompanied them. His concern was liability, and he was not moved by my contention that ponds were made for children and unusual adults like Henry Thoreau. Our grandchildren delighted in frogs, turtles, salamanders, and fish with an enthusiasm that made my own curiosity when I worked as a college student for the Oregon Fish Commission seem world-weary by comparison. Adults, I argued, can sometimes respond aesthetically to a pond when it reflects the vault of heaven and colorful quivering leaves, but to children a pond is the experience of life itself, as though they know in their bones that it all began in a pond.

Our neighbor stood by his legal apprehensions. There would be no ugly metal fence around the pond, he said, but it would be forbidden, and I knew our neighbor's view of private land was widely shared. Our society increasingly chooses private over public. Our love affair with privatization, which heated up in the Reagan years, has been especially torrid for those of us who retreated from cities to suburbia and the rural countryside. We have built houses with front porches too small for sitting and talking with our neighbors, replacing more public porches with private decks, hidden in back yards. Our country and suburban houses tend to be almost unapproachable on foot, the ceremonial front doors usually accessible only from the driveway and across a wide lawn. We have turned increasingly to private malls, where security guards can protect us from contact with homeless people, street musicians, and political activists. And we move about in vehicles that resemble our private homes, both in size and amenities.

So our neighbor's position on the pond was understandable. Why should he share the cool shade and birdsong of his pond in spring and summer any more than he would share his hearth and CD collection in a colder season? And yet it was a disappointment. Forbidden Pond seemed to be a symbol of an approach to country living that values privacy more highly than community. These new country people, traumatized perhaps by crowded sidewalks and thin walls in urban high-rises, seem to wish they had no neighbors at all. In

The Practice of the Wild Gary Snyder says place-centered cultures traditionally distinguish between agricultural land, which can be private property, and wild and sacred land, which should be shared. Our Canaan neighbors, who grew mainly flowers on land that had been agricultural generations ago, seemed to think of the woods around them as a buffer from the rest of civilization. As Nancy and I thought about a vision of the land that seeks to close it off from local people, some of whom have walked on it for generations, we took down the bright orange "No Trespassing" signs we'd inherited with the trees on our 5.31 acres, and we began to think about moving on.

Moving on, after all, is the American way. In *the Unsettling of America*, Wendell Berry says: "As a people, wherever we have been, we have never really intended to be." This pattern, he says, may have begun with Columbus, who found our continent when he was looking for India. One result of our restlessness, according to Berry, is that the real settlers, the people who choose to stay put and nurture land and community, are generally under pressure from folks who want to make a profit, grow bigger, and move on—those *boomers* I mentioned in the Prologue.

We had profited massively when we traded away our cabin near Cannon Beach in Oregon, and now, as we considered exchanging our Canaan property for something else, we stood to make even more money, at least on paper. One of the effects of the fear that swept our country after September 11, 2001, and our subsequent "war on terror" was an increase in property values on rural land north of New York City. When we began to think of moving farther north, we stood to become, like the Halliburton corporation once headed by the man who was then our nation's vice president, war profiteers.

As I reflected on this possibility, I remembered a conversation recorded in my journal on June 22, 1976. I had been talking with a man in our Granville community garden as we wielded our hoes in adjoining plots. He told me he'd gardened in Minnesota and Virginia, but he preferred the soil right there in Ohio. He wanted to own land for gardening when he retired, he said, but then he caught himself and added he didn't really plan to stay in one place very long. He was silent for a while, probably knowing what he was about to say was pretty revealing. He dreamed, he went on after a while, of buying an Airstream trailer. When he visited dealers to look at his dream, salespeople sometimes asked him why he didn't buy one now and enjoy it, but he couldn't see the point of buying a travel trailer for two or three weeks out of the year.

As my fellow gardener and I talked, I realized the Airstream was an end, not a means. I thought of Merle Haggard's country song "The Highway is My Home." It wasn't so much that there were places the gardener wanted to see, but he was drawn to the elegantly streamlined capsule for living on the move, unbound from the chains of the working world. The sleek trailer with its yacht-like interior was a symbol of a self-reliant life. What struck me about that memory of our Airstream conversation as I prepared to move away from Canaan was the irony: the garden where we stood leaning on our hoes was a better symbol of self-reliance than a travel trailer, but in a society that values mobility as highly as ours does, we seem to be fixed on RVs, SUVs, Airstreams, and space capsules, as images of independence. And Nancy and I were about to rent another moving van before we had learned much about gardening in Canaan's rocky soil.

The house we found in Grantham, New Hampshire, four hours northeast of Canaan, wasn't flawless. There was a rip in the screened-in porch big enough for a very large mosquito, and we heard tales of mosquitoes the size of turkey vultures. The railings on the deck were flimsy, and the deck itself showed signs of rot. I had a history of breaking my arms and knocking myself out on decks like that. The kitchen was long and narrow, and like basketball players jockeying for position Nancy and I exchanged elbows when we worked there together. The lawn was not as blessedly small as the postage stamp we had cultivated in Granville.

But daughter Annie was just twenty miles north in Hanover, where her husband was a hematologist and oncologist at the Dartmouth-Hitchcock Medical Center, and she was preparing to have a baby. Soon Judy and her partner, Jannay, who was pregnant now too, bought a place on nearby Eastman Lake, and in the summer of 2004, while our country's war on terror raged on and people were dying in Iraq, our family gathered in New Hampshire for three months of playing music, talking, writing, swimming, kayaking, hiking, and waiting for the births of Jack and Toby. It was a summer so full of wonder and joy that we might have imagined all was right with the world if we hadn't read newspapers.

Chapter Twenty

Looking Back on a Friendship

When an ex-student of mine became a rabbi, I was reminded that the most powerful alternative to hatred is love. In the spring of 2006, Nancy and grandson Nate and I attended Rabbi Michelle Werner's ordination in Cincinnati's beautiful Plum Street Temple, and the words spoken by the congregation struck a resonant chord. "If we can hear the words of our ancestors, then love will flow from us and we shall serve all that is holy with all our intellect and all our passion and all our life." Religious language is sometimes used in public to identify evil and even to justify war. But the language spoken that day in the Plum Street Temple reminded me of Martin Luther King's message of nonviolence in the 1960's, his insistence on the transforming power of love. "If we can serve all that is holy," the congregation continued, "we shall be doing all that humans can to help the rains to flow, the grasses to be green, the grains to grow up golden like the sun, and the rivers to be filled with life once more."

One of the humblest forms of love is friendship. Although we don't have statistics on broken friendships comparable to the numbers we have on broken marriages, some of the same pressures that end marriages almost certainly destroy friendships too. And lost friendships in turn probably have something to do with broken marriages, fragmented communities, our increasing reliance on counseling professions, the ill-tempered and polarized politics of our time, and maybe even our desperate, growing reliance on war as metaphor and policy.

I haven't done particularly well at sustaining friendships, and the break with my oldest friend, Terry, several years ago set me to thinking about what this failure might mean. By the time our friendship appeared to have ended, he had been in prison twice on drug convictions, and his marriage was over.

In the summer of 1996, Terry had reached the end of his second probation period in California, and we agreed to meet in Oregon on Saddle Mountain. Our family planned to be in Oregon, and Terry and I had walked and talked before on Saddle Mountain. We thought it might be a good place to consider what had driven us apart. When Terry didn't arrive on the appointed day, I wasn't altogether surprised. I returned to Ohio a few weeks later to find a letter from him. He had been delayed by car trouble, he said, and then he was arrested with marijuana in his car, not far from Saddle Mountain. Now he faced a long sentence, and he thought he had to leave the country. He was angry about the war on drugs, and he seemed to hold me responsible. He was writing to say a furious goodbye.

When Terry and I met in the first grade, he was one of the smallest kids in our class, but he was by far the fastest runner. His father had once been a jockey, and Terry had the same small, wiry build. In the third grade, he won a scholarship to Portland's Multnomah Athletic Club, and he became a skilled boxer and strong swimmer. My early memories of Terry have a touch of adulation that endured: he lends me a talisman that he carries in his pocket and lets me outrun him; he fights a much bigger kid who grinds out his cigarette on my arm while we're working in bean fields near Eugene; he persists as a running back on his high school football team even though he is too small; he works his way through college by teaching accordion lessons, and a few years later he insists there is something wrong in Vietnam well before the war has fully registered on my consciousness.

I began to sense the importance of our friendship one afternoon in the second grade after our teacher, Miss

Galbreath, left our class in the care of an eighth grade girl. The whole class behaved badly that morning. I was usually a model child, but the eighth grader's diminished authority seemed to release something pent up in me. It may have been an early form of a mating dance, and I went mildly berserk, breaking a vase and distinguishing myself as the wildest member of a very unruly class. After lunch, Miss Galbreath told me to join Terry and a few other boys at the front of the room, where we were the focus of a chilling, detailed indictment. There was something dispassionate and leisurely about Miss Galbreath's review of the eighth grader's report on our behavior. I remember several long, ominous silences.

Well into an afternoon that seemed to stretch on forever Miss Galbreath invited those of us who felt we had paid adequately for our sins to take our seats. It didn't even occur to me to sit down. My strict religious upbringing had kicked in, and I was feeling remorse. As the boys around me slouched toward their desks, I began to imagine the new horrors to be visited on me when I was left alone in front of the class. Then I saw Terry standing beside me, and it felt like an act of great loyalty and courage. I can't remember the punishment that followed, probably nothing much, but I do recall my gratitude, knowing Terry would share it.

When we were in the sixth grade, Terry's family moved away from Portland, first down the Columbia River to Astoria, then south to Eugene. We corresponded, and our parents helped us visit each other during vacations. I lived on their farm west of Eugene the summer before our ninth grade year while we worked as bean pickers.

After high school I went to Park College, a small Presbyterian school in Missouri, and Terry went to the University of Oregon, but we got together in the summers for fishing trips and camping. We both were married the summer after we finished college. I was Terry's best man.

After his wedding, in a variation of the western shivaree tradition, Terry was abducted by male relatives and locked in a bar managed by one of his uncles. I was supposed to find him and return him to his wife, but a young girl, his cousin, performed the rescue while I wandered around southeast Portland looking vainly for my friend. In the next few years, we both did graduate work in English, even though he'd majored in mathematics and I'd completed a pre-med major in science, and he joined me to teach composition for a year at the University of Missouri in the early 1960's. We both had two daughters.

After my wife and daughters and I moved to Ohio in 1966, Terry and his family settled in northern California. We wrote to each other frequently, and every year or so our families got together even before we began planning the project described above in "The Institute." It became increasingly clear that Terry was struggling with depression, and his marriage was falling apart. He worked with a psychiatrist and tried lithium before he began to use the illegal drugs with which, I now believe, he sought to medicate his depression. Later, Terry's use of drugs seemed to be inseparable from his growing commitment to a spiritual vision that would probably have made sense to Transcendentalists like Henry Thoreau and Ralph Waldo Emerson.

By the time Terry went to prison in the mid-1980's, great mutual mistrust had come between us. Over a decade, we exchanged occasional angry letters punctuated by periods of silence. Early in the 1990's we seemed to be finding our way back to each other, and we made the plan to meet on Saddle Mountain in the summer of 1996. And then our long, struggling friendship appeared to end with Terry's angry announcement that he had to leave the country.

In the silence that followed, I tried to imagine where Terry might be. He had traveled earlier in Brazil so

I guessed he might have gone there again. As a musician and mathematician, he would find a way to make a living, I thought. When I read about Curitiba, Brazil, a progressive city where poor people can exchange bags of garbage for food, I began to think of that as a place where he might find a way to move beyond his anger and despair.

Two years later I received a brief letter from Terry with an article from *Synthesis*, an alternative magazine published in Chico, California. The article, "War in the Woods," describes my old friend as "a yoga instructor, massage therapist, and artisan." It includes a photograph of Terry seated in a yoga position and tells of a benefit concert given by several local bands to raise money for his legal defense. Following a description of his arrest for possession of marijuana while camping on federal land, the article quotes his response to the possibility of another drug conviction: "'I pray that the case is dismissed or that a jury finds me not guilty. I will not accept probation and community service. That's a form of slavery. I am a yogi and have explored the differences between physical and spiritual existence. One of my conditions for continuing to live in this material world is that I must be in a place of love. If I am imprisoned, this will prove that the hearts of people are hardened and their love has grown cold. If forced behind those prison walls, I will surely and quickly dissociate myself from the encumbrance of the body and the restless tides of breath.'" In the rigid and sermonic speech that didn't sound much like Terry at all I thought I could read great anger. But I imagined he meant it when he said he'd rather die than live any longer in prison or even under house arrest. Having talked with lifers and corresponded with men in Ohio's harshest prison, the "supermax," I'd been convinced that someone who struggles with depression outside is likely to find prison unendurable. He once wrote to describe several months of living with an electronic bracelet, when he had just two hours free on Saturdays for shopping errands. He was working fulltime and attending required meetings on addiction, and he claimed to have no life. Like prisoners on death row who sometimes "volunteer" for execution, he sounded as though he'd experienced enough incarceration to be certain he would rather die than live in a cell.

I don't know why Terry remained in the country. Although we've exchanged many letters since 1998, when he sent me the *Synthesis* article, I'm not sure of his legal status. Probably there was no room for Terry in California's crowded prison system. Given the budgetary crisis facing the state, it's unlikely they will find the billions of dollars necessary to lock up Terry and all other people who have been charged with marijuana-related drug crimes.

For a few years, Terry moved to Oregon, often taking the train south into California to visit his two daughters and their children. Until his mother died in the spring of 2006, he visited her in Portland too. He spent considerable time translating Hindu texts from Sanskrit, depending on Social Security for his primary source of income. By U.S. standards, he has been poor for several years.

Our struggling, resilient friendship has become a source of considerable comfort to me. Our letters have taken on an unguarded, contemplative quality that reminds me of our correspondence when we were much younger. We focus increasingly on our grandchildren and other sources of hope. "One way both of us seem to be dealing with our intensified sense of mortality," I wrote to Terry in May of 2004, "is by investing our lives in our children and grandchildren." He agreed.

I told Terry about a recent book by Mary Clark, a friend who lives in Oregon. Her *In Search of Human Nature* (2002), I said, seems to me a "quest for hope in the midst of nightmare." By *nightmare*, I meant the dark sense of inevitability many people bring to the great damage we're doing to the earth. Clark's sense of hope comes from her careful examination of research in several disciplines. My comments on Clark's book touched a chord, and Terry wrote back twice about his own search for hope. "What I'm suggesting," he says near the end of the second letter, "is that many people are finding valuable antidotes to the pessimism and helplessness so many of us feel. If we are to change our world and our lives, we need to get past the belief that we are essentially flawed and bad. I think we can—even amidst the dismal scene of war, injustice, and brutality to our environment. It's my heartfelt prayer."

We've become tentative philosophers in our old age, and our friendship begins to feel like an amazing stay against the entropy that seems to whirl so many of us apart.

Chapter Twenty-One

Death by Metaphor

In the summer of 2005 there was a funeral for our 21 year-old relative, Robert, an enemy combatant in our nation's "war on drugs." A freshman at Pittsfield High School six years earlier, Robert had been a starting guard on the basketball team, and he was a good enough catcher that we thought he might have a career in professional baseball. But just about the time that he began to emerge as a gifted athlete, Robert was infected by the heroin plague that rampaged through industrial and farm towns fallen on hard times. It was downhill for him after that although he struggled.

His whole family struggled. Robert's grandfather punched a drug dealer who came to their house one night to collect money, and a few nights later the tires on the family's cars were slit, a surprisingly gentle reminder that Robert and his family were dealing with dangerous people. There were disagreements within the family about how to help Robert. Some thought he had to be allowed to hit bottom, and others wanted to send him away to a resident rehabilitation program. Some thought the youngest members of the family had to be protected from him. Others recalled how gentle and loving he could be with children. The disagreements caused quarrels and opened chasms between family members who had been close for decades, and Nancy and I, our daughters and grandchildren, were part of those battles. But the conflicts disappeared with Robert's death. Friends and relatives gathered around his body to embrace each other.

In our war on drugs, addicts as well as dealers are the enemy, and it's hard for those closest to them to know how to love them without becoming "enablers." Robert went to jail for a while, but he found no rehabilitation there. He attempted suicide, but his stay in the hospital didn't lead to serious treatment. When addicts realize what it means to be the enemy in our war on drugs, they learn to be very secretive, and they learn to lie and steal. If they're out of money and their dealer doesn't trust them, they're totally alone.

Robert was alone when he died. He had fought his way free from heroin for six months, and then something seems to have flipped a switch in his brain. He believed he had to have a fix. There was no one he trusted to tell him he could beat it this time or to say the dose he'd been using months earlier would kill him now. If he'd found his way into a community of recovering addicts, a group like Alcoholics Anonymous, someone he trusted might have been able to encourage him and warn him of the danger, or they might have seen he was in trouble. But when an addict knows he's the enemy, it's difficult to believe in friends.

One of the pallbearers, a young cousin, came back from the funeral with us to New Hampshire. He brought with him a stash of marijuana he'd bought from Robert just a few days before he died. When our daughter Judy found out about it, she told him much of the money we spend in our war on drugs goes for imprisoning people who grow and use marijuana. State troopers with dogs have stopped us at checkpoints on I-91 in Vermont, she said, and they're looking for drugs, as well as illegal immigrants. Our young cousin went home earlier than we had planned, seeming not to understand how easily he could become an enemy in our deadly war on drugs.

Our experience with Robert revealed a blessing in my brother Dave's war experience. He returned from Vietnam with no addictions other than tobacco. It isn't easy for me to admit this, but his experience in combat left Dave with a lasting self-confidence of the kind sometimes seen in athletes who move through the world with the same poise and certainty they show on playing fields. Such confidence might have grown in Robert if he hadn't been captured by addiction and then targeted in our war on drugs. Challenges grounded in the physical world, whether they involve fixing a house, a car, or even a computer, don't intimidate Dave. I've wondered if the confidence and competence I see in my brother help to explain why voters are drawn to politicians with military experience. If so, the wisdom in the impulse seems to be confirmed by our tragic experience in the "war on terror," planned by men and women guided by ideology and fundamentalist belief. Conservative critic Andrew Sullivan summarized the thinking behind the war on terror policies of President George W. Bush, Vice President Dick Cheney, and Secretary of Defense Donald Rumsfeld this way:

> Fundamentalism cannot question; it is not empirical; it is the antithesis of skepticism. Hence this allegedly 'conservative' president attacking conservatism at its philosophical core: its commitment to freedom, to doubt, to constitutional process, to prudence, to limited government, balanced budgets and the rule of law. Faith is to the new conservatism what ideology was to the old leftism: an unquestioned orthodoxy from which all policy flows. Cheney and Rumsfeld, however, do not strike me as the same. They're just bureaucratic brutalists, thrilled to have complete sanction to do as they please because they have the mandate from the leader-of-faith.

I was drawn to Sullivan's reasoning, as a good many critics of our war in Iraq were, but my family's experience doesn't fully bear it out. My own early religious development was consistent with our family's fundamentalist background. When I was eleven, I attended a religious camp chosen by my grandparents, a two-week session devoted primarily to saving campers' souls. I wasn't reborn at any of the camp's many revival meetings, but I remember taking my Bible to an outdoor chapel in the woods and preaching to a cabin mate who then borrowed the book to preach back at me. We seemed to be telling ourselves we were already saved, and we didn't rebel against the camp's fervent godliness. In 1956, when I went off to a small Presbyterian school in Missouri, Park College, I was a conservative young Republican who sometimes led worship services. As a senior, I was an elder in the campus church, where I met the Irish Democrat from Massachusetts who would become my wife.

In the early 1970's, when I'd begun to discuss my religious and political doubts with my parents, they had joined the Bible Study Fellowship, an organization that would be important several years later to George and Laura Bush in Texas. A. Wetherell Johnson, a Baptist missionary who had been ejected from China, founded the Fellowship in 1958. It grew to be more important to my mother than her church. She became a local leader in the organization, structured with a strict chain of command from Small Group Discussion Leaders to Teaching Leaders to Area Coordinators to the Executive Director in San Antonio. My parents, who were living then in a mobile home just outside Portland, Oregon, came to know quite wealthy families in the Bible Study Fellowship. On a visit to Oregon in the mid-1970's, I met one of these women when she invited our family to her beautiful home to use her swimming pool. In her living room was a large red, white, and blue sofa, and above it a large painting the woman had commissioned of her sofa's patriotic floral pattern. I remember my mother's obvious discomfort that day even though she was the woman's Discussion Leader. The uneasiness seemed a result both of their difference in social class and my mother's fear that I might say something to reveal my apostasy.

Although the Fellowship is committed to the Bible's "inerrancy," other fundamentalists have criticized the organization's emphasis on leadership roles for women. "Evangelical feminism" is the phrase they use, and it's meant to be dismissive. Critics from the religious right have argued that the leadership roles assumed by Bible Fellowship women could produce gender role confusion and even homosexuality. This was already a matter of controversy in the 1970's, and I remember my mother's saying that women in the Fellowship were not allowed to assume positions of leadership without seeking their husband's permission. She added that a Christian woman was expected to obey her husband even if she was saved and he was not.

In the last few years before my mother died in 1982, the Bible Study Fellowship had, unpredictably, a liberalizing influence on my parents. In addition to its very limited version of "evangelical feminism," for example, the organization took pride in its ecumenical inclusiveness. In her autobiography, *Created for Commitment* (1983), Johnson tells of Catholic participation in the Fellowship and adds: "Members from Jewish, Christian Science, Jehovah Witness, Mormon and other congregations have become interested in Bible study. Seeing that all denominations are welcome, BSF has a truly ecumenical fellowship." My mother and father seemed to be responding in part to this ecumenism when they moved from their Presbyterian church to join a congregation of conservative Quakers. The pastor of their programmed Quaker meeting encouraged my parents to give me a subscription to *Sojourners Magazine*, published by a progressive, Bible-based community committed to peace and justice.

Remembering this growing openness in my parents' thinking, I also remember telling my wife when my parents were considerably younger than I am now that I feared they were too old and set in their ways to change their thinking about religion and politics. Who could have imagined my mother and father would find their way through the same terrain that seemed to give President George W. Bush a troubling certitude to a more inclusive religious vision and a more genuinely compassionate politics in the last years of their lives?

When fear of enemies and evil is driven home with drumbeat insistence, and we see ourselves fighting a "war on terror," the kind of softening I saw in my parents' worldview during the last years of their lives can still happen, and that possibility is heartening. My parents' growing elasticity would have made them skeptical of the polarized vision that finds order by seeing the world neatly divided into enemies and friends, good and evil.

Chapter Twenty-Two

Return to Fox Creek

Near the end of September in 2006 my brothers and I gathered on *Llandaff,* the sailboat that was John's home in Puget Sound. We were planning an expedition to the Fox Creek forest, and it would be John's first visit. As we motored slowly out of La Conner, Washington, toward the notch that cuts through Whidbey Island and creates Deception Pass, where swirling tidal currents can turn a boat around in seconds, a heavily armed police boat passed us going very fast. Homeland Security, John explained. Lots of boats roared around the Sound with powerful motors and machine guns, he said. So far, they hadn't found much to chase, but they were potent symbols of our war on terror.

There were large patches of fog when we reached open water, and we couldn't see much of the island where every few minutes a Navy jet dropped out of the sky and into fog to land at Whidbey Island Naval Air Station. Dave thought the planes looked like F-111's, high-speed bombers he remembered fondly because he called them in for air support when his patrols ran into trouble in Vietnam, but F-111's had been out of service since 1996, and these were probably F-115's with similar double tails. When the fog disappeared, we watched funny-looking radar planes circle over the Sound. Dave said they might be Prowlers, planes with four crewmen that provide "electronic countermeasures" to baffle enemy radar.

Both of my brothers are skillful sailors. I am not although I thought about boats as an adolescent with nearly same intensity I thought about girls. John's 39-foot Beneteau sloop, the *Llandaff,* a French-built, Welsh-named boat, had sported four elegantly crafted, built-in wine racks when he bought it, but he removed two of them, converted one into a filing cabinet, and made the other into a storage cupboard for cooking utensils. John wanted the *Llandaff* to be a home for two, and there is little space to spare on a boat, especially if you've grown accustomed to living in a house, even a small one.

We were planning our expedition just a few weeks after John had signed papers to divorce Barbara, his wife of more than thirty years, who had left several months earlier to join her sister and brother-in-law in Alaska. Barb and John's grown son and daughter, Aaron and Jessie, moved aboard the *Llandaff* for a while. Aaron, working long hours as an electrician for a local boat builder who was rushing a $5 million yacht toward completion, invited us to visit the 85-foot boat with "Sarasota, Florida" already painted on its beautiful stern. Jessie had just finished nursing school and was providing home care to a family on Whidbey Island while she waited to qualify for a hospital job. Like Aaron, she was accustomed to storing her belongings rather casually, but youthful clutter is a problem aboard a sailboat, and the disorder aboard *Llandaff* had begun to weigh on John by the time we sailed out of La Conner in September. A week after our voyage, they moved to their own digs, and John was alone.

Barb had gone to Alaska in their pick-up truck so John moved to and from work, when he could find it, on a bicycle with a small trailer that carried his equipment for servicing boats. He had considered traveling the U.S. with his bike and trailer, but he loved life aboard the boat, and there were practical reasons for staying at home in La Conner that had much to do with caring for and financing *Llandaff*. I've long understood the love of boats, and I understood better the desire to spend one's life on the water after I read E. B. White's essay "The Sea and the Wind that Blows" in which he describes a primal need that includes more than a touch of fear, linked with a desire to be alone on the water and dependent on one's own skills for survival. Such needs, joined with an expensive commitment to a boat, have ended a good many marriages, and they might have had something to do with Barbara's exodus. But in this case there was also John's increasingly intense battle with depression, the darkness that has haunted other members of our family. Sometimes paralyzed for weeks by despair, he spoke of longing to be out on the sea, especially in bad weather. Combined with his restless movement from one job and its accompanying dreams to another, this must have felt like a never-ending journey on heavy seas to the woman living with him through many shifts in the prevailing winds.

There wasn't enough wind to fill a sail as we headed toward Deception Pass, and Nancy and I used the gentle, motor-driven ride on the *Llandaff* to exhort John to travel with us for a few days after the trip to Fox Creek as we revisited old haunts in Oregon. He'd already agreed to accompany us on the hike to Fox Creek, although he intended to walk in sandals over very rough terrain because he experienced a kind of neurological pain in his feet that made shoes and boots excruciatingly painful. (Just as I had hoped the Fox Creek forest would make Dave comfortable with wilderness again, I thought it might begin to salve the wounds from John's broken marriage even though it was unlikely to help his feet.) To my surprise, John agreed to join us on our Oregon tour.

The tide was coming in when we arrived at Deception Pass, and John had no intention of trying to take us through it toward the Strait of Juan de Fuca. Sailboats with small diesel engines can get through the pass at ebb tide, but when the tides are running, only power boats can make it. However, John wanted us to feel the currents, the churning gray whirlpools boiling near the entrance to the narrows. As he swung *Llandaff* around, we could feel the vibrations of conflicting forces at work on the hull, the keel, and the rudder so that for a few seconds it wasn't clear to me just what the boat would do. Then we found ourselves headed back toward La Conner. John seemed to have meant to remind us all of nature's unforgiving side, which sailors forget at their peril. It was a good reminder to have as we set out for Fox Creek. We'd chosen late September for our expedition, hoping to avoid elk hunters, who have been known to hunt in Saddle Mountain State Park, perhaps intending to drive elk onto logging company land, where they can shoot them legally. But even without hunters, the old growth forest can be dangerous if an early autumn storm comes in from the ocean, and limbs and trees begin to fall.

Our plan was to return the *Llandaff* to its moorage in time to drive five hours south to the place Dave shared with Joan in Vancouver, Washington, where we would spend a short night and rise before dawn to drive seventy miles to Saddle Mountain and meet our guide, Doug Ray. Dave could have led us once more along the labyrinthine elk trails to Fox Creek, as he did on our first walk into the forest, but we asked Doug, another ex-Marine, to guide us because he knew the ancient forest better than anyone else except perhaps biologist Neal Maine, and Doug was one of its protectors. We had a faint hope that Dave's son and daughter, Chris and Kate, might join us at Saddle Mountain too. Neither of them had been back to Fox Creek in the fifteen years since we made our first trip, and we weren't sure they would be eager enough to make the hike again to get up early on a Saturday morning.

In 1994, on Dave's fiftieth birthday, three years after our first hike into the Fox Creek forest, his marriage ended. A few years later, he met Joan, who was an unapproachably beautiful and hip young woman at Franklin High when I was enrolled there in the 1950's as an adolescent nerd. Closing in on her seventies in 2006, Joan was still a beautiful woman. She showed me a letter from the Marine Corps that she had framed and hung on the wall of her study, awarding Dave the Bronze Star and commending him for actions he's never mentioned to me or to anyone I know. Joan and Dave met at an Al-Anon meeting, an offshoot of Alcoholics Anonymous that brings together people whose lives are affected by someone with a drinking problem. She was trying to understand the collapse of a marriage, and he was trying to grasp the failure of a relationship that came apart after he left his marriage.

When Dave became a high school student two years after I graduated from Franklin High, he attended suburban Clackamas High because our family had moved to Milwaukie, a Portland suburb. Instead of playing sports, he backpacked through the Cascades and climbed snow-capped mountains whenever he got a chance, and he remained in the Boy Scouts long after most of his friends had turned to hipper activities.

In the summer of 1994, not long after Dave's marriage ended, Nancy, Dave, and I had walked to Fox Creek with Doug Ray. It was the first time the two ex-Marines had met. Doug seemed to respect Dave's "recon" experience, and Dave was eager to tap Doug's knowledge of temperate rainforests. That day the ancient cedar, spruce, and Douglas fir trees were more beautiful than we remembered, but red plastic ribbons marked a route used a few days earlier by a search and rescue team to recover a body. Every time we saw one of those ribbons, we were reminded of John Licari, a young man from nearby Seaside who, according to observers, had rushed barefoot up the steep and rocky trail to Saddle Mountain's summit three days earlier, covered his eyes with his hands, and leaped 500 feet onto rocks below. Licari's body landed on an almost inaccessible slope high above the Fox Creek forest. The recovery team left ribbons to help them find their way out of the woods, and to me the red ribbons seemed to hang like question marks, asking why Licari chose Saddle Mountain.

In 1997, three years after that grim walk along a route marked by red plastic ribbons, Doug Ray and I had walked out to Fox Creek again, and we were briefly lost on Saddle Mountain. "Not till we are lost," Henry Thoreau said famously in *Walden*, "in other words, not till we have lost the world, do we begin to find ourselves, and realize where we are and the infinite extent of our relations." We were lost on a day of rain and fog, good weather for finding shy mountain elk because water dripping from the canopy covers the sounds of humans, but it was bad weather for finding our way home because we couldn't orient ourselves by seeking glimpses of Saddle Mountain's summit. We resorted to leaving yellow ribbons on branches, much as the team recovering John Licari's body had done three years earlier. Doug, whose father once worked as a logger on the land around Saddle Mountain, was as delighted as I to see the normally elusive elk, and we were soon caught up in the excitement of getting close to them. Once, we came within fifteen feet of a young bull, so close he looked embarrassed when he realized we were there, and he stared at us for a few moments before lunging away. We forgot to leave ribbons for a while, lost our bearings, and tried walking uphill in the hope of finding the base of steep bluffs on the mountain's west side, where Doug expected to recognize a landmark. Instead, when we came out of the trees, we seemed to be below cliffs on the mountain's north side, gazing out into fog and what we surmised must be the Columbia River although we couldn't see it. Our deliverance was a little embarrassing for Doug: we found our way out on a web of logging roads his father helped to build and Doug sometimes criticized.

When we had given up on finding our yellow ribbons and were walking out through a clear-cut recently sprayed with herbicide from a logging company helicopter, Doug began to talk about war. In 1981, he was serving in the Marines at our embassy in El Salvador when Ronald Reagan was President. This was the period when our government's foreign policy was focused on defeating communism in El Salvador, Guatemala, and Nicaragua. As we walked, Doug told stories of violence he witnessed in San Salvador. Then, sweeping his arm to take in the ugly landscape around us, he spoke of our government's defoliation policy in Vietnam. It is one thing to read about defoliation, another to walk among small, dying alder trees as they drop brown leaves in June because a corporation wants to harvest more marketable spruce, fir, and cedar. Walking among ancient trees, Doug generally spoke in a whisper, but as we moved through the clear-cut interspersed with dying alder, his voice grew louder. Herbicides don't kill just plants, he said. The poisons drain into streams and rivers, and soon people are asking what happened to the Coho salmon.

The Fox Creek forest, part of Saddle Mountain State Park, was in less danger than old growth stands in national forests. The second Bush administration had gutted the National Environmental Policy Act, the National Forest Management Act, and the Endangered Species Act. Apparent victories won by environmentalists on behalf of the Northern Spotted Owl in the 1980's and 1990's were overturned. In 1997, as we had walked through land visibly damaged by industrial logging practices, it was hard to feel confident about the forest's future.

In 2006, when we arrived at the Saddle Mountain parking lot for our expedition, Doug Ray was waiting with Neal Maine, his old biology teacher who once taught our daughter Annie. Neal couldn't go with us to Fox Creek, but he wanted to say hello. He'd retired from teaching and was now preparing to retire from his position as

245

Executive Director of the North Coast Land Conservancy, the organization that negotiated a land trade to protect the Fox Creek forest in 1991. He was working furiously to complete several additional land deals. An unanticipated side effect of the successful battle to save the Fox Creek forest had been the growth of the conservancy. While the federal government's forestry policies tended to favor short-term profits over environmental stewardship, Neal explained, private developers had begun to understand that protecting biodiversity could increase the value of building sites, and one result was the expanding opportunity to care for wetlands, watersheds, estuaries, and other wildlife habitat.

We weren't equipped to stay overnight in the Fox Creek forest, as our party had been on our first expedition, so Doug and I had planned to get an early start. But Neal had a lot to tell us about their efforts to protect coastal ecosystems, and it was a good thing he did. Well after the hour when we had agreed to head into the woods, Chris and Kate arrived with Kate's boyfriend, Aaron Fordice. To my surprise and delight, our whole party of nine had gathered. We said goodbye to Neal Maine, who photographed our departing expedition with a camera he normally used to document wild things for the conservancy.

It was the rutting season for elk, and Doug encouraged us to walk quietly and converse in whispers, on the chance we might see a bull elk out looking for an opportunity to send his genes on to another generation, as Doug put it. Within fifteen minutes we were following an elk trail through a mature alder forest, and I knew this was going to be different from earlier visits to Fox Creek. One big difference was the light. We had never been there in early autumn. Bright shafts of golden sunlight filtered through the canopy at unfamiliar angles. The temperature climbed to 80 degrees Fahrenheit on the coast that day, but we experienced sunlight mainly as patches of crystalline radiance on rough bark. We were cool even though we used lots of energy on the steep terrain. The other difference had to do with aging: we took our time as never before, eliciting occasional hints of impatience from members of the younger generation. We stopped to look closely at the damp ground beneath our feet, to search for recent elk sign, and to whisper comments on what we saw. After a bit we took to gathering in a circle occasionally to listen to Doug's whispered commentary on the forest. We saw no elk, but Doug spotted a large alder where a bull had rubbed his antlers lasciviously—and recently, judging from fresh elk scat nearby. The bull left a surprisingly symmetrical etching on the tree that rose as high as my arm could reach.

When we finally came into the old growth, the forest floor that was usually dark was surprisingly colorful in beams of sunlight. Along with cedar, spruce, and younger hemlocks, we saw Douglas fir trees, shortened by wind and lightning, the kind of huge snags that provide nesting places for northern spotted owls.

When we sat down to eat lunch among the ancient trees, my niece's boyfriend, Aaron, pulled out his cell phone and pretended to order a pizza. He told of training at a large Army base in Texas, where a local pizza parlor promised to deliver to even the most remote parts of the base if they were given the proper coordinates. After that, he said, he was stationed in Egypt until two weeks before our troops invaded Iraq in March of 2003, and he mentioned his surprise at finding graffiti and posters in Cairo that roared with disdain for President George W. Bush even before our occupation of Iraq had begun.

Aaron didn't have to call a local pizza parlor. The older generation brought more than enough sandwiches, crackers, cheese, and fruit to feed the expedition, and Doug, an ardent fisherman and hunter, passed around smoked tuna. While we ate and rested, he asked me to read aloud from Eliot Norse's book, *Ancient Forests of the Pacific Northwest* (1990). I chose a passage about elk. Logging company representatives often say clear-cuts produce meadow-like hillsides that are just the ticket for elk. But Norse quotes several biologists who make the case that old forests are almost as important to the survival of elk as they are to Northern Spotted Owls and Marbled Murrelets. The birds find nesting places in the old trees, and elk find winter food that isn't covered by snow.

I was preaching to a captivated choir about the virtue and beauty of ancient forests, but the silence that followed my brief elk sermon set me to thinking about why we were there at Fox Creek. I'd begun to plan the trip long before I knew of John's divorce. Maybe I was hoping we'd get lost out there for a while and "find ourselves," as Thoreau put it, "and realize where we are and the infinite extent of our relations." We weren't lost although some of us, the older ones, wondered if we would have enough energy left to get back to the parking lot. Doug, urging us to watch carefully where we put our feet, told of having to carry his daughter-in-law out of the Fox Creek forest when she injured her ankle and knee. It was likely to be the last walk to Fox Creek for some of us, and I realized our expedition had as much to do with my whimsical dream of being, at least momentarily, our family shaman as it had to do with the forest. Our family might be considered dysfunctional by a professional student of such matters, what with our broken marriages, our bitter political and religious disputes, and our failure to stay in touch. Of our four Northwestern nephews and nieces, I had seen only Kate in the last decade, and we seldom corresponded with the younger members of the family. Except for my Uncle George, who had devoted much of his adult life to working for Jerry Falwell and who in 2006 lived alone in Idaho, I was our *patriarch*, a title unlikely to be accepted in the family's western branch let alone on the east coast, where my wife, daughters, and granddaughter were sure to laugh at such language. But in organizing our walk into Fox Creek, I had pulled together a gathering that might be as close as we would come to a family reunion, and I wanted it to be a healing ceremony.

Although I told Doug Ray none of this, he must have sensed it. On our walk out of the forest, which was even slower than our very deliberate entry, he encouraged us to gather in a circle as we did for his nature talks going in. But he withdrew from our circle and was silent, and we began to catch up on the lives of Chris, a civil engineer; Kate, who worked fulltime and studied to become a nurse practitioner; and Aaron, who majored in political science with the thought of attending law school. Dave was unusually silent on our return, but he seemed to take pleasure in hearing the young people talk about their lives. When he spoke, it was usually to register a delighted sense of familiarity with landmarks along our way, leading Doug to remark that he'd never walked to Fox Creek with someone so at ease with the confusing topography, and I felt pride in Dave's reconnaissance skills. By the time we were back in the Saddle Mountain parking lot, our expedition felt more like a family.

There was a single disappointment for me in our return to Fox Creek: I had wanted to include my old friend Terry, who was then living 150 miles southeast of Saddle Mountain. In 2006 he was back in Eugene, where as a youth he worked on his family's farm, taught accordion, and attended the University of Oregon, majoring in mathematics. We planned to visit him in Eugene, which was home to John and Barbara in the early years of their married life. During the summers of my college years, I had worked for the Oregon Fish Commission in Oakridge, a logging town east of Eugene.

Of all the places where I've lived, Oakridge seemed the least likely to be featured in the *New York Times*, but a few weeks before we headed west to revisit Fox Creek, an Oakridge profile, "Rural Oregon Town Feels Pinch of Poverty," appeared in the *Times*. The blue-collar mountain town had fallen on hard times, and it had a pretty hard edge when I worked there. I recalled a night in the summer of 1959 when a fish hatchery worker I knew got a phone call from a bar in town telling him a logger was coming out to his house to beat him up because of something he'd said. When the logger drove into his driveway, the hatchery man met him and beat him unconscious before he could get out of his car. About the same time, another hatchery worker got tired of waiting for his wife to have their first baby and took her out driving in his old pick-up on rough mountain roads.

There was no such thing as deer season in Oakridge when I lived there. Local hunters borrowed radio-equipped pick-ups from a logging company and drove the back roads at night in spread-out threesomes. Hunters with spotlights and rifles were in the middle truck, and if anyone came along, the hunters got a radio warning from one of the other two trucks. Afterwards, they stored their venison in the freezer at the state fish hatchery.

The most memorable hatchery worker I knew was Joe, who claimed he fled a Pennsylvania mining town when he was young. The night before he left Pennsylvania, Joe said, he was sharing a bed with his older brother, who had knocked him around once too often. Joe waited until his brother was asleep, punched him hard in the jaw, lay back down and pretended to be asleep. He left town in the morning. Joe worked as a logger in Oregon for several years, until he injured his back, and then he came to the hatchery. When I knew him, he awoke at five each morning, drank a pot of coffee, and smoked a pack of cigarettes before work. If he caught a cold, he drank a pint of whiskey and wrapped himself in blankets for a night of sweating and refused to take a day off. Working with him was like trying to keep up with a machine that runs only at full speed. Joe moved to a hatchery over on the coast when word got around Oakridge that a logger whose wife Joe had been meeting in a bar wanted to kill him.

Lots of people in Oakridge seemed to be influenced by the town's frontier ferocity. A local lawyer spotted me walking out to the hatchery from the bus station one Sunday afternoon with my tennis racket and challenged me to a match the next morning before work. When I beat him, he was so angry we didn't play again. A hatchery biologist told me one day how he planned to kill his family and himself if Communists took over the country, and later that week a hatchery man, invited me to go with him when he drove the Oakridge ambulance to a car accident in the mountains. Loggers are notorious for taking mountain curves on two wheels, but his driving was considered crazy even by Oakridge standards, and I told him I suffered from motion sickness.

Those were the good old days in Oakridge, when "poverty meant you didn't have an RV or a boat," according to the *Times*. The Oakridge I remembered was replaced by a town where some people lived in campers in the forest and looked for jobs in other towns, blaming environmentalists and the Forest Service because the lumber mills shut down. This happened before the recession that began in 2008. What really happened to the town's prosperity is complicated, of course, and it has a lot to do with the fact that logging companies squandered the trees as though they would last forever.

Instead of visiting Oakridge while we were in Eugene, Nancy and I decided to head south to Cottage Grove and introduce my brother John and my old friend Terry to Mary Clark, a biologist who wrote two books that offer hard-earned hope in a time of difficult challenges:

251

Ariadne's Thread: The Search for New Modes of Thinking (1989) and *In Search of Human Nature* (2002), which I mentioned in Chapter 20. In the first book, Clark provides an interdisciplinary analysis of a predicament she describes this way: "We live in a world undergoing multiple large, rapid and mostly unprecedented changes, in the face of which most of us feel utterly helpless. . . . Tensions rise; debts mount; the arms race, despite recent token treaties, continues to grow, not decline." Our sense of helplessness, Clark suggests, has much to do with what we've come to believe about human nature, and in the second book she explores this question: "Who do we think we are?" She would have preferred that question for her title, she says, rather than *In Search of Human Nature*. The question captures Clark's feisty side, for her heavily documented hymn to hope is also an attack on ideas that have been important in much modern scientific and social thought. She provides evidence, for example, that undercuts the idea of a "selfish gene," a concept that assumes individualism is rooted in our DNA. "To entice you into this huge tome," Clark says at the beginning of *In Search of Human Nature*, "I will tell you now that I believe our true natures are far more lovable and positive than we in the West currently believe them to be. There is indeed hope for us after all." She sets out to show that the impulse toward community, stewardship, and sustainability may be more "natural" than most of us assume, describing communities that have set themselves against environmental and social destruction.

As we drove into Eugene on Highway 126, just north of Willow Creek Farm, where I used to visit Terry, I was more nervous than I'd been since my days as a college administrator. It had been well over a decade since Terry and I had seen each other. In the interim he had been in and out of prison twice, and almost been sent there to stay. Our friendship, like the Oakridge economy, had fallen on hard times. Although our recent correspondence had seemed to restore trust and affection, I wondered if our friendship could survive now only in writing. Both of us resisted the fast-track prose that goes with email and texting although we occasionally emailed when Terry visited one of his daughters or used a library computer. In our correspondence we looked for areas of agreement, and we steered leisurely paths, avoiding subjects that had touched off our anger. Would we be able to maneuver so warily in an actual conversation, I wondered, and if we did, would it feel as though we hadn't actually met at all?

Terry was living in an old house with several musicians from local bands. He has been drawn for years to musicians and had lived in a "band house" in Chico, California, too. But even though he can play the accordion, banjo, guitar, and piano, Terry hasn't performed music in years. His lack of instruments undoubtedly has something to do with his poverty, but I've wondered if he avoids playing music much as Dave shunned the woods for many years after Vietnam because terrain like that he'd loved had been a location for great pain. Terry had found an old electric piano to set up in his room, but it had mechanical problems, and he hadn't been able to play it. I'd told him more than once that playing the guitar helps to keep me sane even though I'm a much less accomplished musician than he is. The thought appeared to resonate with him, but he preferred to listen.

Terry was waiting on the porch when John, Nancy, and I drove up. Nancy and I had recently attended a 50th high school reunion so I was prepared for large changes in Terry's appearance, but aside from being gaunt in a way I didn't remember, he seemed unchanged. He wore no earrings and had no tattoos that I could see. His thinning hair didn't hang down to his shoulders. There was no stoop in his posture, and at 68, he still moved with the grace of an athlete.

We ate lunch in a rose-filled park next to a heavily used bike path, and I could see he had difficulty chewing. He mentioned to Nancy that he was about to have quite a lot of dental work done. But he appeared to have recovered from a bad case of shingles that had knocked him down a few years earlier. Our conversation was effortless, and it was filled with laughter that didn't seem nervous at all.

Terry's room could have been a monk's cell: a mattress on the floor was made up neatly; there were a few books, the silent electric piano, and some colorful artwork based on Terry's reading in Buddhism. Near the door, he had posted a list of people who could be called if something happened to him, and he mentioned that this was something new. His younger sister was dying of lung cancer, and he was feeling his mortality.

Approaching eighty, Mary Clark was surely feeling her mortality too, but you wouldn't have known it from talking with her or reading her prose. She was a mountain climber as a young woman, and old climbing injuries had begun to take their toll. She had recently dislocated a hip while working in her garden, an incident that might have turned out badly if she hadn't been carrying her cell phone.

After a career in biology, much of it in England and then at San Diego State University, Clark moved into the social sciences, focusing on conflict-resolution for a few years at George Mason University before she retired to Cottage Grove in Oregon to write *In Search of Human Nature*, among other things. Her recent experience in the social sciences is part of what led her to write a large book about what it means to be human.

Clark is a grandmotherly woman who can be very warm with strangers, and she quickly seemed to make John and Terry feel welcome. But as soon as we walked into her living room, her intense, scholarly side emerged. Piles of articles and letters, neatly labeled, were lined up on the floor, and she spent some time explaining them. When we walked upstairs to her study, there were piles of books on a large table with pages marked, more material she was gathering for a project she summed up with a question she asked a few days later in an email: "How do we self-criticize without shaming, pointing fingers of guilt, or otherwise exacerbating the psychological malaise that already permeates our society and all too many others?"

Terry had just finished reading *In Search of Human Nature*, and Clark's responses to his questions converged on a concept I hadn't heard her mention before, "the public imagination," a phrase that seemed important in a letter she mentioned writing to Senator Hillary Clinton. She was trying to answer the question about self-criticism, and she was thinking about presidential politics. A few days after our visit, she sent me a copy of the letter she'd written to Senator Clinton, a letter that put in perspective much she'd been saying as we walked in her garden and talked around her table. She'd been thinking about the American public's failure to see the consequences of our disastrous economic, environmental, and foreign policies. And she was troubled by the Democratic Party's inability to help citizens imagine, not only the catastrophes our policies were likely to cause, but also the likelihood that alternative policies could make things better. Clark chose to write Senator Clinton because she was then the front-runner for the Democratic presidential nomination. Within weeks she had sent a similar letter to Senator Obama.

"The last thing the future world will need is an unstable, greedy, hegemonic United States, struggling to grasp for itself the last drops of oil and water!" Clark wrote. As she neared the end of her long letter, she indicted our war on terror:

This "war on terrorism" makes even less sense than a "war on viruses" or on "tsunamis." "Terror" is a state of mind – not a physical object. And to fix "states of mind" requires not tanks, and bombs and concepts of "shock and awe" to cure them. Indeed, these are counter-productive, only serving to reinforce such antagonistic "states of mind." In the eyes of all too many others, we are the world's terrorists! That's a hard sell, I realize, but at least the government must understand it, even if it feels unable to publicize it!! Indeed, given the technologies now available to our species, wars for any reason are no longer useful, if they ever, ever were.

Mary Clark chose Cottage Grove for her retirement, hoping to become a founding member of an intentional community there. Her teaching and research about our destruction of the environment convinced her of something Bill McKibben says in *Deep Economy* (2007) about communities that work. It's not possible to suggest a perfect size or shape for a community, McKibben concludes, but "it's enough to say that, for reasons of ecological sustainability and human satisfaction, our systems and economies have gotten too large, and that we need to start building them back down. What we need is a new trajectory, toward the smaller and more local." Like the Institute we dreamed of with our friends in the 1970's, Clark's intentional community failed to materialize, but she stayed in Cottage Grove and became an active citizen there while she continued to write about the importance of building peaceful connections with each other and with the Earth itself

Epilogue

In October of 2013, Nancy and I drove from New Hampshire to Oregon on our way to Fox Creek. It was a leisurely journey with visits to several friends and relatives along the way, and in a cold motel room in Prineville, Oregon, I received an email from an old Ohio friend, Harry Heft, who asked if I would help Viki McCabe, a writer about to publish an important book, *Coming to Our Senses: Perceiving Complexity to Avoid Catastrophe*. Although I wouldn't understand this for several months, Heft's request probably helped to shape what I learned when we hiked once more to the Fox Creek forest.

Our plan was to visit Fox Creek with daughter Judy and granddaughter Ana. Judy, who was about to develop a non-profit, Artists for Soup, in La Paz Centro, Nicaragua, flew in from New York. Ana, who would soon leave for more than a year of study in Brazil, rode a bus in from Seattle, where she had just attended a memorial service for her other grandmother, Betty Orians.

After tune-up hikes on Cape Falcon, Neahkahnie Mountain, and the trail to Saddle Mountain's summit, we walked into the Fox Creek forest on October 17th with our guide, Doug Ray, and Judy Sorrel, another member of the North Coast Land Conservancy. It was a beautiful autumn day but still very rugged terrain, and Nancy and I felt our years. We found our way into the Fox Creek old growth but stopped short of Fox Creek itself. Doug Ray, whose love of Oregon's coastal mountains and wetlands is joined with the zeal of a fine teacher, realized Ana was both tireless and disappointed. If she continued walking for a few minutes in the same direction, he quietly suggested, she might find her way to Fox Creek. The rest of us could sit down, have a bite to eat, rest, and talk while we waited for Ana. We had been walking in several directions, it seemed to me, and I remembered getting lost in the Fox Creek forest with Doug on a foggy, rainy day. But Ana, who once tried to ride her bike up the stone stairs of the Vassar College chapel in a race with her older brother and who makes friends with strangers more quickly than anyone else I know, jumped at Doug's suggestion. Judy, who has probably inherited from me an ability to find silver linings only after imagining terrible possibilities, has also learned to mute her grim imaginings. She encouraged her daughter with a nervous smile, and Ana took off.

We sat down for quiet conversation while we waited. By the time Ana returned, her feet wet from Fox Creek, I already knew my understanding of the place was changing. In Don Berry's fine novel *Moontrap*, set in 1850, Saddle Mountain is a powerfully evoked mountain man's world, and in my own *York's Journal: A Novel* about the Lewis and Clark Expedition it's a place where Clatsop and Chinook boys go to seek their tribal identity. In *Fleeing Ohio*, another novel, I tell the tale of a father who breaks his son out of a "supermax" prison in 1998, and they hide in the Fox Creek forest. It has been for me a man's world and a place of escape.

Like her other mother, Jannay Morrow, and her younger brother, Toby, Ana is Jewish, but we celebrate Christmas, as well as Hanukkah, and three months after our return Ana gave Nancy and me a book of photographs to remember our hike into the Fox Creek forest. Among the pictures of beautiful landscapes and our hiking group there is a shot of me with a tall pink and white granola-berry-yogurt parfait, which I ordered at Camp 18, a restaurant near Saddle Mountain that was built from magnificent logs and surrounded by antique logging machinery. Celebrating the troubled industry that has been crucial to the Pacific Northwest, Camp 18 proudly serves breakfasts that would be welcome in any logging camp. In a book of photographs with very little written text, Ana has placed beneath the picture of me and my parfait the words from a song I sang very quietly at breakfast so as not to offend the leather-clad bikers at the next table: "I see that you are a logger/ And not just a common bum/ 'Cause nobody but a logger/ Stirs his coffee with his thumb." That song and my defiant parfait order at Camp 18, where large stacks of pancakes are the usual fare, were side-effects of my much-delayed Fox Creek epiphany.

Years ago, when Nancy drove my father, my brothers, and me out of a living room where we were accustomed to read the newspaper after church, suggesting that we lend a hand with dinner, I should have known already women would help me find Fox Creek. Maybe I began to glimpse the answer when I was unable to help Viki McCabe, who needed assistance because she had discovered she was very ill. Her book, *Coming to Our Senses*, makes a persuasive case that we fail to respond effectively to climate change and growing inequality partly because we rely too heavily on words and theories, not enough on our senses. As an illustration of our commonly neglected ability to understand our surroundings on the basis of sensory experience, she tells of watching a film that displays a black screen dotted with tiny lights. The lights begin to move and coalesce into patterns, revealing themselves as people walking, dancing, and doing push-ups. Their faces and bodies have been blacked out, and reflective bicycle tape fastened to each performer's six major joints reflects light onto the screen. Their movements are visible and understandable from the illuminated patterns they produce. Surprisingly, observers who know the performers recognize individuals on the screen based solely on their distinctive movements because each person's unique proportions produce identifiable body movements.

In *Coming to Our Senses* Viki McCabe encourages us to trust the complex knowledge we gain from sensory perception instead of theories or ideologies, which often obscure reality. Such abstractions, she argues, are partly responsible for our political paralysis in the face of climate change. McCabe's argument is hopeful because if she is right, our failures to address problems such as climate change and inequality result from our failure to trust our perceptions. When Harry Heft, an environmental psychologist, contacted me, he said McCabe was seeking someone to help her write a second book that would address more directly the politics of our environmental crisis. I corresponded with McCabe and talked with her on the phone, but for reasons I may never understand I was unable to help her. Still, my failed attempt to work with her set me to thinking about other women who find hope in the most formidable problems we face.

I mentioned above the hope biologist Mary Clark provides in *Ariadne's Thread* and In *Search of Human Nature*, and I think of Rachel Carson's *Silent Spring* (1962), often considered a founding document for the modern environmental movement. Setting herself against a chemical industry that tried hard to destroy her credibility, Carson revealed why anyone who looked out the window in the spring and listened with care might find evidence that chemicals developed as weapons during World War II and used increasingly to control pests on our farms were destroying bird populations. Her last chapter, "The Other Road," described ways we could save our crops without killing birds and ultimately poisoning ourselves. Far from provoking pessimism, *Silent Spring* inspired hope and energized the environmental movement.

A book by Rebecca Solnit, *A Paradise Built in Hell: The Extraordinary Communities That Arise in Disaster* (2009) also fits the pattern I'm describing. Solnit studies disasters, including San Francisco's 1906 earthquake and the destruction of the World Trade Center on 9/11, and she finds examples of resourcefulness and unselfishness in grass roots responses to calamity. Authorities fearful of social chaos, Solnit points out, often work against this kind of communal self-help, as in the police killings in New Orleans after Katrina. Like Mary Clark's *In Search of Human Nature*, Solnit's book provides evidence of our human capacity to act in ways that are, as she puts it, "resilient, resourceful, generous, empathetic, and brave."

Ann Hagedorn has written *The Invisible Soldiers: How America Outsourced Our Security* (2014), revealing the likely long-term consequences of privatizing our military. She describes a barely visible shift in 2012 from a traditional military to "a mix of Special Forces and private military and security companies that together would provide the backbone of national security and defense." Uncovering stories of the rapidly multiplying businesses that succeed partly by being clandestine and ruthless, Hagedorn makes a case that profitability is likely to figure importantly in the lobbying that leads us into wars. She explores, for example, the likely influence on foreign policy of our growing dependence on drones. Like Carson's *Silent Spring*, *The Invisible Soldiers* invites us to address a grim reality that is very hard to see and hear. Hagedorn tries to make possible a debate that could be crucial to our survival as a free society.

After I retired from Denison University in 1998, I taught writing classes at Dartmouth College for a few years, focusing on environmental issues. As the time approached when it seemed right to re-retire, I wanted to invite my students to read a book that might surprise them, maybe even change their lives, and I chose Michelle Alexander's *The New Jim Crow: Mass Incarceration in the Age of Colorblindness* (2010). Although I'd served several years on a criminal justice committee in Ohio with the American Friends Service

Committee and written about the increasing use of isolation in our prisons, I was shocked by revelations in *The New Jim Crow*. Alexander shows how our country's criminal justice system has been transformed by the "war on drugs" to a system of racial control. In the Prologue I mention that *Finding Fox Creek* is a story of great privilege, and Alexander emphasizes the danger in such white privilege, showing how the "war on drugs" has decimated communities of color.

Of the books I've mentioned, perhaps only *Silent Spring* has, so far, had greater influence than *The New Jim Crow*. There appears to be a bi-partisan movement against mass incarceration growing as I write although it is not yet the mass movement Alexander believes will be necessary. And she provides this warning:

> But if the movement that emerges to end mass incarceration does not meaningfully address the racial divisions and resentments that gave rise to mass incarceration, and if it fails to cultivate an ethic of genuine care, compassion and concern for every human being—of every class, race, and nationality—within our borders, including poor whites, who are often pitted against poor people of color, the collapse of mass incarceration will not mean the death of racial caste in America. Inevitably a new system of racialized social control will emerge—one that we cannot foresee, just as the current system of mass incarceration was not predicted by anyone thirty years ago.

The New Jim Crow calls for a new social movement, and there are encouraging signs that Michelle Alexander has struck a chord.

It is probably no coincidence that these compelling invitations to work for social and political change, embedded in unflinching descriptions of very grim realities, are written by women. A recent *New Yorker* essay about climate change by the novelist Jonathan Franzen, "Carbon Capture: Environmentalism vs. Conservation" might unintentionally reveal why this is so. Franzen shows why climate change denial is more complicated than the story of Oklahoma Senator Jim Imhofe, who brought a snowball to the Senate floor as a way of summing up his position in a debate that barely exists. As you might expect from a terrific writer of fiction, Franzen imagines his way into the mind of a man—the novelist himself—who acts as though he denies the grim conclusions of climate scientists even though he fully accepts their evidence that our Earth is in deep trouble.

This is the heart of Franzen's approach to climate change denial: "Climate change is everyone's fault—in other words, no one's. We can all feel good about deploring it." (He might have added what also seems to be true: we can all feel pretty good about ignoring it, which most of us do most of the time.) It is a fatalistic position. Believing global climate change is inevitable no matter what we do, Franzen argues for local conservation: "Only an appreciation of nature as a collection of specific threatened habitats, rather than as an abstract thing that is 'dying,' can avert the complete denaturing of the world."

In a society already severely polarized, Franzen claims environmentalism is in conflict with conservation. He describes conservation projects such as the impressive work of Daniel Janzen and Winnie Hallwachs in Costa Rica and says: "At every turn, the smallness contrasts with the vastness of climate-change projects— the mammoth wind turbines, the horizon-reaching solar farms, the globe-circling clouds of reflective particles that geoengineers envision." As his primary authority on the existence of a conflict between humble conservation and large-scale, ultimately futile environmentalism, Franzen quotes Jim Williams, a blogger for the Minneapolis *Star Tribune*. Williams dismisses as "nothing" the deaths of the few thousand birds likely to crash into the glass walls of the Twin Cities' proposed football stadium when set against the National Audubon Society's recent prediction that "nearly half" of North American bird species are likely to lose their habitat by 2080 as a result of climate change.

Taken together, Franzen and Williams remind me of the two students I described in "Battling Boredom" who seemed determined to show how much more terrifying and inevitable was the future they imagined than anything Jonathan Schell described in his chilling book on the implications of our Mutually Assured Destruction policy, *The Fate of the Earth*. Like my own view of the Fox Creek forest as a man's world where one can escape for a while from an increasingly denatured Earth, Franzen's fatalism seems to me an example of the machismo imagination at work on predicting the Earth's future.

In Naomi Klein's book *This Changes Everything: Capitalism vs. The Climate* (2014) a compelling response to Franzen's dismal "Carbon Capture" appeared before the essay was published. Klein, who takes down geoengineering and criticizes several flamboyant, large-scale approaches to combatting climate change, describes activists' efforts to protect local ecosystems and communities as part of a global movement to resist climate change. And she describes her own decision to have a baby and how it moved her beyond experiencing nature by "grieving its inevitable loss."

Franzen believes local conservation projects are the best we can do—a palliative treatment, as he puts it, for an Earth with terminal cancer.

Klein disagrees, insisting that people who work against fracking or for affordable public transportation or for increased public ownership of energy and water are working against climate change. She shows how local efforts to protect indigenous land rights are part of the much larger resistance movement. And most heartening of all, Klein argues, if people began to realize they were collaborating in their varied work for conservation and justice as part of a global movement, it "would help to end grotesque levels of inequality within our nations and between them."

Franzen's fatalistic essay makes explicit an attitude, or perhaps a conviction, that seems to be widely shared. It is close to a position taken by my old reporter friend, Fred Bruning, who forty years ago registered his skepticism regarding the idea of the Institute discussed in Chapter Eight. Fred acknowledges the grim climate science but believes activists who oppose the Keystone Pipeline, Big Oil, or fracking won't resolve the crisis. His argument against those actions rests heavily on his conviction that poor people will pay the price for reducing the availability of cheap fossil fuel while prosperous Americans—some in the environmental movement—continue our privileged way of life. He also has faith in human ingenuity, believing technology can save the day, a prospect Franzen considers only in passing when he mentions the possibility of "a miracle cure like fusion energy."

More openly than Bruning and most people who throw up their hands when someone speaks of addressing climate change, Franzen says bluntly that the Earth's goose is cooked and the best we can do is temporarily protect islands of biodiversity. He is especially concerned about bird populations. Naomi Klein, who would probably say Franzen's desire to protect birds and their habitat makes him part of the movement resisting climate change, decided to bear a child despite her own fear of the Earth's ecological collapse. That choice seemed to invest her imagination fully in the welfare of coming generations. She quotes Katsi Cook, a Mohawk midwife: "At the breast of women, the generations are nourished. From the bodies of women flows the relationship of those generations both to society and to the natural world. In this way is the earth our mother, the old people tell us. In this way, we as women are earth." This hope-filled link with the generations who come after us may be what the brave women who shaped my changing view of Fox Creek have in common.

We'll need great humility, imagination, and hope to avoid environmental disaster, and those same virtues might help us see the absurdity in making wars, including metaphorical ones. Admittedly, there's irony at work in the story I've told here about our family's suffering in wars real and imagined. It would have been a much darker story if we lived in almost any European country, Vietnam, Somalia, Nicaragua, El Salvador, Afghanistan, Rwanda, Colombia, Pakistan, or other developing countries. As I've acknowledged, our native land has been essentially untouched by war since 1865, and with a few exceptions, our nation has been on the side of the "winners," sometimes even the aggressors. Yet we've also been victims. This irony reminds me of something the anthropologist Colin Turnbull once said about capital punishment. He'd been studying the influence of executions in our society and learned they poison the lives of people quite distant from the principals, including family members and friends of the guards and the murder victim, as well as people connected with the person executed.

In the spring of 2000 I met a truck driver whose son worked as a correction officer in the Ohio State Penitentiary (OSP) in Youngstown, the state's "supermax." At breakfast in a restaurant a friend and I were talking about the recent suicide of Richard Pitts, a prisoner at the OSP. The truck driver overheard and asked if he could join us. He wanted to talk about his son, who had come out of the Army and found a job at the OSP when it opened in 1998. He'd taken his work in criminal justice very seriously, his father said, and he'd become enough of an expert on the influence of gangs that he was sometimes asked to give talks on the subject at other prisons. His son, he said, was on duty when Richard Pitts committed suicide, and here the truck driver had difficulty continuing because he was crying. His son told his family the death of Pitts, a man he didn't know at all, was "good riddance to bad rubbish." When his son came out of the Army two years earlier, the driver said, he wouldn't have talked that way, but he'd begun to express only contempt for the prisoners in his charge. He spoke of them, his father said, as though they weren't human. The truck driver said he knew there were some evil men in the supermax who deserved to be severely punished, but he saw in his son something frightening, a growing bitterness that made him abusive to his wife and children. His family was collateral damage in our wars on crime and drugs. There is no escape to Fox Creek, no prospect of durable healing, until we "cultivate an ethic of genuine care, compassion and concern for every human being," as Michelle Alexander says. It must be the kind of love that takes into account grandchildren, maybe even the grandchildren of grandchildren.